#86/639

D0609377

I dedicate my
to Elisabeth, my very
much valued friends.
Cordially

Dion Newton
June 1987

lot Inscribed & SIGNED 30"

Dione and Richard Neutra at his seventy-fifth birthday celebration in 1967.
Dione holds their wedding picture taken in 1922.

# Richard Neutra
# Promise and Fulfillment
# 1919–1932

Selections from the Letters
and Diaries of
Richard and Dione Neutra

*Compiled and Translated by Dione Neutra*

*Southern Illinois University Press*
*Carbondale and Edwardsville*

Copyright © 1986 by the Board of Trustees, Southern Illinois University
All rights reserved
Printed in the United States of America
Edited by Teresa White
Designed by Quentin Fiore
Production supervised by Kathleen Giencke

"Frank Lloyd Wright to Dione" (Taliesin, March 1925), "Frank Lloyd Wright to Richard" (Taliesin, August 1929), and "Frank Lloyd Wright to Richard and Dione" (Taliesin, August 1929) Copyright © The Frank Lloyd Wright Foundation 1985.

*Library of Congress Cataloging in Publication Data*

Neutra, Richard Joseph, 1892–1970.
  Richard Neutra, promise and fulfillment, 1919–1932.
  Includes index.
  1. Neutra, Richard Joseph, 1892–1970. 2. Architects—United States—Correspondence. 3. Neutra, Dione, 1901– . 4. Wives—United States—Correspondence.
I. Neutra, Dione, 1901– . II. Title. NA737.N4A3 1985     720′.92′4  [B]
845-2245
ISBN 0-8093-1228-X
89 88 87 86 85  5 4 3 2 1

# Contents

——————

Illustrations

The marriage of Dione and Richard Neutra was not simply an unusual duet. It was a whole orchestra. In the early years of their marriage, Richard was the conductor, composer, and concertmaster. Dione, talented and adoring, was his student. Over the years of their long marriage, however, Dione became not only a mature artist but also a composer and impresario.

Together they created an extraordinary repertoire. They each composed solos, accompaniments, arias, lyrical songs, dirges, lieder, and each wrote and wrote—to each other, to their children, to their friends, and to the world. The selection of their correspondence in this book illuminates the development of both of these artists and the remarkable themes of their lives together.

Their interdependencies, their tempests, tranquilities, joys and despairs, affected not only their own lives but that of their children, Frank, Dion, and Raymond. Frank, brain-damaged from birth, was for many years a tragedy for them. But in more recent years Frank's modest progress is a comfort to Dione. Dion became a gifted architect in his own right, and Raymond, who left the architectural scene altogether, is a distinguished epidemiologist.

Richard was unquestionably a genius. He had a symphonic view of all life, art, architecture, botany, biology, zoology, ecology, and history. He wove these elements into harmonies, with wit and style, in stone, steel, wood, glass, plants, and words. But without Dione, Richard's music might have been heard not at all or only faintly during his life or now. It was Dione who managed all the troubles and details of daily living. It was she who sang away his despairs and pains, who planned the tours, made all the arrangements, typed the lists, the speeches, and itineraries (multilingually), often sitting with a typewriter in her lap while flying with Richard around the world. Despite his tremendous intellectual gifts, Richard was always a needy man. He needed the abiding love, the tender care, and the constant emotional support Dione always gave him, and Dione always knew it.

I early admired them both. But over the years of deepening friendship, I came to cherish each of them—Richard with his crystalline insights and Dione with her indomitable spirit. Even when Dione lost the other half of herself, when Richard died, she was not daunted. Dione continues to spend each day of her life learning something new. She continues her cello, voice, concertizing, learning new languages, writing, and lecturing. She is a devoted mother and grandmother. Through all of the years, she has retained those rare and special attributes of spontaneous and unselfconscious curiosity and joy. Most of us lose those elusive qualities when we are no longer children, but we recognize and admire them when we see them glowingly alive in another.

These letters open to all the minds and hearts of Dione and Richard Neutra, as they lived their lives together.

The letters evoke for me many memories of them. I recall the evenings, with Richard conducting an opening verbal prelude, followed by Dione's playing her cello and singing. All of us would be completely absorbed by her music. When her concert was over, Dione would serve a lovely dinner.

Once again, Richard would lead a conversational opus, calling upon different guests to produce solos and counterpoint. Dione would contribute grace notes.

Hours with the Neutras, as the readers of this book will learn, are rediscoveries of the voyages of the mind, of life as it should be, and life as it is.

Historians have told me that my late husband, the architect Richard Neutra, is, or will become, a significant historical figure because he played a vital part in the development of modern architecture and is considered one of its most important pioneers. This seems to have come to pass, as recently demonstrated in Thomas Hines's book *Richard Neutra and the Search for Modern Architecture: A Biography and History*[1] and with the exhibition "The Architecture of Richard Neutra: From International Style to California Modern," which was created in 1982 for the Museum of Modern Art in New York by Arthur Drexler and Thomas Hines. It traveled to Vienna, Barcelona, and West Berlin in 1983, continuing on to Los Angeles (UCLA) and Houston (Blaffer Gallery) in 1984.

When Richard died in April 1970 many of the more than seven hundred letters of condolences I received, while expressing the contributions Richard had made to twentieth-century architecture, insisted that I had a contribution to make—to write a book about our life together, "otherwise so much would be lost and you are the only one who can do it." Some mentioned the role they felt I had played in his life, the influence I had had on his success. For instance, there was this from the Swiss architect Robert von der Muehll, whom we had known for many years: "How was it possible for a man of such caliber to radiate to the fullest extent and in so many ways? . . . When we reflect on how you lived and worked together with him so intimately over a long life-span, day and night, it seems that it was this combined force that made his life's work possible, that enabled him to endure so many burdens, struggles, and difficulties. . . . Your steady presence and your devotion to him and his work were, therefore, of immeasurable value."

Yes, it is true that Richard lovingly and enthusiastically let me share in his thoughts and ideals, and they became my ideals too. Here was the architect called "one of the world's best and most influential moderns,"[2] and I was with him from the beginning of his formative years as an architect, with him during those crucial career years of struggle and finally first success. I certainly did have a unique perspective from which to tell Richard's story. But where to start? And how?

Weeks went by without inspiration. But then, while going through some storage boxes in the basement of our house—I have long since forgotten why, but it proved providential—I discovered a box of correspondence labeled "Dione to read when old." There, neatly bundled, were the letters, spanning more than a decade, that I had started writing as an eighteen-year-old girl to the dashing twenty-seven-year-old Viennese architect.

Richard's letters I had always carefully preserved, as I considered them to be one of my greatest treasures. My own letters, however, had been forgotten for nearly fifty years. Reading them after all of this time, I realized that my letters combined with Richard's were in themselves a history of our early life together, before and during our marriage—a dialogue in Richard's own words and mine, as well as those of my parents and our

---

1. New York: Oxford University Press, 1982.

2. "New Shells," *Time*, 15 August 1949, pp. 58–66.

friends, and other architects such as Mendelsohn, Schindler, Wright, that provided a narration and documentation of Richard's developing concepts, approaches, and attitudes, his frustrations and achievements.

Here was how I could "write" the Richard-Dione story. Settings range from imperial Vienna to imperial Japan, from the nightmare of Ellis Island to a dreamhouse in Los Angeles. And the time covered is considered one of the most important periods in European and American socio-cultural history—the early twentieth century during the reconstruction after World War I, a time of struggle for young artists and architects on both sides of the Atlantic.

However, these letters tell the story of not only the making of an architectural career but also the making of a lasting marriage, for many of these letters were first and foremost love letters that span our meeting, our courtship, and the first ten years of our marriage. They represent the establishment of a line of communication that both formed the foundation of a marriage and helped it to endure for forty-eight years, vital and productive to the end.

*A Note on the Text*   Dates in the headings of the letters have been standardized to show only month and year. I used this device to solve the problem of narrative flow. Because of the nature of the mails, especially when Richard was in the United States and I in Europe, sometimes a question asked in one letter could be answered only after two or three other letters had intervened. Simple month and year dating allowed me to arrange the letters according to subject matter within a given month, so that, when needed, each letter had its answer. Maintaining the flow of the narrative seemed more important to me than a pedantic adherence to individual dates.

In those letters that I have translated from the German, spellings and punctuation have been emended to conform to modern English usage.

No attempt has been made to reproduce typographically the appearance of any of the letters; where, for example, in Frank Lloyd Wright's letters to Richard there was canceled type.

Word or words originally underlined in the letters appear in italic type. I am grateful for the help given to me by Lilly Schorr and Thelma Ginzler in correcting the English translation of the letters. I also acknowledge with thanks the editorial help of Kit Morgan and Meredith Stricker. I would also like to thank The Frank Lloyd Wright Foundation for granting permission to use the following letters: "Frank Lloyd Wright to Dione" (Taliesin, March 1925), "Frank Lloyd Wright to Richard" (Taliesin, August 1929), and "Frank Lloyd Wright to Richard and Dione" (Taliesin, August 1929).

In the mid-1970s, I decided for two major reasons to write a biography of Richard Neutra. First, I believed that his work constituted a significant, though underappreciated, achievement in the development of the Modern Movement in architecture. Second, I was certain that Neutra's personal life experience was an equally trenchant reflection of important currents in European and American cultural history.

Though I had first encountered Neutra in the mid-1960s in architectural history courses at the University of Wisconsin, my interest in him was confirmed when I began to teach at the University of California, Los Angeles, in 1968. I quickly visited his most noted buildings in southern California, and in early 1970, my wife and I became tenants in his Strathmore Apartments (1937) near the UCLA campus.

Shortly after we moved in, Neutra, his wife, Dione, and his sister-in-law Regula Thorston paid us a visit, and we talked for several hours on a variety of topics—including, of course, Neutra's life and work. This was my only meeting with him, for he died several months later on a visit to Germany in April 1970.

The experience of living at Strathmore in the years following Neutra's death further stimulated my interest in his work. As I got to know his wife and family and his friends and enemies and as I explored the archive of papers and drawings Neutra had left to UCLA, I became convinced that I should write a book about him. Believing that history at its best is analytical narrative, where the "methodology" pervades but never engulfs the "story," I saw in Neutra's experience a powerful story with significant implications: the search, via architecture, of Neutra and his generation for the promise and meaning of the twentieth century. The new architecture, which they agreed to call "modern," would express, define, and shape the new century.

In reconstructing Neutra's early life in Vienna, I relied chiefly on the unpublished diaries of his youth, but in treating his development after World War I, my most important sources were his and Dione's letters to each other and to relatives and friends. These included the couple's early "love letters"—following their initial, postwar meeting in Switzerland—while Neutra was constructing a career in Vienna, Berlin, New York, and Chicago. Equally significant were the Neutras' reports from Berlin, Chicago, Wisconsin, and Los Angeles to their relatives in Europe, particularly Dione's parents, Alfred and Lilly Niedermann.

While I drew heavily from these letters for my understanding and explication of the Neutras' lives in the 1920s and 1930s, I regretted that large amounts of fascinating material in them had necessarily to be left out of my book. Therefore, I was delighted when the Southern Illinois University Press decided to publish this edition of the letters, thus complementing the narrative I had written in 1982. That the letters were saved, translated, and collected is due to Dione Neutra's keen sense of history and to her loyal devotion to the Neutra legacy. Their publication is a tribute to her and to him.

It was also fortuitous that the final manuscript, which I had asked to see, arrived during my sabbatical year abroad just as I was leaving to spend a week in Berlin. Each day of my visit in that poignantly divided city, I reread another section of the letters. They were ideal companions to my architectural explorations, particularly as I visited two of Neutra's earliest works—buildings of 1922 and 1923, upon which he collaborated with his mentor, Erich Mendelsohn. One of these projects was the group of four, relatively unaltered houses in the prosperous, middle-class Zehlendorf section of West Berlin. The other Mendelsohn-Neutra example still standing in Berlin—the "Mossehaus," or *Berliner Tageblatt* building— was more difficult to find since the name of one of the streets on which it was located had been changed after World War II from Schützenstrasse to Reinhold-Huhnstrasse. It stands in what is now East Berlin at the corner of Jerusalemerstrasse, a few hundred yards from the Berlin Wall. By visiting East Berlin or by looking over the Wall from the elevated platform at the end of Lindenstrasse, West Berlin, one can see the altered, but still recognizable, "modern" corner entrance of the building as renovated after the wartime bombing.

In rereading these letters, I recalled the nostalgia they had earlier evoked for the Germany I had visited in the early 1960s. Then, as I read on past the German sections of the letters into the American period of the 1920s and 1930s, I began to feel—*in* Berlin, ironically—an equally great nostalgia for New York, Chicago, Wisconsin, and Los Angeles, the American places that are also evoked so well. But the letters describe not only times and places past. They also document the lives and achievements of extraordinary people, particularly of their authors, Richard and Dione Neutra. It is good to have the Neutra letters as a permanent companion.

T.S.H.
Berlin
March 1985

*The Neutras*    Richard Neutra was born April 8, 1892, in imperial Vienna, Austria, the son of an artisan-industrialist who owned a small factory that produced metal products, including cowbells. Though of Jewish heritage, Richard's father had been for many years a secular agnostic. Richard's mother was forty-two when he was born, the last of four children. She died of breast cancer when he was sixteen. The eldest brother Wilhelm ("Willy"), fourteen years older than Richard, was a medical student. Through him Richard became interested in natural history. The second brother, Siegfried, twelve years Richard's senior, studied engineering. Richard's sister Josephine ("Pepi"), six years older, was a painter and sculptress. She eventually married Arpad Weixlgärtner, a renowned art historian, who introduced Richard to the world of art. Weixlgärtner was for a time the director of the famous Kunsthistorisches Museum.

Though he graduated summa cum laude with the degree of architect-engineer from Vienna Technische Hochschule, Richard's all-around education was also a humanistic one that included six years of Greek and eight years of Latin.

While serving as a cavalry officer in the Balkans during World War I, Richard met a fellow officer who gave him the address of an aunt, Nurse Elsa Teleky, who ran a guest home in Switzerland in the small village of Stäfa bordering Lake Zurich. After the end of the war, Richard managed to leave war-torn Vienna and come to Stäfa in the spring of 1919. There he tried in vain to find a job in an architect's office. Finally he was accepted as an apprentice in Europe's acclaimed nursery and landscaping firm, Otto Froebel's Erben, which was located in Zurich. Under the expert guidance of the famous Gustav Ammann, Richard was introduced into the world of plants and trees and site planning, which would have a profound influence on his later development as an architect.

One of the frequent luncheon guests at Elsa Teleky's, where Richard was staying, was old Alfred Niedermann, painter, xylographer, poet, and novelist.

*The Niedermanns*    Alfred Niedermann's son, also named Alfred ("Vaterli"), was an engineer by profession and a chamber music player and excellent pianist by avocation. His wife, Lilly Mueller Niedermann ("Muetterli"), grew up in Ostfriesland on the North Sea. Compassionate, warm, and intelligent, she was the center of a talented and charming family that consisted of four daughters. Dione, the eldest, was born April 14, 1901.

Named after the heroine in her grandfather's first novel, *Dione Peutinger, the Physician of Ingoldstadt,* Dione had just celebrated her eighteenth birthday when in the spring of 1919 she met Richard Neutra. At this stage of her life, Dione was a diligent music student and accomplished musician. Music and the perfection of it filled her whole being. She had started to play the piano at seven and often played four hands with her father. When she was fourteen, her father decided she should also learn to play the cello, since he often had difficulty finding a cellist for his chamber music ensembles. Thus, she received a cello for her fourteenth birthday.

Dione's sister Vreneli, sixteen, attended high school and studied Latin. Doris, fourteen, also played the piano. Regula, the youngest of the family, was the darling of Nurse Teleky and a frequent visitor to the guest home with her grandfather, where she met Richard. Regula, eleven at the time, pleaded with her mother to invite the exciting and handsome foreigner for a visit.

Richard was immediately captivated by this enchanting family, particularly, in the beginning, by the beautiful Lilly who at forty-five was in the bloom of her womanhood.

*Chronology*

1919　Richard tries to find work in Zurich, Switzerland.

1920　Richard meets and falls in love with Dione Niedermann.

1921　Richard corresponds with Dione in Niederweningen, Switzerland, from Vienna, Berlin, and Luckenwalde.

1922　Richard works in Erich Mendelsohn's office in Berlin. Dione studies cello in Berlin. They marry in December.

1923　Richard leaves for the United States in the fall. Dione remains with her parents in Hagen, Germany.

1924　Dione bears a son and joins Richard in June. They stay with Frank Lloyd Wright at Taliesin for three months.

1925　Life in California begins. They live in R. M. Schindler's house in West Los Angeles for five years.

1926　Richard completes his first book, *How America Builds*. He and Schindler work on drawings for an international competition for the League of Nations Palace in Geneva.

1927　*How America Builds* is published. Richard signs a contract to design the town house for Dr. Philip Lovell, called the "Health House."

1928　Richard teaches at the Academy of Modern Art and concentrates on the design and supervision of the Lovell Health House.

1929　Richard becomes a citizen. The Lovell Health House is visited by 1,500 persons.

1930　Richard Neutra travels to Europe by way of the Orient. After receiving her citizenship, Dione and the two boys meet him in London.

Richard returns to the United States in the fall, while Dione stays on with her parents in Switzerland for half a year.

1931　Richard designs buses for the White Motors Company in Cleveland and lectures in New York and Chicago. Dione joins him in June.

1932    Richard succeeds in bringing the "Modern Architecture" show of the New York Museum of Modern Art to Los Angeles. His work is featured along with, among others, Wright, Mies, Gropius, and Le Corbusier.

A benefactor gives him a loan and he designs his own house and office.

Neutra as a youth.

Neutra in 1917 toward the end of the war.

Alfred Niedermann, Jr. (Dione's father), called "Vaterli."

The four Niedermann sisters. *Left to right*: Regula, Dione, Vreneli, Doris.

Dione on her eighteenth birthday.

Lilly Niedermann (Dione's mother), called "Muetterli."

*Richard leaves war-torn Austria, reaching Switzerland in April, where he stays at the rest home of Nurse Elsa Teleky in Stäfa near Zurich.*

*He is introduced to the Niedermann family.*

*Unable to find work in an architect's office, Richard accepts a job as an apprentice in a tree nursery in Zurich.*

*Dione persuades her mother to let her vacation in Stäfa, where the closeness to Richard develops into a romance.*

*Noticing with alarm the growing attachment of Dione to Richard, who has no money and no apparent future, her parents send her to Vienna to continue her cello studies, hoping she will forget him.*

*Richard finds an architectural job in Waedenswil.*

*1919*

*From Richard's Diary*
*after Meeting Dione*

Dione Niedermann, her legs clad in light blue stockings, looking west. I look at her and my impression is "blue stocking," a little princess, somewhat stilted. Another impression: oldest daughter of the house, the most important one. A music student, I hear. Complexion not quite perfect. Quite thin, perhaps seventeen or eighteen years old. Full lips, not very red. Avoids looking straight at you. Hair loose, held by a ribbon, blue I think. Her hair covers her ears. I observe her but do not speak with her.

Later, I ask her: "Do you take singing lessons?" "No, I only listen while a lesson is being given to someone else, in order to learn. I practice the cello, but I would much rather have singing lessons." She sighs. I speak with casual politeness, as a grown-up. After all, I am twenty-seven and she is eighteen.

Dear Mrs. Niedermann                    Zurich, March 1919

*Richard to Muetterli*

Tomorrow, around noon, I shall be at the university. Instead of visiting you after lunch, which might be inconvenient, I'd better write you this letter.

Taking everything into account, I am sorry to find so little occasion to seek a refuge in your family, as I am such a lost fellow, and was always so grateful for all your kind and friendly attitude towards me. (For this I would immediately promise you God's blessing, if I only could believe in your religiosity.)

In this connection, I suddenly pose a question (a question which you have not absolutely to take seriously). Would you permit me, once a week, to be your boarder for lunch? I beg you to take my following sentences quite seriously. Please decline this daredevil proposition if the acceptance poses the least problem to you, so that I could not rejoice without anxiety if you agree. I am not so foolish not to realize that this may pose problems to you at the present time. That I might involve you in a conflict of questionable outcome with nurse Elsa, regarding ration cards. Also, you will have to figure out your costs so that you do not suffer any loss, and permit that I come from work without having a chance to change, and perhaps, occasionally, might arrive in a despondent mood. You will not hurt my feelings if you decline because I hope, in any case, to keep in your good graces. I beg you to give Mr. Niedermann my respects, and remain your devoted

Richard Neutra

*During the spring the sisters and Richard hiked over the mountains from Stäfa to Zurich. They danced, sang, and unanimously voted to elect him an honorary brother, as they had no brother of their own. Late that evening when they returned, Muetterli exclaimed: "Dear me, you all have fallen in love with Richard!" Dione wrote him a letter asking him whom he liked best in the family, hoping he would mention her,*

*Richard to Dione*

Dear Dionerl                                                      Stäfa, May 1919

Such mistrust! Cry shame, I hate it! (Knock my forehead with the back of my left hand.) Oh! Constancy, constancy to the last coda to the very last phrase of the very last spring, this is my burning ambition!! (Those sentences to be read with rushing breath and heaving breast.) Girls, I am all yours! You say it is tiresome that I like you all! I am devoted to all of you, each one in your family and all together as an ensemble, but I am capable of topping it yet. . . . It is your Muetterli I love most of all. I will remain to all of you,                                                      Your Richard

*From Richard's Diary*

Stäfa, May 1919

A quarter of a year has passed since I lived in Zurich. In Trencin, I escaped from the Czechs. I was the last Austrian-Hungarian officer in Slovenia. In the railway car, a peasant discovered my identity (underneath my overcoat), and an Italian legionnaire, with his bayonet, cut off my insignia and publicly made mince-meat of it, at the same time asking my pardon: "Scusi, Signore . . ."

I wandered about in Bruenn for a while, until I reached Vienna via Vlaza Pass. In Vienna, I spent an exhausting month, running from one public office to the next, with one goal in mind: Switzerland. Inland revenue office, police commission, county physician, city hall, consulate, police physician, rate of exchange, bank, giro bank, Swiss consulate, exchange office, tax office, and back again, in the same rotation—the pack is half crazy, dances on its head, and trills on top of it. At no time was it possible to see such an agglomeration of extravagant females and entrancing luxury articles, so that they may stay in fashion.

For weeks I had no lunch, for months really. My shoes are torn, my hat is greasy. For days on end, I ran indefatigably through watery slush, unkempt, without a meal, to look for work, answering newspaper ads, tugging desperately at the aching umbilical cord of our expiring currency.

I suffer all the agony of a senseless lost wanderer, with empty pockets, a beginner who cannot find the beginning.

I am sure that no one has such ragged shoes and wet feet at this early morning hour. I stare into the mass of snowflakes. Is it not absurd that a diligent young person cannot find work while the whole world is in need of work? Housing shortage and slumbering construction offices—how can it be explained? Listlessly I wander about, without a goal, exhausted. No work, no money, no home, no resting place. Lying awake in my bed, during a holiday, from 5:30 on, and gazing through the morning haze into the blue sky beyond, something wells up in me which transcends all that is known or nameable. Quite unforeseen, my self-doubts vanish, and I feel sure of myself, even if I should perish tomorrow. One has to be quite alone to find such communion with the universe. Alone—what a sweet expression—"al-one"!

Stäfa, September 1919

What you are reading in the papers does not give you an accurate picture concerning the European crisis. The building trade is stagnant, as it is everywhere. I know that also in America things are difficult. But here it is beyond description. In addition—in contrast to America—every state here is autocratic, has no raw materials or consumer articles, the turnover is strangled through the horrible inflation, the prohibitions of export and import, the closing of frontiers, and an unimaginable railroad misery which you cannot fathom in your wildest imaginations. For one semester, I took the course with Professor Moser,[2] at the Zurich Polytechnic. I worked in a tree nursery. Here I have found joy of heart, and happiness that will last me for a lifetime. I have worked with the poor, have listened with understanding to what there was to learn here in this nursery. As an artist, I have gained an outlook hardly to be guessed.

Finally, I had a chance to make a start in my profession; I am no longer a bloody beginner.

I understand that in some moments you are tired of the United States, as most people get tired of monotonous situations which they know through and through. But that you contemplate changing for the situation here could only be done out of ignorance. Perhaps Europe is ahead of the United States in its tradition, in a finer and more developed class structure,

---

1. Rudolph M. Schindler (nickname RMS) had studied with Austrian pioneer architect Otto Wagner. Richard met Schindler at the evening seminar of Adolph Loos, another innovator, who had a great influence on Richard's thinking about architecture.
2. Professor Karl Moser taught architecture at Eidgenoessische Technische Hochschule in Zurich.

pragmatism, conservation, treatment of all cultural values, a more spiritual, less hectic life which was the result of a certain affluence. All of this has disappeared, is discredited, refuted.

If only I could get to the United States! How I wish I could! If only to get together with you! But I believe it is impossible to get a visa, and the trip is expensive. Could you give me advice? Could you help me?

*From Richard's Diary*                                    Stäfa, November 1919

I walk through the frosty air to my ugly basement room in Waedenswil. Five different tasks to work on. All empty, cheerless drafting, without rhyme or reason. The façades disgust me, I don't understand the sections, but all has to be carefully copied, like a treasure for posterity. Not even on the floor plan do I detect a creative idea. Everything seems a nightmare. Five years of pointlessness have undermined my ability to see any purpose. Here vitality has vanished. Of what use is all this drafting? Where and to what does it lead? To nothing! Thus I spend my days, glad that at least I am not freezing.

I have learned to work long hours, and so could overcome the deadness of the soul, and I was able to persevere. Although I have been for five years a commanding officer, giving orders, sitting on a horse, day after day, it does not hurt me to be a subordinate, sitting well behaved on a drafting stool.

*Richard to Dione*                                    New York, December 1923
*Four Years Later*

I don't think that I ever before felt so depressed as during these months in Waedenswil. I loved you in deep desperation. I could not, could not see any path, any possibility to get nearer to you. I could not even make a modest start in my profession. Everything seemed to humiliate me. While I sat at my drawing board, behind my boss, I was shaken, tearless, by a terrible inward spasm of silent sobbing. When I opened up the office in the early morning hours, lighted the stove, swept out papers and debris, I rolled on the floor, filled with despair. Writing this, I now can hardly fathom it. I suffered from unspeakable loneliness, exactly at the moment where I had found you and most probably had to lose you again.

This desperation had a physiological foundation, while I incessantly thought of you without any hope whatsoever. I also tried to find consoling reasons why it might be best that we should not get together. But nothing mitigated my passion which did not give me peace for a second—for months—not a second. I often thought of suicide, especially when I saw and heard the evening express train thundering by and disappearing in the distance, after I had worked like a coolie for eleven hours with no hope of coming nearer to my goal. During one supper I had to leave the room precipitously to vomit. A sign, how my nerves were down.

This evening however, provided a certain turning point, because I clearly realized that my end had come if I did not help myself. My wretched condition was not only a sorrowful one, I was not only hopelessly in love, but really ill. I prescribed for myself a certain cure to divert my mind from circling around my constant sorrow and to start thinking of something else. A neighbor had allowed us to use his outhouse as a W.C. From our office we had to walk a few steps through the fresh winter air and up six to eight steps. I used to vault them in two jumps thinking simultaneously, as if planned and somehow as a cure for my illness, of a ship's ladder. I repeated inwardly twice and in some kind of a commando tone, joyfully: "CALI-FORNIA CALLS YOU." "This is the way you will jump onto the boat that will carry you to California," I thought to myself. The words "California calls you" I had seen and read on a lighted advertising sign on Zurich's main street. I kept it in my heart as a suggestive formulation. I thought to myself: "What one wishes ardently has to be repeated in a pregnant sentence and ever so often repeated over and over again."

Stäfa, January 1920

*Richard to Muetterli*

It is now a year that I am in Switzerland. I practically have forgotten all the hardships it took to get here. Only those of the war remain an ever festering wound, because they culminated in a horrible, senseless debacle.

Now I have many acquaintances who take an active interest in my fate and are so kind to me that I don't know how I can ever show my gratitude. But above all, I have found you and your circle . . . I have not had a home since my mother rests in her grave . . .

*While Dione is in Vienna, Richard continues to visit the Niedermanns.*

*Richard is summoned to Vienna to his father's deathbed. Before he leaves he tells Muetterli of his love for Dione and asks permission to visit her while he is in Vienna. Muetterli consents with the proviso that he treat her like a sister.*

*After four weeks of enjoying Vienna with Richard, Dione returns to her parents, who now live in Niederweningen, a small rural village near Zurich.*

*Richard finds a job with the Society of Friends, where he meets an American social worker, Frances Toplitz, with whom he develops a lifelong friendship.*

*In September Richard finds an architectural job in Berlin, but the firm is forced to let him go when it loses a large design commission. In the meantime, Dione and Muetterli visit him.*

*Richard to Muetterli*

Dione came to see us for five minutes, during a streetcar change. She wore her little hat, decorated with a red ribbon, which is so becoming to her. She wore it today while she was photographed together with Korngold.[1] Now she has two more days in Vienna, and then something new starts for her, and her Muetterli. Heaven will help her that all will turn out well, because we so ardently wish for it. Is it not so, Muetterli?

I am proud that I was worthy of the good opinion she has about me, and I shall be in need to have it from many others. This I wish to be my basis for everything else. It is no small prayer, since I am convinced that it contains the essence of inner *and* outer success. Opportunities await us that should be seized, while others better be ignored; vexations shall test our resistence; small successes and temptations prepare us for the inevitable disappointments. Much practice is needed to learn resignation.

Vienna, March 1920   *Richard to Muetterli*

I had the great thrill to hear Erich Korngold. I understand perfectly well all the objections one could voice against him.

"Die Neue Freie Presse" is indeed his paternal home. His exuberance, his wit, which he richly mixes with his pathos, originate from the same source. But he *is* a human being. I am happy to have had a chance not

---

1. Erich Korngold was a "wunderkind," wrote several operas, and became a well-known composer.

only to hear him but to see him, and there was for me a lot to observe—from his divergent starry eyes to his pale corpulence, which penetrates the instrument by fits and starts to dissolve into a languid loosening up of tension. His roaring agitation produces a thin thread of spittle dropping from his wide open mouth. This is not beautiful but, strangely, does not seem abhorrent to the beholder. At first he played wonderfully from Mahler's "Lied von der Erde." Perhaps I was even more fascinated and spellbound, as it was the first time for me that I had ever heard anything like it. I even forgot that all this emanates after all from an ordinary piano. I am sure you will deride me if I confess that I, finally, even fell in love with his voice, which he mistreats so outrageously. Once harsh, puffed up, then strident and overturning into a pitiful falsetto.

*From Richard's Diary*                                                 Vienna, April 1920

I suffer from an agonizing depression. I have lost interest in my job at the Society of Friends, but cannot exist without this job. I am too tired to wish for anything. These depressions follow each other faster and faster. I have lost my best time, my best strength. I shall not be able to achieve anything worthwhile. The obstacles are insurmountable. I am supposed to make decisions and choose between matters of indifference. I don't want to, I am no longer able to. For six years I have been held back from any worthwhile work. I am frightfully isolated—I don't want company. I have no social contacts. No work, no soul, no friend, no outlook. I shall go to bed.

I only see drudgery in front of me, no breath of fresh air. It appears that my fearful misgivings have not deceived me, and I shall founder. I am without strength, I feel childish, like crying. I feel somewhat relieved to write it down in legible letters.

*Dione to Richard*                                                Niederweningen, May 1920

You always told me that you wanted to make me happy. Now you have done it. You have given me SO many worthwhile things to think about on my way back to Muetterli. I feel so enriched! Everybody tells me how happy I look. I can give something to everybody. Does it not make you glad to know that you are improving my character? Oh, my dear Richard, how delighted I am in the thought that one day we shall finally be together, that I will be able to tell you everything with no one to disturb us. In Vienna I was often too restless, too concerned, thinking of our separation.

*Richard to Dione*                                                     Vienna, May 1920

After we had experienced a beautiful, tiring day, as usual, we took the streetcar. The spring was still quite new, lilacs blooming in the park. There is no shadow on me because I was able to keep a tight rein on myself. (Oh, God, I could imagine how I would feel unfettered, dear Dionerl.) Even if you cannot quite understand it now, I hope you realize that I treated you properly and so my conscience is clear. I knew it precisely and am sure you will later comprehend it along with me. Then you will have an altogether lucid and lighthearted memory of that time.

Niederweningen, May 1920 *From Dione's Diary*

I rack my brain to recall a moment in which Richard told me that he loved me. But it is in vain. When I hear the love songs of Schumann or of other composers, I always think how different he is: so sensible, so controlled, reserved. Why should I not imagine that in reality it is Muetterli whom he loves, while he only likes me? After all, I am her daughter. But I am not quite sure. Perhaps he is reserved because everything is so insecure. Perhaps he would be very different once we were married, or does my imagination play tricks on me because I hope for romance? I simply don't know.

Zurich, May 1920 *Dione to Richard*

I was in town today and had a singing lesson. Afterwards I visited Wille,[2] my mother's physician. She always wants me to talk about you. I told her about my apprehensions regarding your being so reserved. She thought this was a sign of great devotion, that you did not want to make me unhappy for a period that might be of long duration and that there are few men in this world who would be capable of such restraint. Instinctively I felt this to be true but was afraid that my hope was illusory and to my own advantage. I thought it was too presumptuous of me to assume that you restrained yourself out of love for me. My talk with Wille was very comforting to me.

Vienna, May 1920 *Richard to Dione*

Pentecost: I took the steam tramway to Mödling but when I came home in the evening—how do you think I felt that night as I went to bed, dear Dionerl? I don't want to spend my time writing about it. But the fact that I have to steal the time from work to write you (in the evening as an exhausted man I don't want to write) must show you that the conducive order and beneficial strength to demand the best in us is threatened.

I was so happy to notice that you are *completely* aware of not only how you must write to me but what you must strive to become. No dissembling of anxious tears on account of me; you *must* not shed them. *Never* must sorrowful thoughts about me cause you to resort to either idle diversions or even work in order to deflect these thoughts. If we have any right to think about each other, then our reflections must be *bright*. They must be thoughts that intensify happy moments and ease hard work. Look at me, dear Dione. If it is ever true that any situation is only as we comprehend it, certainly in our case it *is* so! *This is not a time for sorrowing, this is a time*

---

2. Wille—Dr. Wildenow, a gynecologist—was Muetterli's physician and a friend of the family.

*for aspiring*. It is a time full of hope, a time in which we concentrate all our energies, which must not be deflected uselessly but joyfully built into the future.

Observe a certain regularity and never forget there is *no* danger, no critical mishap, for anyone whose nerves remain steady. This, one can achieve with diligence and purpose, a little good health assumed, but especially if there is a human being around who ardently wishes it. Without actually becoming secretive, I would advise you to keep more to yourself. Also, Dionerl, do not indulge in your dreams too much. Not that they are sinful, but perhaps they are not quite fair. These are all precepts which *I* am supposed to fulfill, *I* who struggle so hard in order to make a beginning. Don't you notice that you make demands from one who has his own hands full, who has to get the mortification out of his own mind, that he is powerless? Can I keep silent as if this, your attitude was harmless? If you believe that you are building castles in the air, don't you believe that it is *I* who should realize them, that you in the final analysis may only be weaving a lovely ornament around them? This is not sensible talk to someone in my situation.

*Richard to Dione*                                                    Vienna, May 1920

I can no longer stomach it. Again you write me that what concerns you is not important to me. Before that, you wrote me that I left you in limbo or something similar. Did I treat you badly by chance? Without hesitating one heartbeat I would have given you my blood to drink on that evening when you sobbingly told me that I did not want to make you happy on that day or any subsequent one. No, I have never forgotten you for one moment, not even in my present turmoil.

But you wrote me that you preferred a man who had no work in town but instead had a lovely little house in the country, which, however, requires a lot of money. Is it harsh when I demonstrate through my silence that I do not concur with your castles in the air that become ever more costly, like villas in the country or leisure time? It is not enough that you put aside your automobile goggles for the time being or the thought of driving a car. Your castles in the air are a mockery of my present situation and, thus, I reject them. If this is harsh for you, it is at least honest and I do not want by silence to encourage you to invent ever more agreeable material underpinnings for your happiness. Nobody shall ever be able to say that I had allowed you to ignore my circumstances.

I know money does not interest you and that you do not have a man with money in mind, but you are not aware that what you wish for does indeed cost money. I can picture the man who can fulfill your dreams, what you call "castles in the air." He looks very different from me and surely has at least 150,000 francs at his disposal. Do not speak of misunderstandings! This is no misunderstanding. In no case does it make your personality better and more generous, not for me, not for others, when you wish for yourself the agreeable, even when tastefully conceived. Think thus of the future: I want to bring sacrifices, sacrifices, sacrifices, one *sweeter* than the other and thus no sacrifice at all. Give up all trifles and keep things in hand. I can no longer stand the thought that you do not joyfully recognize that I want the best for you and that to some extent I have succeeded. You understand me better with your heart than with your mind.

Dear, dear Dionerl, all of this no longer bothers me because you love me and you want the best for me. This is my unshakable conviction. If you err occasionally in your tone, I blame myself for it. This, however, should not concern us. If one has love for an instrument, one learns how to handle it. The finer it is, the more patience and devotion it requires. When I watched you playing the cello, darling Dione, I often speculated how much more difficult and demanding it is to learn to know a human being.

If you think of the future, think of it in terms of sacrifice. Do not think of a comfortable life.

It is right that you praise my endeavors. Keep on praising. It does my soul good. *You* should always divine the good in me. (You are not as yet so sophisticated as to be able to criticise me.)

Vienna, June 1920

Be calm, my Dionerl. I can see that your heart pains you; how else could you write me that I would a priori not side with you and other such sad nonsense as that for my sake you would give up all thoughts of beautiful dresses. "Must I also give this up?" you ask in a tearful voice. Come on, darling, hug me, give me a kiss, and have no imaginary sorrow. It's already out of mind, is it not? I thank you for every line you write. Just recently I have been thinking how I would like to dress you beautifully. I hit upon plissé and flounces, which would be lovely for you as long as your dress remains unpretentious. *That* it should always be, even if the material is very expensive. Buy all the shoes your heart desires. Don't imagine that I want to hamper your free life and drive.

Vienna, June 1920

Dione, I don't know if it can really be as you describe your castles in the air, whether you can enjoy them in fantasy, without their becoming reality. I strongly believe—can you see how I look at you threateningly, dear heart—that you are in earnest when you say that an industrious life interests you more than any beautiful castle. *I believe you, Dione.* You in turn must believe me when I say that such an attitude can only be useful to you. If there is something wonderful to wish for, surely it is I who wish it for you. I wish you all the best and would be surprised if you disagreed. Of course, wishing alone is not enough and so you have decided that you yourself will dig in to dig yourself out.

Vienna, June 1920

I simply cannot tell you how much I felt with you in everything you wrote in your last two letters. I was very moved with the way in which you

15

described how you miss me and when you ask how I know that you do not suffer any privations. My dear girl, look, I know what I know and beg you with all my heart to keep peace with yourself. That you have a mild temperament which will not fling you into painful crossroads is a blessing. Don't believe in a frenzied transport for you or for anybody else. Real love will also have in its greatest glow a quiet inner core and a sensitive awareness of self and not "après nous le deluge" for our souls.

*Richard to Dione*                                                    Vienna, July 1920

To get something else than music and "castles in the air" into your head, I have figured out another task for you. You will have something real to dream about, namely construction of a room, the furnishing of a space. A floor plan can be marvelous, or intimate, simple, tricky, thought out grandly into the smallest detail, or narrow-minded. It can even by joyful or comical.

I enclose a floorplan, one of many which I figured out for an Englishman who has many continental tendencies. (Unfortunately, it will not be realized as I cannot travel there.) You and Muetterli have now so much time that you can concentrate fully on this little sketch which I have translated for you into German. The compass card, in the right lower corner, shows you the wind directions. The red arrow shows you how you reach the entrance over a few steps. The entrance is protected against the weather by a low protruding wall, and a tree. Are you in the picture? It would give me a great joy. Every proper female is at heart a small-house architect. The diagonal pencil drawings show the swing of the doors. Through an entrance foyer that shields from the wind, you enter the kitchen at right, and at left the hall. Here is a door to the W.C., a stairway to the upper floor; there also is a clothes closet, window seat and a bench between a cupboard holding flower pots. From here, another entrance, into the owner's study. Bookshelves surround the writing desk; then there is the piano room with a corner window seat. From here, or from the other side of the hall, one enters the dining room, which in addition has a lovely fireplace corner with upholstered chairs, opening onto a terrace protected by trees.

Because of the kitchen smells, there is no direct connection between dining room and kitchen. Kitchen stove and fireplace are placed back to back on account of their joint chimney.

In order not to frighten you too much, I am not sending you the floor plans showing the basement with laundry, or the upper floor with bath and bedrooms, so not to deter you from a real study of the first floor. To make a real study means to become as familiar with the house as if one were living there oneself. Imagine the placing of the furniture, the relationship of window areas and the light influx. How the inhabitants might be distributed at 11 A.M., 3 P.M., or 7 P.M. The ceiling is only 250 centimeters above the floor. One has also to imagine winter and summer. Perhaps you would like to make practical suggestions about rearranging the furniture? Put a transparent paper over the drawing and try to make changes. I shall be most grateful to Muetterli if she gives it a thorough scrutiny. (Eventually I will let her know what I think of her suggestions.)

Your letter gave me enormous pleasure. Where shall I begin? In any case, I shall write in depth. First, about the house plans. This line signifies a two-minute pause of reflection. Reflection whether I, as an adopted son, can allow myself to be free and easy with you. Dear Muetterli, you are a splendid woman. Your proposals gave me such pleasure and I listened to them with pointed ears. Your sound proposals illuminate my brain and heart. Not so much that they contain something shatteringly new, but that we can understand each other so uncommonly well in this matter, dear Muetterli.

However, now come with me, and let's look at the plans. Thus: Windowsill to be wide, the lower part of the window frame high, to accommodate a bottle with a stopper, so that when opening the window, it does not have to be removed? How shall we treat the surface—where do you want to put flowerpots, and water them? Perhaps with sheet metal and gravel over it, or what else? Oh, Muetterli, I shall be so glad to consider a sewing room! Does one absolutely sew more often during winter than summer? Muetterli, I expected that you would criticize the position of the range. Very good. The light influx is bad, but how you positioned it, it is no better; also, the swing of the door is unfavorable, and might bother the cook, even if opening the door into the dining room which surely would be incorrect. Furthermore kitchen odors would invade the dining room. There is no vent. Don't you like a free-standing range? Is it detrimental to the pantry if two flues run up in a wall? Is my drainboard not much too far from the dining room? It is impossible to have the toilet door open directly into this much used hall. The wardrobe must be situated between entrance door and hall, on account of winter weather. The writing desk must never be placed in such a way that the writer has a door at his back, and thus an entering visitor can surprise him. Dear Muetterli and Dione, it is true that a grand piano could suffer if placed alongside a badly insulated wall. However, as you have placed it now, the player cannot see his score as he faces the bright window. The wide, low couch is wonderful, darling Muetterli; I put a blanket over you, assuming you have already removed your shoes?

The dining room might not get enough light if you place a covered glazed porch in front of it. A modern dining room must be light, and not dark like a gothic one. To be sure, I would love to enjoy the morning sun in your porch at breakfast time. Washed and brushed from navel to toe, ever so smoothly shaved, wearing a fresh white shirt and a gay necktie beneath a head free of worries, Dionerl being the one to serve breakfast.

But Muetterli. such a long bench has its drawbacks when everybody has to rise and strain to make room for a latecomer. For the one sitting, comfortably opposite on a chair, this must be a comical spectacle. To place the older, portly ladies on the chairs prevents the younger girls to give a hand, jump up, to get the forgotten bread, if they sit squeezed in between others. Where do we place the lady of the house? Such a cozy dining corner with bench cries out for a sedate mistress of the house. No? Or is it just right for a young and lovely one? Oh, Muetterli! One could make the cushion covers so colorful that they cry out for a children's party. However, not only children, also a few grown-ups would fit excellently. My Muetterli, you are a true female, and immediately you adopt the plan with body and soul as if you were living in this air-castle. However, we architects have to wreck our brain for others. For you, dear Muetterli, I would work very cheaply, just cover my costs, but first I have to have the chance to thoroughly design for a few other people.

*Richard to Dione*

Vienna, July 1920.

I have not forgotten your repeated question to explain to you three-dimensional effectiveness of a building, but wanted to delay the answer. However, in order not to test the durability of your thirst for knowledge, briefly this: A well-designed house affects our entire sense of space. It is composed of many ingredients as I explained to you on one of our walks. A sense of smell, of touch, of hearing, of temperature *and* the eye, also an obscure sense for materials. This sense guesses whether a third dimension is filled with green cottage cheese or green marble, even if the surface appears to be similar. A current of air, a draft, a breeze, felt when strolling through the gallery of a cloister, or the rising air in the Dome of Milan, the exhalation of plaster, stone, heated by the sun, a musty basement, or underground water odor in a crypt; a scent of iron, laquer, wood stains, the deposits of water vapor on window panes, the reverberation of my steps, the echo from tapestries or flagstones, the faint, steady stream of air through a perforated tower, all this affects the heart more than a view. The coolness, the dryness, their opposites, and dear God, how much else, speak to our sense of space, and to our eyes besides. The well of a staircase in Genoa can be magnificent for a layman, but *never* so in a photograph, in a drawing. A space affects the senses three-dimensionally, not as pitifully drawn on a flat surface. A garden too is a space. A hundred objects look beautiful on a photograph, a thousand others are *different* in reality. An apple tree seen while ascending a path on a certain spot, five meters before climbing over a summit, can be a greater mystery than all ghosts taken together. What is it that moves one so deeply everytime one reaches that certain spot?

I believe that space has validity, because I am an architect, and even more, because I am a human being. But believe me, dear Dione, there is more to it. More to space and time as externally perceived.

*Richard to Dione*

Vienna, July 1920

Another Sunday, and I stayed in all day. Only towards the evening did I go to the Schönbrunn Park, where I spent an hour in the Botanical Garden. Dear Dione, when I read the names of plants, the time in Zurich became very vivid in my memory. Names play a great role in our recollections. I thought of small occurrences and facts which make you come alive for me. Would you like to write down what you remember of our time together in Vienna? I wish it may have been a beautiful and hopeful memory, my child. These were rich weeks considering external happenings too.

I walked towards Mödling. I did not take one of the main park arteries, but went around a huge hanging beech tree that rose up like a mountain towards a minor part of the park. Are you listening, Dione? What I am now going to recount is not a fairy tale. I suddenly had an unfathomable experience. It was after a sultry rain, towards evening, similar to when I lifted you up onto a stone bench near the Volière. Can you remember this evening, quietly and surely? Dione, I walked for an hour into the evening, always through unknown parts of the park, always along paths that were as foreign to my foot as they were to my memory, until my limbs were exhausted. Occasionally I traversed a main artery which, however, also looked strange to me in this context. Otherwise, I wandered through a marvelous foreign park, foreign by magic, *foreign like by magic*! Dione.

For an hour I walked on a path I had never seen before, between three-meter-high beech hedges. On a diagonal path, arched over, and ending into green enclosures, an unending variety, richer and more manifold than I am capable of describing it. The evening light illuminated one side of these trimmed masses of foliage, while the other side stood in dark blue shadow, while night fell. I walked and walked through quite a wide avenue, vaulted over by trees, on a path between hedges that were double a man's height, and I continued for about 300 feet more. From a labyrinth of dwarfed paths, I suddenly came to a wide open space, surrounded by high cut beech hedges, and a piece of lawn of about 60 by 100 feet, under a tremendous evening sky towards which the scent of sweet hay rose from various spots. I continued walking, again on small paths into narrow enclosures. An entanglement of green paths and enclosures which only a bird could understand, flying over it. I wandered on with open eyes, in various directions, full of wonder and astonishment. I came to a place surrounded by huge chestnut trees. In the center, a stone basin full of water, and in the middle, a baroque stone figure of a child, naked and joyful. Dione, imagine, there is in Schönbrunn Park a huge eliptical water pond of 20–25 feet *and I have never seen it before*. My Dionerl, just as if one walked daily, inattentively, along a wall, past a little door, without noticing it, until one happy hour one found this door open, and one could look into a fairy garden. Or, as if a treasure started to glow mildly in a heart near one. As if today I had fulfilled some kind of condition, had absolved some kind of debt, so that suddenly this garden became visible to me and let me enter.

Oh my Dionerl, that you could not experience this with me! So I can only tell you about it. This was no coincidence, it means something, and the interpretation grew by itself out of my soul.

Vienna, July 1920

*Richard to Dione*

I gladly imagine how you submerged yourself in playing the Mozart sonata. I want to tell you how submerged in music I am myself, more than since many years. Dear Dione, remember: Whenever you make beautiful music, you do it for me, too, at least I thank you for it. I imagine with delight how marvelous it must be to have someone who, in order to please me, would play something so many times, until I know every note by heart. In this respect I am very slow, just like trying to look at a painting.

To see it once never satisfies me. Next Sunday, I shall go again to hear church music.

*Richard to Dione*

Vienna, July 1920

Sunday I heard Mozart in St. Peter's. Such a tremendous domed church of such height can rarely be acoustically perfect and still; such an interior is the fitting frame for this music as far as a human mind can long for it. Often one has compared the art of music with the art of architecture and vice versa. Is it necessary to look for similarities in order to understand how these powerful soul impacts can melt into each other? Slight reverberations retard the movement and significant form of the melody, as if one tone was reluctant to follow the next, or give way to it. This produces a solemn weightiness. How the soul must soar when one stands on the choir loft, sings down into this wonderous space and up into the dome. After the "Ite Mina Est" the organ starts to bellow its wild dissonances so that everything vibrates. To the eye nothing is visible, but suddenly the space seems to be filled with demonic fumes. Then the service ends and the mundane Sunday has the word. A quiet Sunday makes me so happy after seven days of work. Leisure is marvelous, as is work, and one cannot exist without the other. For the one who rests from his labors, the scent of the linden tree fills his soul more stirringly and gives it passionate strength and stillness at the same time. As one lives, balancing on a razor's edge, it is better to look up than down and to be convinced that a downward tumble is not at all possible.

*Richard to Dione*

Vienna, September 1920

It is approximately the same hour as at that time and I lie on the ground, on the same spot on the grass, you know, dear Dione, on our meadow. I came on the same path as at that time. Only for minutes did it seem strange to me, but then I recognized many stones, trees, views from the side, bends in the road, descents and ascents. If you could look at me now, there would be no need to say anything, but now I must write it and tell you: Dione, be very *serious*, I have this to tell you. I don't want to conjure any sentimental memories in your soul, I mean it quite differently. Continue reading. Here are the same molehills and the meadow near me swells up. But, of course, the myriads of anemone flowers are gone and in their stead are meadow saffrons and autumn crocuses. But not as many as our spring flowers, before summer, half a year ago. Many of the deciduous trees at the lower edge of the meadow have yellowed; the outline of the mountains in the background, which we observed through our binoculars, embrace this beautiful scene as peacefully as it did then. At that time a birch tree and a fir, as well as some beech shrubs, stood in the foreground. Now I lie before them, dear Dione. Also today the sun disappears behind the trees, so that I must move, just as we had to move. When I rise I see also now over the lower edge of the meadow to the left suddenly a street crossing and above it further still the distant mountains. Of noises I hear, I notice first the wind in the foliage near me. It moves along the timberline; it murmurs through the more distant copses and rustles full and steady through the distant slopes. A cricket. Two crickets. A big fly buzzes around my head and I see her shadow on my white paper. Passing bird sounds, also out of the forest.

It is hazy and warm and has rained. There are more flies, several birds are singing and chirping. Hardly any movement of air. I walked on our path, quite frequently with eyes closed. Dear Dione, at that time I was happy in my innermost soul, not only now in my memory. Meanwhile I am sure you have understood that to know the good in me we need a quiet space of time rather than short hectic weeks. This is probably also true regarding my shortcomings.

This I wanted to tell you: Every human being can experience all sorts of things, either by accident or by inquisitive striving, but only *certain things lie clearly on the inner track* and are interconnected through a beautiful continuity which in memory appears to be a wholesome totality. Only this! First of all only *this* is in a higher sense experienced and through this can the lovely harmony be fulfilled which may never be found in a total rough-hewn whole life.

Berlin, October 1920

I think of you with all my heart. And my deep wish is that Dione remains healthy. I kiss your hand.

Last month I worked very hard, and was really able to get for myself a two weeks vacation, for the end of September. In order to get it, I had worked beyond my endurance, and so my boss made it possible. At the same time, I had received a vague offer from a furniture factory. I was already on my way to the streetcar, suitcase in hand, to start my vacation in my brother's sanatorium in Baden, when an urgent phone call brought me back. I was told I could get a position in a central heating firm, which I had tried to get for half a year. I would be in a somewhat leading position, and the work seemed interesting. I begged them to let me first take my vacation.

I went to Baden, spent three days there, during which I ate like a cannibal without ever filling up. I bet you never saw anybody gorge himself like that. Soon everybody thought I started to bloom and lose my haggard looks. Then my brother Siegfried phoned from Vienna that he had received a telegram from my friend Ernst Freud[3] in Berlin: "Position available in Berlin. Telegraph if interested." An hour later, I answered him: "Will take position, wire date."

I had no visa, no German money, had not given up my position at the Mission, and was out of Vienna. I wrote a letter to Ernst Freud. Meanwhile, another telegram arrived from him: "Start work immediately." Early the next morning, I went to Vienna, ran to the American consulate,

3. Ernst Freud was the son of Sigmund Freud. Ernst and Richard went to college together and remained lifelong friends.

visited the central heating firm, packed all my things, went to see my sister, did a hundred other errands, bought a railway ticket, spent two nights on the train, missed a connection, and five days after the first telegram, I presented myself to my new bosses.

*Muetterli and Dione visit Richard in Berlin for a few days.*

*Richard to Muetterli and Dione*

Berlin, October 1920

After bringing you to your train, I walked back, mounted the stairs, heavy-footed, entered my room, turned on the light, sat down, took off my coat, and went to bed. It was about 7:30 P.M. Is it your impression that grief is a good sleeping remedy? Perhaps so, but my mind started to mull around. Here I was, without work, without a job, without an acquaintance, without a friend in this tremendous metropolis, with no money or any prospects. Also winter was standing before the door, cold and sinister. When, oh, when shall I ever find a pursuit approximately near my *inner* path?

All these thoughts crossed my mind. Here it was already three years after the war. In Albania and a thousand other godforsaken places, I had waited for four years for the war's ending, ill and powerless. While I was waiting, I had accomplished crazy tasks with youthful enthusiasm; I pulled the covers over my head and said to myself: "At the moment your life is not endangered, but the human beings, whom you treasure most, have now left."

True—I was alone, but in no life danger. True—I also had a bed and was not afoot since forty-eight hours, with five cannons and eighty horses, trying to worm my way upward in deepest darkness and pouring rain, while once the dawn broke, the sun shone, the enemy on the opposite ridge started to shell us. As one completely exhausted, I was indifferent to any danger. I gave my orders quietly, helped to pull the heavy howitzer, while the weapon carrier lay already in the ditch. When I heard the whistling of the approaching shells, I bellowed, "Cover," in order to show my people that I had not yet lost my mind. Of course, the wheel-driver with his two horses could not jump behind a rock and the poor critters put their heads together. A few detonations fell right in front of us. I shouted, "Pull, get going," because for heaven's sake, here we could not linger. We had not slept for thirty-six hours, had not a stitch of dry clothing on us and just now the damned, so often mended shafts broke again. This happened on the mountain Glumina, 900 meters above Trebinschitza Gorge in Albania.

But now I was lying in my own bed and, come morning, could walk up and down endless streets to look for work.

Then came a very desperate period. I knew that I was not forsaken, but still 100,000 minutes were solitary ones and at this stage of life I am ready to give and receive love.

*Dione to Richard after Visit to Berlin*

Niederweningen, October 1920

I would like you to find a greeting from me before you go to sleep. Try to imagine how Muetterli and I sit in the train thinking of you with closed eyes as we travel farther and farther away from you. When you fall asleep, we shall still be sitting in the train. No unwashed Dionerl will come to bring breakfast into your room. For you it will be like a dream because your usual life will continue, at least for the time being. But I shall have a few agitated days in front of me before I am able to settle down, taking time to reflect upon everything.

When you warmed my feet one evening, you asked me whether I did not have a great bodily longing for you. While in Vienna, yes, and in the beginning in Niederweningen likewise, but not anymore. When I am together with you, my heart feels at peace and I am happy. This is surely preferable to the terrible restlessness I feel when we are apart. A longing to commune with your soul I always have, but this is not distressing, it is rather a blessing.

Berlin, October 1920

*Richard to Dione*

I found your letter only Thursday morning in the pocket of my night-shirt. To be lonely is not so terrible for me. Half of my conscious life I have been lonely. I separate myself from exterior happenings, choosing locations and times that are beautiful, enticing. I immerse myself in long stretches of enjoyable work. You are somewhat aware that many things have come into my life with and against my will, although I am not that old. They have enlarged my horizon, my outlook. They stand around me like many vessels into which I can pour whatever I can scoop up from my inner being. I want to confide in you and you must keep it to yourself. (Do you understand?) As a human being I do not think of myself in a modest or halfhearted manner. I alone know how my heart and spirit can soar and cover a wide span of time. I believe that the starry sky does not represent a canvas with light-holes in it, a shadow, not the night, a wall, not a wall. I consider myself a wise and superior soul, higher than any exterior calling. However, it is prudent to view strength and steadfastness as something relative and always to be aware that there are greater powers beyond them. Also, my present situation is surely not one to produce suspicion that I might be presumptuous. As to my future, I must and will think of it only with diffidence. This I have learned in the past six years, important years in which I might have learned something more useful if my hands and head had not been inhibited. Even if I should be a complete failure, my belief in myself is unshakable. I believe my parents or a divine providence have given me a valuable ability, but that on the other hand, there is no defense against exterior circumstances.

Dear Dione, I hope you will not be sad when I tell you that I love your hair long, even if you put it up during the day. I tell you this only because it is your right to thus make me happy and you repeatedly said that you wanted to please my flesh and blood. In return, however, I am unable to promise what sort of form I may eventually assume.

Niederweningen, October 1920

*Dione to Richard*

I am so glad to be home again. I know you want me to be a nimble spirit, always ready to be off and on the move. Although it is wonderful to have mobility, to be able to leave a certain place without a pang in order to see a new piece of the world, I still find solace in the thought that somewhere there should be a place where I could seek refuge. It is, of course, possible that I think thus momentarily because I now feel traveling from one spot to another may become too tiring. Right now I notice it especially because I am so relieved to be home again.

I am not at all sad, if I don't please you with my hair cut short, on the contrary. But I am sad that you do not want to savor human beauty also with your soul. Altogether I do not understand how you can separate body and soul. If you asked me whether I did not love your soul more than your body, I would not know how to answer you, because how should I know it? I don't know whether this is so, especially as far as you are concerned, or whether it is a male characteristic that they make this distinction as far as women are concerned? With me surely one flows into the other and I *always* love body and soul *together*. When I made breakfast for you, I did not speculate that I did this for your body, but simply for Richard. When I sang a song for you, I did not think of your soul, but simply of Richard. When I kissed you, I did not think of your body, but again about my dear Richard, who is always a body with a soul, never only one or the other. To separate the two, I can only then understand when the soul wants to soar. Have you never thought about it, whether my soul can soar with yours, or at least not pull it down? As yet, I don't want to think about it.

*Richard to Dione*

Berlin, October 1920

Now the moon is already half full again. When you came to see me, it was full. Do you see it through your window?

Before you came to Berlin, you begged me beforehand in writing not to take you to the art museum, while I, meanwhile, had looked at every painting with you in mind and happy in this thought. Just as your mother could only see it as a troublesome "program," that I wanted to take you to a church concert.

She supposedly told you it did not matter what I told you or what I begged you to do, as it was too cumbersome. What would happen, if in the course of time I had to subject you to difficulties or even risks? Are you then going to tell me: "I thought about it and that must suffice you, my darling, because I was told . . ." Dear Dione, in certain matters nobody can advise you; not even what is important or unimportant. If you now think that here lies the slightest reproach for your mother, then you would have misunderstood me completely. It is *you*, to whom I am directing these words. Yes, imagine! It is you, whom it concerns! You have the most wonderful mother whom you can emulate. You cannot be thankful enough that so far you can live in her house. Pray for it that she remains palpable and tangible. But how you should deal with your beloved, *that* you have to find out for yourself and there even the best mother might overlook something and if she is as fun loving as yours, might take certain things not seriously enough.

My dear Dione, don't be for one minute downhearted about all this.

I told you from the beginning that I have full confidence in you and the best I can give you is to learn to have confidence in yourself. Believe in yourself, as I believe in you.

Here in Berlin it was as wonderful to be together again as always when it was granted to us, whether here, there or anywhere. Woe onto me should I ever forget it. How could I tell you this, if I wanted to nag you unnecessarily? What kind of an influence is this when I say: "Develop, be yourself, *my* Dione Niedermann, which I want to honor more than any other person?"

Can you feel it, that *because* I honor you so highly, I have some value for you? To love you only, would be little in comparison. Can you remember when I told you on the return from our night excursion: "For love alone one need not be grateful"? Also don't believe that I am a particularly complicated person; I have no more secrets for you than any other.

Dear, dear Dione, now I want to tell you that those minutes we sat in that hall and you gazed towards Botticelli's *Madonna* that this was a marvelous moment for me. I felt so strongly that I had succeeded to lead you somehow in front of an opening, through which you could see another world, the real world, forgetting all the misery around us. How could your mother or anybody else possibly understand what this means to me or to us? Perhaps they imagine I want to discuss art history with you or educate your taste. However, if one only passes through a city, if one has only a few days time, to be together, is it, therefore, not exaggerated, even perhaps pedantic, to insist? How does one expect a young girl to be interested or have eyes for buildings, spaces, pictures, or what have you? Oh, my dear Dione, what if my memory holds just such moments most strongly? To the devil with art history! Your mother believes I would cherish a friend, educated in art history, but you know that I care a damn about such training in this real honest-to-goodness world of art, real art. One can discuss it endlessly, but only after loving and experiencing it through long periods. Even if I can see it with you only for a fraction of time, it must suffice for the vast, mysterious illumination it can bring.

Did I perhaps want to discuss with you that Botticelli was not the greatest artist? From where he came, and who followed him? No. But I wanted you to recognize that this was one wonderful voice in the symphony of a million voices that constitute the *real* world. Believe me, dear Dione, I mean well, and that whoever believes I am exaggerating to take you to such experiences does not give you good advice. I am now completely in the sphere of influence of the old Italian masters with their melodic harmonies and their eternal devout innocence. It should be wonderful to build a structure to house these choirs as the Greeks did. Sometimes, I believe you too will be able to see this. Don't fret, I surely will find the way back, enriched without having lost my path. The unreal life, I mean the "practical" one which is in reality quite impractical, keeps one in balance. In the seventeenth century it happened for the first time that the art and culture of the baroque period touched all the people in the world. Surely today something *decisive* in the way of thinking and expression has validity, where real people live in the real today and harbor the future. All nationalism is only a delusion, a romantic love for home and country in that moment where it resists the first pregnant idea of world citizenship. All politics is a shadow play, only that it casts terrible shadows. All stock-exchange vortexes are brilliant fireworks that cremate the skeletons of millions of individuals while beyond that other events take their course.

. . . Despite the disgust with our period we have to say *yes* to it and recognize that it is brimfull of possibilities (which logically grow out of it), as they did at *all* times. Let's give a toast to understanding, kindness, and *love*!

*Dione to Richard*

Niederweningen, October 1920

Your reproach is very justified and I have made a firm resolution to be more flexible in the future, as this seems to be the point in question.

I *love* to go with you to museums. I cannot now imagine why I wrote you in the negative. By the way, I find it remarkable that everything you propose is always wonderful. So I can calmly let you take the lead. Muetterli calls this being completely "your creature," my always agreeing with what you propose. If I am convinced that what you propose is right, then why should it mean that I have no free will of my own? By the way, I smile inwardly when I hear such opinions expressed.

I must continually ponder over a statement you once made to Muetterli, namely that you needed a stupid wife. I wonder what you would do with such a one! Occasionally I smile wondering how a stupid wife would have reacted to your explanation of Einstein's relativity theory, when even I, and I don't believe one could consider me downright stupid, was wretchedly desolate because I could not follow you.

*Richard to Dione*

Berlin, October 1920

You asked me to describe to you how I spend my day. My day is this: While my room is put in order, I take a half-hour walk. Today I read your loving letter in the Kleistpark. Then, I work in my room until noon, have lunch, and continue working. When it gets dark, I go to the library near the Potsdamer Platz, a thirty-five minute walk. At a quarter-to-nine I return, have supper. I am not allowed to use light after that time. Thursday I took the streetcar at 7:30 P.M. to hear a Bach concert.

May God be with you Dionerl!

*Dione to Richard*

Niederweningen, December 1920

Now I always rise at 7:15 A.M. It is very cold when I wash myself in the laundry room. Occasionally I balk, but because I have decided to do it, I stick to it. Today I hurried in order to get away at 8:30 to fetch the morning milk. Outside it was foggy and rainy and I needed my heavy boots. One can see our little house from a kilometer's distance. When I was five hundred meters away, I saw a white square in the window. Coming nearer, I realized that my family had hung your letter there so I would be sure to see it.

Berlin, December 1920

Have a happy festive holiday. Be completely happy. Occasionally lie down warmly covered. Imagine that I sit beside you, talk with you, be silent with you.

Niederweningen, December 1920

You write: "Be completely happy." I tell you that I am *very* content. Since I met you, I have learned the meaning of the word "happy" and that I am *very* seldom without you—perhaps when I hear or perform wonderful music, or when I experience a marvelous nature scene. Otherwise I am content and that is already very much.

If I say "I am happy," then it is as if my heart would burst because it is loaded to the brim with overwhelming emotion. It is impossible to float always above the clouds and when I am together with you, it is not always this way. But no other human being can *move* me thus, only good music and now pictorial art. Occasionally, like lightening, when I remember a meaningful moment we had together, my heart overflows and then I am happy. I still don't understand how you could tell me in Berlin: "These coming years may be the happiest for you." This is simply incomprehensible. I acknowledge to be lucky to have such a loving mother, a wonderful home, and a chance to study. Perhaps one could call that being "happy." However, *how* shall I call the emotion that floods over me when I am together with you? If I call *this* emotion "happy," I must call my present existence a satisfying, contented, harmonious, protected, and aspiring one. Do you understand me?

Berlin, December 1920

Of course you cannot be continously happy. To be happy once a month is inconceivably much. Altogether happiness cannot be measured by a clock or meter. Happiness is timeless, independent of space, and, according to its depth, unfathomable, boundless. It moves unconsciously and continuously like a "cantus firmus," and for moments *everything* around us seems to be in harmony. That's how it is. It cannot be otherwise. I don't want it any other way. How and when "happiness" appears and how it suddenly manifests itself at unexpected moments, eluding all programmed exertions, make it clear to me that it is perfect nonsense to reach for "happiness."

Happiness is a concomitant symptom that may occur when doing something constructive. Probably it is the best life can offer us. However, one cannot aspire to catch it, because it is elusive. It has to appear all by itself. This is a knowledge known by the most learned heads since a hundred thousand years.

To begin with, one has to have the great good fortune to find worthwhile and wonderful human beings and mysteriously fuse with them; then the possibility exists that this magic side phenomenon, "happiness," easily manifests itself again and again. However, one surely should not loll around waiting for it but decide to become the kind of person who has the capacity to respond to the love that surrounds one and this surely will in any case deepen one's inner core. Often it seems to me that I am less gifted for this than you, my treasure, but then I console myself and reflect that this gives you a better chance to practice on me and thus become a real saint!

One thing is certain: The "Gods" play a fascinating game with the talent and endowment they have bestowed on us. The best way to answer them is to have a combination of irokese-stake endurance, Christian-Socratic superiority, a good-humored frame of mind, and an indulgent smile.


*Dione to Richard*

Niederweningen, December 1920

In one of your last letters you mentioned a strange experience that puzzled you.

Dear friend, I want to tell you that I shall never probe or ask you about your past, if I ever should get the faintest inkling that you do not like me to. I know many women who could not desist, who would want to know everything. Fortunately, I am not one of them. On the other hand, nothing could give me a greater joy than to know all about you. I mean I would like to have a clear picture of your former life. All is very dark and unclear and I know only a little about the war years. If you never tell me about them, I shall assume you have your good reasons. On the other hand, I also understand that only after living together a long time do heart and soul open up towards each other when confidence has been earned. But don't believe I am not interested if I don't ask. Oh, I think I comprehend it, but shyness closes my lips.

*Richard takes a job as an extra in an operetta.*

*In March Richard becomes city architect in Luckenwalde, East Prussia.*

*In October he starts work in the office of Erich Mendelsohn in Berlin—one of the most famous of the avant-garde architects in Germany.*

*In the fall the Niedermanns move to Hagen, Germany, where Vaterli has been offered an excellent job.*

*Richard asks Muetterli's permission that Dione visit him in Berlin after more than a year's separation.*

*1921*

*Richard finds a job at the Metropol Theater as an extra in an operetta.*

Berlin, January 1921       *From Richard's Diary*

End of the performance. After I climbed the narrow staircase with my fellow stand-ins, I learned not to shudder when I put on my makeup above a dirty shirt. . . . Together with others remove the makeup, use the same powder puff, enter the iron stage door. I am a soldier, white uniform with purple lapels, long frock coat with golden buttons, lace collar around the neck, white wig with side curls, black silk leggings, a Prussian headgear, smartly put on. Don't be afraid of the many high officers behind the wings in the darkness, they belong to the next scene.

My colleague and I enter first the empty stage and stand in front of the double columns of the court ballroom. Erect, rifle near foot, gaze over the footlights towards the spectators.

I take off my makeup with grease and a paper napkin. I use an outside faucet and a bar of carbolic acid soap to wash myself. Through the iron door of the stage house I hear singing and dancing, hay he, hay ho, in Holland they dance so. I take my jacket and overcoat, say good night, descend the stairs, pass the dark courtyard, the caretaker room and wend my way to the subway. I have stomach cramps. I feel miserable and I look it. I have earned five marks and thus starts the new year.

*Richard to Dione*

By the way, to speak about myself: For instance, should I be a failure, you can assume without a doubt that nevertheless I was worth something, because there is no doubt that hundreds of thousands have reached a happy haven who were less diligent and had lesser gifts than I have.

Also one cannot say that I am a moonstruck dreamer, wooden-headed in wordly matters.

To be a genius in our profession one has to have a sincere and unalloyed conviction. Anything else is a shadow play of talent that may however be ten times more successful.

To build cities for human beings needs a man whom God loves—one who is conciliatory, has much experience, and one in whose soul dwells a benevolent intention stronger than himself and the thousand obstacles he will have to overcome.

Today, when I dipped the spoon into my soup, I imagined that you sat opposite me. I looked fixedly at the chair as if you sat in it. I thought that to be a real human being is primary and one's occupation is secondary.

Lately I have been trying to find a new job without success. For the last two months I have been working in the heartwarming, light, and comfortable library of the art museum. If you are interested, I shall gladly tell you what can be seen there. Never fear that I want to burden you with a total education. Be only all around. I go among books if I cannot go among trees. Spring will come again.

*Dione to Richard*

Niederweningen, January 1921

I was especially pleased with the sentence in your letter in which you said: "Today I felt that being a full-fledged human being is the most important thing and that a profession takes second place." Since I know and esteem you, I rather had the impression that with you it did come first. Silently I have tried to absorb this fact, to have it become second nature to think thus. This has now occupied my mind for a long time.

When I think of my life as being intertwined with yours, I always imagine that your art will take precedence, although I know that you love me very much. In the beginning it was very difficult for me to get accustomed to this concept, but now no more.

As far as I can see, I shall always understand whatever decisions you make to get nearer to your goal. Fortunately, I have my own artistic activity, and thus it would be deplorable to burden you instead of trying to alleviate your burdens.

Naturally, I shall have setbacks, but whoever strives valiantly will finally succeed!

Every woman hopes to be most important in her husband's life. Only because I've tried to tell myself for a year that I am only second in line has this become a natural conclusion. I would now find it quite unnatural if it were not so. I am, in the truest sense, terribly ambitious for you, not to gain fame and fortune, but to finally get a chance to build. If I now tell you it was occasionally difficult for me to reason thus, then I must admit that this is only relative. Is there anything that concerns me deeply? If so, I allow it to get hold of me only for minutes. It is seldom that I let anything bother me for much longer. I have few conflicts. Vaterli is the same way and apparently he has no conflicts. The deluded mother maintains that I have inherited the best traits from each parent. If I subsequently confirm that anything is difficult for me, then it must have happened in my subconscious and not with knowledge and reflection. When I read in one of my old letters that something proved difficult for me, I am rather surprised not to have noticed it. It must be true, how else would I write about it?

I am so glad that I can quickly rise above negative thoughts, especially that I can sing them away. It is unbelievable what effect my own singing has on my soul. I can adjust the song to my mood. "For the musician there is eternal spring." I like that saying.

Niederweningen, January 1921

*Dione to Richard*

Surely I don't presume to know you the best. Perhaps in some instances better than other people, but nurse Elsa in Stäfa, who saw you daily for two years should know you better than I who has spent only five weeks together with you. I say "should"! All who knew you during this period, even Regula, tell me that you were unbearable. I can tell them in fullest sincerity, that I fully understand you. Considering your life at that time in that miserable hole of an office in Waedenswil and the long working hours, could anyone expect you to be a gallant and witty cavalier and entertain the ladies of the rest home? I would have loved to tell them: "Should he have come to me, he surely would not have been disagreeable but would have found solace for a few hours and strength for the next morning."

Berlin, January 1921

*Richard to Dione*

The situation is lamentable. I have visited a number of people. Impossible to find a job. Immediately everybody starts talking, just to take away one's courage. It looks as though I must go back to Vienna. Also R. M. Schindler writes hopelessly. My money gives out; I sit now every morning, morning after morning without work, and when my bosses appear, the situation is most uncanny. It seems only a matter of days now. The weather is gray and gloomy. It is so contemptible to let outside situations depress you.

Niederweningen, January 1921

*Dione to Richard*

In Berlin you said to Muetterli: "Your Dionerl will be of good cheer most of the time but occasionally full of longing. That will not hurt her a bit." Naturally, I cannot always be in a good mood. However, as I promised myself not to write to you when I feel downcast or feel like complaining, I better tear up such a letter. You cannot possibly believe that I could part from you without a qualm. You don't, do you? Only because I want to be reasonable, I try to be gay. But occasionally I am *not* reasonable and weep. Then I feel ashamed, thinking of you and try to be gay again.

You would have more reason to be sad but then you can live easier without me than I can . . .

Should I die early, that would be all right. It would be much more terrible for me if you should die first. After all, you have your profession and your art. This is most important for a man. A woman, on the other hand, loses herself completely in her love.

I think I can now understand when you suffer from depression. The most important thing, however, is not that I *understand* but that my understanding helps you.

There is nothing I wish more than to be able to understand and feel with you, whatever concerns or motivates you. I pray my being has the power to lighten your burden and alleviate all bitterness. Because I wish so much for this and because I love you, I hope, God willing, it will be possible. In what other way could I have meaning for you?

*Dione to Richard*

Niederweningen, January 1921

. . . I do not have an easy time with your letters. You know how lovingly and intimately we all live together, how everything is discussed by every family member. Everytime I get a letter from you, Muetterli asks me whether she may read it. Of course I don't give in but instead read those portions of it that are of general interest, keeping most of it to myself. However, occasionally I have to make a sacrifice. Don't believe this is so easy for me when I see Muetterli's sad face and hear her say: "This is the fate of a mother. Here she bears children, cares for them, works for them, and brings them up. Then a man shows up, tells them the egg is round and they believe it blindly, while the mother tries to cope with this new situation." Do you think this is agreeable if one loves one's mother and would rather give her pleasure than displeasure?

*Dione to Richard*

Niederweningen, February 1921

Sometimes I am deeply sorry that I had not the chance to meet your mother. The picture I saw of her in your sister's apartment is so clearly in my mind. I know I would have loved her very much. For a long time you have told me that I may express a wish. I hope that in the future you will tell me as much about your parents as you can remember. I hope you do not rue your promise. First I thought I would ask you to write me about them when you found time. But during the night I realized how much more beautiful it would be if you could tell me at night while I lay quietly beside you in the darkness, my face turned towards yours so as not to miss a word. You would whisper to me.

Of course I will tell you about my parents. Both of them surely were above me as far as character and ethics are concerned. I wanted to write you about my father's steadfastness. You know that he was a metal worker. Picture yourself entering a high dark hall, open to the rafters. Much of the space is filled with the workers who extract, with long metal thongs, the red glowing containers filled with white gleamy metal that pours nearly like smoking thick milk, only 2,000 degrees hotter. Two or three of the workers pour this mixture, carefully and systematically, into the ready forms, until a little lake is formed inside the sand. While it cooled slowly, it became iridescent and started, fairylike, to change color. Glowing green, violet, rose-colored, yellow little lakes in this dark hall. If a form was especially complicated, my father had to bend forward somewhat awkwardly (his hand was ten times steadier than my own), bend forward ever more to empty the whole container. Once a little glowing stream escaped and ran over his apron, which blazed and ran glowing hot over his trouser leg and over his shoe. He and his helpers kept pouring, let burn what burnt, let pain what pained, and tore what burnt off only after the form was saved. One had to cut the liquified shoe off his foot. He quickly made himself a compress of petroleum (he fervently believed it would cure burns). He had all sorts of remedies and panaceas by which he swore. Oh Dionerl, what a boon a real handicraft can be. My father had a wonderful occupation and understood it to the last dot on the "i."

As a young man, he had to cast many bells, especially those for the lead animal. He mentioned how difficult it was to adjust the well-timed bells to a certain tone, so that they may sound clear and true and over long distances. They also had to have certain definite intervals. He could tell in a very amusing manner how some of the herdsmen came as buyers, what experts some of them were, and how they made tone experiments at a distance.

I was thinking of my mother this morning, when she was a young girl, thus this recollection. My mother's name was Betty Glaser. Elisabeth Glaser. Only superficially can I imitate her signature. She always wrote in Latin script and very steep and not flowing. I have many testimonies of how admired she was. She fitted the saying, "Salt and bread makes the cheeks red."

I guess she married at twenty-four. It is a lovely but also slightly funny story how she met my father, and he courted her. He told it to me ten years after her death. Because my brother Willy was her firstborn, she was to the end deeply attached to him. He was named after my grandfather Dr. Wilhelm Neutra. She told more of his infancy than she did about her later children. I think this child Willerl reminded her of her first years of marriage, which she treasured. My parent's marriage was, as far as I could see, *without any clouds*, except perhaps financial worries. Quite early it became clear to me that however unhappy I myself might become, beautiful and blessed marriages, full of love, *do* exist, and not between zeros but between beautiful, hale, and hearty human beings. Whatever other people may babble, or even what I may experience myself, does not change my childlike conviction. Just like my sister, my mother became weak and pale in her thirtieth year, and judging from photographs, she must have looked quite miserable.

When she reached forty, she became the robust and healthy woman I remember, with dazzling hair and red cheeks. When she was forty-one, she gave birth to me. You know what flattering things my sister tells about her. I weighed three and a half kilo, and was so fat that one now must be amazed. But that would be silly and I have stopped being amazed. Dear Dione, that I was once a child and a boy is not a lost paradise. Much of it will live on .in me even though I become gray. From you, dear heart, nothing has to be hidden.

*From Dione's Diary*                                   Niederweningen, February 1921

In former times I thought my parents were happily married. In a way they are; nevertheless, I don't want such a marriage. I don't want to have to tell myself as Muetterli does: "Is this all there is to it?" I think Vaterli is completely happy but Muetterli only occasionally. She understands him much better than vice versa and sometimes she is very downcast and does not find any understanding. I fear in our case it would be the reverse.

It really would be much more beautiful if being married does not become a habit, taken for granted, but always is a source of joy and strength. I am not at all clear whether this is a feasible ideal, whether such a marriage, as I picture it, is possible, as I have never seen one. To live all the time in ecstasy is, of course, impossible and there must be periods of depression. However, is it thinkable that one can ever forget what one so ardently wished for and that one day it might be immaterial? I cannot imagine, however, that such a marriage is not possible, especially when both partners diligently work towards it.

. . . I think that everybody has to follow her own inner laws. Should I experience the misfortune that during my marriage another man would impress me, I would try to manage this misfortune alone. That's how I think now. How I would act in reality I, of course, do not know. For a very passionate nature it might be the best to follow her inclinations. It just proves to me more and more that one cannot condemn anybody. If my beloved husband should die, I would find it very natural to uphold his memory, while other women, who might have loved as ardently as I do, would find something new in another relationship, would be incapable of living alone. How often one can observe this among artists. Was the pianist A. Albert not married five times? I find this awful, but he probably acted according to his needs.

What really constitutes happiness? Why are there so few happy people? And why? I don't know anybody among my acquaintances who considers himself happy. Why is this? Because they all look for it too far afield. I can be immeasurably happy, seeing a beautiful sunset, a few wonderful clouds which are here nearly the most magnificent phenomenon, a beautiful flower, a scent, and so many innumerable moments that fill my heart with delight. All this everybody can experience except perhaps the very poor who cannot get into nature. Come to think of it, my happiness is mostly interlinked with nature.

Berlin, February 1921                       *Richard to Dione*

You are in error to assume I am able to fulfill any task given to me. It does not make me sad to acknowledge that this is an illusion. I cannot be put just anywhere. I don't want it, and cannot do it. However, I have proven to myself that I can master many varied tasks, as you know, and as you have observed. To be sure, they have taken their toll, as you also know, because my poor brain is in constant exertion to free itself from my present situation. All this effort, however, comes to naught, my dear child. I am not only lonely, without wholesome, interesting work, being a foreigner with no work permit . . . Dear Dionerl, something in me is nevertheless independent. I finally start to be impervious to disapproval, or approval. Your approval I have, my dear Dione. True, I have worries but often enough I am cheerful. This you have observed too, my Dione. Also, I can laugh like a twelve-year-old, without a trace of bitterness. I do not hate anybody. If only I may keep my health, then I shall be happy and even share my happiness with others, oh, my Dionerl!

I would have had so many opportunities if this damn war had not turned everything around me into shambles.

Every true inner experience lies close and intimately connected on our own individual path. Perhaps in the beginning this inner experience might look fruitful, be bound within a sheaf, be threshed, then break off, and disappear without a trace like chaff and husks.

Berlin, February 1921                       *Richard to Dione*

To conceive the design of a house is not a juvenile art but rather the exercise of a very mature man who has led a difficult and consistent life filled with sorrow and beauty. The greatest architects have produced their best between their seventieth and ninetieth year. One has to be fully developed, more so than to compose a song or write a poem.

For instance, it is very difficult for your Muetterli to understand the true consistency of my character. This is interwoven in myself ad nauseam. It is not so that I speak differently today than I did yesterday. Instead there is a clear connection. To ignore this and simply and playfully follow the agenda, is not possible without hurting my feelings. If I conceive any plan of action, it does not come to me overnight. I don't mention it prematurely, I don't compound it the next night. Here, one cannot speak of *a good quality or a deficiency*. It is simply part of my character out of which flow all sorts of advantages and disadvantages as I have noticed.

*Richard to Dione*

Berlin, February 1921

I hope you are in very good spirits. During the last weeks, I have again been looking for work, a cause for weariness and disappointment. Dear Dione, if I don't burden you with these worries, it is, because you are so young and should be able to develop freely and without any burdens on your shoulders, except those that are your very own. But I have *every* confidence in you, and once you are capable of bearing a load and are as willing as you are now, then I may be permitted to lean on you. Nothing will be further from my mind than to consider you a clinging vine and to spare you.

*Dione to Richard*

Niederweningen, February 1921

Do you believe that one loves a person on account of their good attributes? I have now given myself the answer, why you love me despite all my flaws. I think it thus: Usually one is unaware why one loves a person. One simply loves, forgetting flaws and good attributes. If, however, the flaws are so marked that they preclude a harmonious living together, I would find it quite natural that by and by love cools off. If one lover notices, however, with what valiant effort the other one tries to overcome his or her shortcomings, then the warm feelings remain alive.

Don't you think I now cause you less grief than I did in my letters from Vienna? I have learned to suppress writing what might make you unhappy, thus I cause you no unhappiness. Is that not so?

When you look earnestly into my eyes, I hope it does not pain you to see a background that is still too bright. Would you wish that I, too, had experienced all that you have had to endure? For a girl this would be awful. I imagine that you would prefer to be the one to start writing on the empty pages of my life instead of finding them scribbled over by others, even though I might have missed all sorts of experiences and thus lack the understanding provided by them. . . .

*Dione to Richard*

Niederweningen, February 1921

My dear friend, you asked me whether you had ever found a fault with me. Oh yes! I remember, but you were perfectly right! It is simply awful how little understanding I had for your situation in Stäfa, Zurich, Vienna, and how I ignored your ideas about art and what you hoped for. I always burst forth with whatever came into my mind without considering how I might hurt your feelings. When I was in Vienna, so often I wrote you thoughtlessly and superficially so that on the whole our correspondence was not a fruitful one. The difference between then and now is tremendous. At that time I was so unsure of you. I felt so inferior to you in comparison to now. . . .

You are for me the ideal for everything beautiful, worthwhile, and noble. Seeming misunderstandings cannot disquiet me. I always believe everything can be straightened out. For this reason you must not be astonished if I don't believe that your parents were superior to you in character and morality. That surely does not demean them, because I revere them so much but I still believe what I write. Do you call this adulation?

Berlin, February 1921

Before I left Zurich we took a walk together. Finally I said to you in a whining tone: "For heavens sake, from where shall I take the substance and keep the sublime posture Dione expects of me? How can I possibly forever stand on a pedestal to be admired by her? She will have to suffer a terrible disappointment." You answered in a short and superior tone: "It *is* possible!"

My dear good Muetterli, I was *very* happy with your decisive answer, stopped questioning and have never forgotten it. I understand that I asked out of chickenheartedness, as one without experience, as one who had heard from here or there that certain things are impossible to achieve. When I intimate to Dione that she henpecks me, she thinks that's a funny joke. I give God thanks that you do not have a cunning daughter, who might treat me quite differently. She insists on seeing me as a hero, and if one whispers something contrary into one ear, then she simply is deaf in *that* one. Occasionally therefore, when I am in a morose mood, I posture myself with a deep sigh in front of a mirror and practice. If I succeed to portray a halfway acceptable half-God, despite my unshaven and undernourished cheeks, I hold this position for half a minute and forty seconds, expel a sigh of relief and sit down.

One has to have a cheerful belief and outlook regarding one's own, God-given nature because this *is* our constitutive principle that knows to help itself occasionally in such a manner that our mouth is agape. This I know again from experience. Only foolish people pride themselves that their procedures are always wise. Therefore everything is O.K. as far as I am concerned.

Niederweningen, February 1921

Muetterli sent me the letter you wrote her which I had forwarded to her some weeks ago when she was in Zurich. It made me so happy in one way, astonishing me at the same time. It had never entered my mind that I pushed you into a role incompatible with you. I am not quite sure that you are right. Of course, I will always want you to impress me. At the same time I can be understanding when you are tired and dispirited. In such instance I would surely behave in such a way as to make you feel comforted and watched over.

Oh, when I picture myself how you practice before the mirror! Is this not a poetical invention? But to me you write: "When I look into the mirror, I ask myself whether your promises are meant for me or to an illusion." Do you believe my promises are meant to someone else and not for you?

*Richard to Dione*

Berlin, February 1921

Yes, you are really writing to *me* and I must have boundless confidence in you. I cannot thank you enough from my solitary island. Dear, dear Dione, your letter made me so happy.

I enclose the program of a wonderful concert. The playing of the viola da gamba would have touched your heart. It is the precursor of the cello. It sounded marvelous and my friend of last year played the flute again very well.

Your inner peace and certainty, acquired in your quiet and rural surroundings, may not be permanent, may often be disrupted. Don't let it frighten you! Everything has to take its time and on account of that proves durable. You will experience many reversals. However, the art of contemplation acquired earlier may prove a lasting benefit. Don't be frightened by such truths. Every human being decides for himself how he views success. This you will recognize and feel yourself. It will slowly come to fruition and need not be a painful birth. Don't let setbacks frighten you. A clear direction will always triumph.

*Dione to Richard*

Niederweningen, February 1921

Dear Richard, my heart is full of confidence and I feel capable of knowing what I should be to you because I pray for this knowledge every night. I shall improve and know how to do it better and better, friendship, comradeship, motherly solicitude, for your solitary years. These are only promises on paper but did we not understand each other when we were together?

The other day I again read the letter you wrote me last year on Pentecost from Vienna. Do you remember it? Since then you have not found it necessary to give me so many admonitions. Don't you think I have evolved in the direction you hoped for? Are you in some measure satisfied with me? I really tried hard.

*Muetterli to Richard*

Niederweningen, February 1921

Dione has become a true angel. Again she has the happiness-producing effect which she radiated as a small child.

At the age of ten to fifteen I enjoyed her less. Now that she is developing so beautifully and selflessly under your influence, I am again truly delighted with her.

*Dione to Richard*

Niederweningen, February 1921

I was walking upstairs light-footed and lost in thought when I suddenly heard my name. Involuntarily I stopped and heard Vreneli continue her sentence, saying: "But surely Dione is not a personality." Muetterli answered: "No, she is a self-sacrificing, devoted being. Just consider how unbelievably she has transformed her character to her advantage since her acquaintance with Richard. She tries in everything to adjust her thinking to his. I am sure she would be indignant if I were to tell her this, but it is a sign of how great her love is." They continued talking while I ascended, very much ashamed of eavesdropping, thinking of what had been said about the "self-sacrificing, devoted being" and "my great love" for you. So this is how my family thinks of me!

Occasionally I ask myself whether it really is with adulation that I perceive you, whether I will have to pay for it with bitterness later on. However, I cannot feel otherwise towards you now and you must know in your own heart whether or not I am mistaken. You have already acquired much wisdom. I, on the other hand, only slowly grow to maturity.

All staid grown-ups tell me that I look at the world through rose-tinted glasses and therefore, will suffer disappointments. This does not prevent me to think in secret: "Even if I should be the first human being, whose illusions are not shattered, I shall believe in them until at my life's end I would sadly have to admit they all were right to warn me." On the other hand, I would have lived for many years with these illusions and as far as I am concerned, nobody can destroy them.

Niederweningen, March 1921

*Dione to Richard*

Ever so often a reputable business has to declare bankruptcy. All around us are people who cannot find work and have to economize. You should witness with what good humor we stand up to this situation. We no longer eat butter, cheese, or meat. We economize wherever it is possible and have fun doing it.

I don't know of any family that laughs as much as we do. I have to admit that Regula and I are often the butt of merriment, but so is Vaterli. Do you remember that I asked you during an evening walk whether the glowworm would not burn your hand if you held it? For such remarks I am the laughing stock of the family. Why not? I laugh with them wholeheartedly.

Niederweningen, March 1921

*Dione to Richard*

One morning Muetterli told Doris and me that we would have to try to find employment in order to earn some money. I was not surprised and immediately started to think how to go about it.

I am not advanced enough to give music lessons, lacking knowledge of harmony and theory. So all that is left is to try to find a position with a family as a mother's helper. What does this mean? One becomes part of the family, does not earn anything, but has to work like a servant. If I were to do this for the next half year, I would have to give up my music completely. Along these lines I have thought out the following: There is a great dearth of good household help in Germany and everybody is glad to get whatever help is offered.

I therefore am going to write to the following singers: Lilly Lehmann, Berlin; Sigfried Hoffman-Ohnegin, Stuttgart; Maria Ivoguen, Munich.[1]

---

1. All were famous singers of the period.

I would offer them the following services: I can cook, can keep things in order, serve a meal, sew, repair clothes, and take care of children. I can do all this very well, better than a servant could, because I love to work and can work intelligently. For these services I would ask for a weekly singing lesson and a daily hour of practicing, as well as ten marks a month so I could write to my dear Richard. It seems to me that such a proposal should be acceptable to at least one of these singers. I would thereby profit and would not have to give up my music. I must admit that it is a somewhat unusual and daring proposal. But I shall write very politely and earnestly.

One could feel disdainful thinking of being a servant, but as I love to wash dishes, keep house, and polish floors, I challenge anyone to despise me! At the moment I have nothing else to offer. In seven years the situation will be different. At the same time we have fun and are in good spirits. For heaven's sake, let us never be rich. I feel in my bones this would be my ruin. Of course, one should not have to worry where money for the next day comes from. One should have just enough to be able to afford occasional pleasures.

*Richard to Dione*                                                   Berlin, March 1921

I want to comment on your plans. They are all good as long as purposefully pursued. I don't know what dangers or what luck may befall or await you. I don't know how to counsel you because I do not know all the circumstances.

Paris is an extraordinary city. What this city would offer me I shall not mention. But for women it is surely a kind of paradise. Any frivolity, scandalous or innocent, is here first assured of being marketable and accepted in high society from Biarritz to Palm Beach, from Trouville to the California seacoast. Everything exotic is made palatable. True, the raw materials of an idea come from elsewhere, but in Paris all feminine trifles are enhanced.

As far as architecture is concerned, it is trash at the moment. I believe that you, as a woman, can gain much there and I have confidence that you will not be dragged down.

I find your proposal to write to various singers a possible solution. In this way you would be in good musical surroundings, would learn a lot and you would be appreciated on account of your good work rather than on account of your smile or "elbows." But *don't* ask for ten marks. That would unnecessarily demean your position, and, as long as you want to write me despite association with high society (this is, of course, a joke), I could swing the postage.

So you have good connections in England? The English are well-to-do in comparison with us ruined Viennese. They put on fresh shirts daily, take hot baths, and apply eau de cologne to their faces. In addition, they surround their houses with lovely fresh gardens where, from April to October, perennial plant beds bloom.

You write me that to be rich would be your downfall. I do not think it would be so for you, but it might be somewhat of a peril for others. To become accustomed to a life of leisure, even if only for a short span of time, either as a guest, teacher, companion, or the like, by participating in the life of an affluent household would not affect you. *For you all will turn out well, I am wholly convinced.* You will meet good and decent people.

Niederweningen, March 1921

The older I become, the more I abhor the complicated and perverse in life as well as in literature. For this reason I do not understand the Russians. I liked the *Insulted and Injured* by Dostoyevsky quite well, but only objectively. I really cannot say that I profited from the reading. Why do you think one reads books? What is the purpose? As far as I am concerned, I expect a book to elevate me.

Yesterday Muetterli gave me the book by Nietzsche that you want me to read. I look at it with utmost mixed feelings. To start with, I am very happy that you were thinking of me. Then I feel very honored that you think me capable of understanding it. However, my overriding emotion is one of uneasiness because I am convinced I will not grasp it. I shall do my utmost to understand it, but don't count on it.

Will I ever understand Nietzsche? Dear Richard, you cannot be in earnest! If only I could be Vreneli. She could answer you beautifully, point by point, which I am incapable of doing. I admit it with a deep sigh. That I had to interrupt my schooling in order to have more time for my music, was given only private lessons, never was forced to concentrate, may account for my present lack of concentration. What I want to express surges like a fog from one part of the brain to the other and when I try to follow I am exhausted. I have to pause and finally admit that I am *STUPID*, just as you wrote once you would like your wife to be.

You should have heard the outcry of indignation among the family when I told them that only once, laughingly and as a joke, to make you appear more clever, did you mention you wanted a stupid wife.

Berlin, March 1921

I used to sing to ease my mind when I was elated or alone in the forest. But now I no longer sing since you told me I do not have a good voice. You surely did not enrich me in this respect. (Not that I was ambitious in any way about my voice, even on these lonely walks.) Do you think I would ever have turned up my nose if you had attempted in fun to make a drawing? A man has more forebearance than a woman, also he knows better.

I helped myself by whistling. Most probably I did not sound like a flute as I whistled a song from Hugo Wolf as well as a Swiss folk song.

Niederweningen, March 1921

You write me that you no longer sing because I dislike your voice, and therefore, I have not enriched your life. It hurts my feelings to have you think thus. It does not fit your clear-sighted and generous nature to be influenced by me and to abstain from doing something that gives you joy. Now watch how one can treat this theme quite differently. To make it easier on you, let's assume that we undertook an excursion together, that you started to sing but then suddenly stopped because you remembered my critical remarks. You would look at me for a moment and say, "Ha!" This "ha" sounds to others, as well as to me, so convincing that I feel annihilated. Hence you say: "Ha, silly girl, you imagine that I don't sing well? What's the matter with your hearing? Do I not have an agreeable voice? Do I not know lots of songs and sing them with feeling and expression? You must be mistaken. Listen carefully once more and then judge." Surely you could have convinced me.

*Richard to Dione*                                              Berlin, March 1921

I want to tell you of a beautiful walk I took during which I quietly watched a woodpecker belaboring a tree trunk. I kept on walking parallel with the telephone and telegraph lines that for thirty-five kilometers lead toward Berlin, their clusters of white porcelain insulators hanging down. I was on my way to the cloister of Chorin. It is as beautiful as it is famous. The church and the church patio are in ruins. The colonnade with its gothic window openings in the warm brick façade is covered with green lichens and with many-branched ivy. I was all alone for a long time except for the geese and chickens. I made a drawing, walked through the old cemetery and through the imposing church interior whose roof had collapsed a long time ago, perhaps in the Thirty Years' War. The choir windows are immense apertures from top to bottom. This decayed building stands in all its enchantment in a wild, green garden full of bush cypresses and underbrush that came to us out of the not so dark Middle Ages.

*Richard to Muetterli*                                    Luckenwalde, April 1921

I have experienced a great success, I am so glad to be able to tell you about it and embrace you. How did you know beforehand that I am not simply going to go under? What a soothsayer you are!

Through a lucky break, I was able to apply a day earlier than twenty others for a job in Luckenwalde, and I was accepted. But now comes the improbable. When I informed my current boss, Straumer, that I was leaving and only wanted to complete what I had started, he absolutely refused to let me go. Imagine that, dear Muetterli! He asked why I had not given him a chance to reflect. He increased with 1,600 marks the salary with which my position had been confirmed by a telegram, and did not want to listen to my explanations.

I told him I had obligated myself already. Writing it all down makes it seem even more incredible to me.

Luckenwalde, April 1921

And now, for the time being, I have advanced from an unwanted foreigner to a commercial bureaucrat in Brandenburg. Here in Luckenwalde, the community is building a lot and much of it is half completed. A railway station, hospital, three or four housing projects. I am supposed to develop a master plan for this city of 26,000 inhabitants, as well as for a forest cemetery, inside the city planning department. I am also supposed to give advice to the private building sector. I also was happy to get out of Berlin's unhealthy hubbub and into the country. In fact, the magistrate has put me up in a housing project at the edge of a forest, and only ten minutes away from my office.

Luckenwalde, April 1921

Sunday morning at six I have washed this whole fellow thoroughly and thought you would be satisfied that my contours are filling out since I drink more milk. I love milk, dear Dionerl. Yes, naked I have the appearance of a *David* by Verrocchio. He is lithe and lean, an impudent shepherd boy. The young *David* of Donatello, wearing a little hat as his only garment, is softer and more "beautiful." But a body is damned ephemeral and David changed into a fat king, to fit into the escutcheon of the meistersinger. But he never gave quite up singing to the harp. You see, Dione, *this* is the hope: A well-built body, also when once long forfeited, leaves a memory, a fulfillment, an imprint, on old souls eternally lost to others.

Thus everything ephemeral has an eternal nucleus and ongoing generating germ. Where are the moths that consumed Antinous's tufted hair? And yet—outside is a magnificent promising Sunday morning, sun glittering on the birch leaves while their trunks are reflected in the pond. What is her promise to me? I don't need any promises. I am happy to write you on a Sunday morning, rested and washed. On Sundays I often think how I would like to be with you. But if it cannot be? Why can it not be? It does not depend on our will but on our being and can long remain constant.

A story exists in which a man can surmount all obstacles, because he possesses a magnificent clump of gold. Whenever he encounters an obstacle, he first throws it over and then suddenly the steepest and most slippery wall is surmountable. It may be difficult for me to reach a place or a situation, but when I know you expect me there, my strength would grow tenfold, my dear, intelligent, gold-heart Dionerl. This morning while I walked over the fields to my office, I thought so clearly about it—how you are capable of finding the path that brings me forward, and this is true from the physical to the most imponderable.

Niederweningen, April 1921

What you write about the clump of gold has moved me so much that tears came to my eyes; how much would I like to accept your invitation to rest my head against your hard collarbone. I've almost forgotten how it feels. This is all very strange and I don't think it is the simplest thing in the world. However, when I am with you, it seems simple natural, but at a distance it seems wonderful and surprising.

*Richard to Dione*                                    Luckenwalde, April 1921

Why should you be indignant that the American government does not admit an alien officer? It is a new sacrifice I have to pay for this German escapade. You know very well that it is only one of many—wealth, shaken health, my best years. The "Austrian participation" soon vanished from our consciousness during the war. But nobody gives a hoot to grant me, or people like me, any benefits. I don't want to enlarge on it, *I ask for nothing*, but keep my own judgment. It does not help much to speculate about it.

That I now, after such a prolonged enforced idleness, must move ahead with all the strength that is still in me surely has your approval, along with the fact that I cannot be satisfied with a first, second, and third mediocre success. Should I have to resign, I hope you will feel with me and help me nevertheless to find strength and contentment. . . .

*Dione to Richard*                                  Niederweningen, May 1921

On Sunday was the concert in the church. It was cause for much reflection. Naturally, everybody seemed delighted. The review will appear next week. It will probably be a bad one because the reviewer's daughter wanted to sing by herself. She wanted to be the soloist. However, it would be unworthy of me to be influenced by a review. When I stood on the pulpit looking down at the sea of faces, smiling and unconcerned, I realized that I really don't care whether I please or not. May God grant me that I never forget that I am not responsible for having a beautiful voice, that I am not proud of it, only thankful. I never want to sing just to please, never for fame or success, but only for the praise of God and art.

Although I have to write to you late at night in bed, I want to send you a few words. Today was an eventful day for me, not externally but internally. What I have tried to achieve on the cello for a year, what I have worked for without daring to attempt, the most difficult exercises, I suddenly achieved. It is the springing bow which hovers over the strings and jumps without making spiral movements with the wrist. Probably you will not be quite able to share this joy with me. But I am so happy because I found it all out by myself, without the help of a teacher. Altogether my playing goes excellently and I am glad that I persevered and bravely kept going despite adversity. I now see that I can also advance without lessons. I wish so much that I could play something for you.

Today I was in excellent form and sang beautifully. Sometimes my vocal cords do my bidding. Then I can express the soul of a song. But that happens only once in six months. For this reason I am happy today. Now I go to sleep.

Niederweningen, May 1921

How often I had to think of you this Sunday! It was again one of our wonderful musical Sundays. You would have enjoyed everything while lying stretched out on the couch listening with your eyes closed. We played from early afternoon until 6:30 in the evening.

After our elaborate Sunday breakfast we took a walk over the meadows and through the forest. You cannot imagine how wonderful it has now been for the last few days.

One thing I would beg of you, that is never to criticize me after a song. I know this is a weakness in my makeup. Even before the ending of a song I am afraid someone will say: "Too bad, this you have sung better on other occasions" or "You have been in better voice," after I have done my best.

Dear Richard, if you would consider this failing, it would be for your own good, because then I could with full abandon immerse myself into a song.

Luckenwalde, May 1921

Dear Dione, surely I would never hurt your feelings by cold criticism if you would be kind enough to sing for me. Surely you do not fear that I would ever do this to you. You know very well how happy I am to hear your beloved voice, to feel that this time you sing for me alone.

Niederweningen, May 1921

I will now tell you what it was that I hoped for so ardently. True, no answer has yet come and now I am convinced none will. I had written to Lilly Lehmann in Berlin offering my services in return for singing lessons. I wrote a friend asking him to forward the letter. After two weeks I wrote him a card begging him to give me her address. After another two weeks I wrote again, sending it to Wille who in turn sent it to friends of hers who are also friends of Lilly Lehmann. They forwarded my letter accompanied by their own warm letter of recommendation. This was four weeks ago. By now I have given up hopes of receiving a reply.

That was the main reason for my dejection, because I would have been so unspeakably happy to see you again; I could have visited you for a few days in Luckenwalde, inspected everything, and in Berlin we could have seen each other from time to time. I pictured everything in my mind, even how I would mend your socks! All this has now come to naught. But, at least, I was very happy for two weeks imagining it and that shall be my comfort. This experience has taught me not to build castles in the air. They prove too expensive for me and it was stupid of me to hope for something so intangible.

Luckenwalde, May 1921

I beg you to wait patiently when you feel dejected. One can hardly escape such moods and occasionally they last a long time. The reasons for them are unending. Just imagine how complicated a human body is with its life and soul. Even the mechanics of it are only the dot on the "i." We have here the most intricate interplay of liquids, electrically connected atoms, stress differentials in the leading and distributing organs, and a million other unfathomable occurences for which "science" has not yet found a nomenclature. Just imagine how difficult it is to get a quartet of four instruments harmonized. One has to take with composure the times when something within us is put off its track. If you feel downcast, *mistrust* your own self-evaluation even more than your other gifts. Defer your self-critique and the outlook for your future development for at least four days. Make yourself comfortable during a fruitless period and wait until it again speaks out of you. I, your Richard, can assure you that it will come back strongly and magnificently. Believe me also that I am with you in such periods and all my strength and soul want to help you. I would hope that you would want to help me thus in a similar dejected mood. I don't know whether I can comfort you, but if you also have to pass through such periods you will be able to understand me much better. After that your joyfulness will be more surely grounded. I cannot foresee the future, but this I know without delusion: You will be able to sing, sing as your earnest heart desires, and I with it. Struggle and setbacks, rapid interludes are the only and correct way to a worthwhile goal.

*Richard to Dione*                              Luckenwalde, June 1921

. . . Your recent letters are full of your own germinating ideas. I do not want to flatter myself that my influence, which I have tried to keep to a minimum, has helped you, and will continue to help you, stand on your own two feet. But just imagining it is marvelous for me.

I told you from the beginning that I have full confidence in you and the best advice I can give you is to learn to have confidence in yourself. Believe in yourselve as I believe in you. . . .

*Richard to Muetterli*                    Luckenwalde, September 1921

As you are such an excellent reader of the unconscious, explain to me why I glisten like one smeared with butter when your daughter writes me in Swiss? Well—?

Yesterday I let my co-worker Peter tell me what he imbibed in Juteborg for his Sunday meal. Marvelous! You would like Peter too. He has a small blond moustache which takes on a blue hue during blueberry time, which is now. All lips are blue and the light cambric dresses contrast joyfully with the blue-tinted pearls of teeth laid bare by a silvery giggle when one passes a group of girls on a bicycle. I do not bicycle for pleasure but in the line of duty, also on a Sunday. I am concerned with forestry matters, look at and buy wood wholesale. Sunday I visited the forester, also a forester's house deep in the forest. Both have excellent daughters, which does not surprise me considering that they grew up in the forest where no child can be perverted. The forester is stone deaf. His daughter Anneliese had to scream terribly to make herself understood, which sounded funny to me.

Dionerl can surely tell you what I am doing. (Whatever other secrets I confide to her she naturally has to keep to herself!) I am already at cross-purposes with half the town and really should carry a Belgian revolver when I go out at night. Why? On account of my building consultations. Naturally, I shall accept protective custody but stick to my insistance that clients and contractors show good taste. The butcher's wife even wanted to bribe me with a sausage. I did not see what kind it was, as it was wrapped in paper, but I swear that it did not get into my hands!

*Richard to Dione*

Luckenwalde, October 1921

After some headaches, I have decided to terminate my present employment and work in Berlin this winter. As soon as I know more, I will write particulars. Now I have to look again for a room, fight to get a resident permit, transfer all my stuff for which I do not have enough suitcases, and work furiously from now on to the end of my employment.

To leave my present employment was a decision that took me four hours, after I had noticed a certain advertisement in a Berlin newspaper. Just on that day, I had to take the train to Berlin to supervise my garden projects in Dahlem. From the railroad station, I made a phone call to that particular office, and I was hired without having any drawings to show. This description is, however, incomplete, and I shall complete it when I know more about my new boss. It is Erich Mendelsohn, who is considered here *the* avant-garde architect. I had become aware of Mendelsohn after reading about him, especially in the leading New York magazine the *Dial*, which published an extensive article. Sometime ago one could see in all the cigar stores, as well as on the title page of the *Berliner Illustrierte*, his new experimental neophysical building called the Einstein Tower.[2] He is a fashionable young man with one eye of glass. What kind of a human being he is, I cannot say yet. In any event, he is self-willed, does not adhere to mere common sense under whose banner some atrocities are perpetrated in the building sector.

Everything I undertook succeeded yesterday, like in a dream. I was on foot from 6:00 A.M. to midnight. Everything went so smoothly that I started to notice how strangely everything seemed to fall in place. Every streetcar needed was there. I kept all appointments as well as every phone conversation. I was on the lookout for a mishap, but none occurred. I had a decisive interview and must have shown an uncommon power of persuasion. Why, how come, what for, is beyond me. Despite my tremendous effort, from 6:00 A.M. until 8:00 P.M., I was only slightly tired and went to a *magnificent* concert to which my old friends had invited me. In my next letter, I shall describe what happened.

*Richard to Dione*

Luckenwalde, October 1921

I promised to tell you what transpired yesterday.

I gave Mendelsohn no time for reflection. Everything happened so fast but orderly, not pell-mell. He liked me so much that he threw his intention

2. Observatory named in Albert Einstein's honor and dedicated to carrying on his research.

to hire a chief draftsman into the winds and took me instead, although he had advertised for one. I had nothing along to show him, but told him I had a concert ticket, was already late, tomorrow was the last possible day to give notice in Luckenwalde; he should engage me for three months, let me know immediately, and now tell me what streetcar to take to reach the concert hall speedily, as the concert started at 8:00 P.M. He said, "Take the 'U,'" but otherwise was at his wits end. I said: "Mr. Mendelsohn, please telephone me tomorrow. I can give notice before noon. Good-bye!"

I flew down the stairs, jumped into a streetcar that came by, and missed only one song.

The next morning Mendelsohn phoned. All he said was, "I repeat my proposal," and I replied, "Very well," lay down the receiver, went to the director's office, and gave my notice.

A few houses of my design will have to be completed after my departure, and nothing should be countermanded after I leave. But all of this takes a backseat to the task of the forest cemetery. The forest cemetery is my baby, and for seven months, I exerted all my effort to defend it against its enemies and their stupidity. When I decided to discontinue the work, I experienced a soul crisis that penetrated my very marrow. I remorsefully called myself even a murderer.

After a few days, I got over it, and started the rescue. I had to win over completely all decisive personalities. I bicycled to the forester's home, drank coffee with his wife, a nice older woman, who took my side. In the evening I visited the city gardener and told him about my life and described my intentions in glowing colors. I pulled all the registers of my superiority but at the same time put myself amicably on an equal footing. He is a good fellow, and hopefully knows his job as well as I believe he does. I gave him books about the newest ideas in gardening and instructed that others be purchased for him. He caught on. From day to day, I made him more enthusiastic and livelier. I ordered plants and saw to it that the letters ordering them were speedily expedited. I sped to Rathenau, pulled the forester with me, telling him stories and buying his breakfast. There, I bought plants on the spot, and hurried their delivery. I advertised in the garden journal and bought plants all over Germany, carefully selecting them. I drew telling and suggestive plans that were supposed to speak long after I can speak no more. Plans and more plans. I suggested to councilman Jahn to start a tree nursery for the use of only the cemetery forest in order to determine for twenty years to come the species of the plants and to preserve the plant unity, preventing the mixing in of a foreign body. I got the funds from another source, as the monies destined for the forest cemetery were already exhausted. I explained that if one buys young plants, grafts them, propagates them, they are at hand when needed, in the correct sizes for a minimum of cost, at all times whenever the continuing planting schedule necessitates it; in the desirable quality with the same exact orientation as one can find it in a tree nursery, thus also in the cemetery. My principal consideration, however, was to produce planting material in two weeks that would be useful in twenty years hence. I counted heavily on the growing interest of the city gardener whose significance through this task would grow, and whose involvement would most likely stay with a project that had decidedly started. I was able to persuade all those in power, and ordered the plant material from three sources. I ordered fire insurance for the cemetery; I ordered the afforestation of the bare south zone in such a manner that the future layout with paths and trees became visible. I ordered clearings for the next ten years, with the necessary and exact plant selections, and, meanwhile, planted with a newly engaged workforce whatever new plants that had been ordered, arrived. I was able to enthuse the city gardener ever more with gestures, glances, and expressions by trying to paint for him, as a magician, what I envisioned would happen on that spot. I helped personally to plant, rake, dig, and bicycled continually to take care of the many other tasks.

Dear Dione, if you could have listened to me, you must understand that a forest cemetery can be as magnificent as wonderful music, or a piece of art, underneath the sky with a colorful and silver gray carpet of plants; its terraces, redberry bushes, and junipers on its slopes; clearings planted full of heather; and a symphony of a thousand individual plant voices with their through-vistas, spaces, trees, paths. I completed the plans for the entrance buildings. Meanwhile, I worked also intensely on my gardens in Dahlem, on the museum project, housing units; had important building consultations, photographic representations, correspondence.

I was able to gain the goodwill of most of the crucial ones. Despite all haste, I spoke quietly and in a friendly way to all. I found the time to recommend those who especially exerted themselves. The work mounted and with it the task. I wanted to start everything during these few weeks and influence everything in a decisive manner; the planning director long ago had given me a free hand.

Must I go to Mendelsohn? Is he my man? I really don't think so, but one has to experience many things. The civil service is foreign to me. However, where is the company I would like to keep? I long for a free world with occasional individuals in it, just as you do. I work for one more week in Luckenwalde, and then manage my change of dwelling, and the start of my new employment.

Berlin-Eichkamp, November 1921                                        *Richard to Dione*

When I awoke yesterday morning, I suddenly perceived you extremely well focused. It looked as though you had just escaped from a crowd and were running towards me with great excitement, wearing your winter coat, your nose-tip reddened. I saw it all vividly. Then suddenly you were dressed in summer clothes, white stockings, and half shoes. I clearly observed the creases which developed in your shoes as they bent, noticing with sharpness your gait. While I walked to my work, I was filled with this image.

A day earlier, walking towards a church, lost in thought, I suddenly perceived you clearly in a crowd, saw you bend your head half threateningly, half jokingly, and heard you say half laughingly, "Just wait and see what I am going to do to you!" Then you lifted one eyebrow (I often saw you do this, dear Dionerl), laughed out loud as if astonished with your own behavior and your threat. The expression on your face was such as you might have had if you had dropped a worthless teacup or something that might have fallen with a crash or exploded, but not dangerously. (It had no relevance to your threat, only to your laughing countenance.) . . .

*Richard to Muetterli*                                          Berlin, December 1921

I want to prepare you for a great request. May Dione visit me in Berlin for Christmas? Now I have managed to say it and it has become a question. Surely your first reaction will be to say no. But this need not be so. I would be in seventh heaven if Dione would be satisfied with me. Muetterli, I just spoke to my landlady, Mrs. Boldin.[3] She and her husbad are retired restaurant people. All this time they have been very friendly to me. They live in a five-room house and have a piano. I would give Dione my room which is next to their master bedroom and could be properly heated for her. I would sleep in the attic. In the evening she would eat with me and the Boldins, and for the noon meal she could join me where I regularly lunch at the boarding house of Mrs. Von. Truetzschler.

On one thing, however, I have to insist. Please do not torment Dione by discussing expenses with me or any such thing. Dear Muetterli, I do not have the peace of mind to write anything else and beg you fervently to answer me soon. How are matters developing for you?

*Muetterli to Richard*                                         Hagen, December 1921

I guess I have to say yes to your proposal. I am glad to observe that for once I notice a longing for Dione in you. Usually one is glad to be aware of one's self-control, but occasionally one could do without it, especially after spending three days with nurse Elsa in Stäfa. She kept dinning in my ear that "Mr. Engineer could have chosen Vreneli or Doris. It would have made no difference to him." I repeat, hearing this for three days in a row, I finally get the feeling that Dione is getting the short end. So, as far as I am concerned, I say yes. I am not overjoyed with your proposition but do not have the heart to deny Dione this visit.

I give you clear sailing. You, together with Dione decide what you would like to do. You have had so many obstacles in your life that in this instance I do not care to build additional ones for you. Did Dione make this proposal by any chance, or was it your idea? If so, it is suspiciously unlike you. As you wish, I will not mention it to Dione who intends to come here anyway.

*Richard to Dione*                                             Berlin, December 1921

I have asked Muetterli's permission, Dione, for you to visit me during the Christmas holidays. A few moments ago I read her letter and she agrees. I shall now go to bed and pray with all my heart that you will expe-

3. The Boldins rented a room to Richard in Eichkamp while he worked for Mendelsohn.

## 1919–1925

Neutra in 1919. "He walked erect as if he had swallowed a stick."

Dione and sister Vreneli (*left*) in the Niederweningen forests, 1921.

Neutra sketch of himself as an extra dressed as a Prussian soldier for his performance in an operetta. Berlin, 1920.

Neutra sketch of sailboats on the Baltic Sea
made during an Easter holiday. Wick. 1922.

Neutra sketch of the Baltic Sea made during
an Easter holiday. Wick, 1922.

Neutra sketch of trees along the Baltic Sea
made during an Easter holiday. Wick. 1922.

Neutra sketch of Dione playing a sonata by Eccles. Berlin, 1922.

Neutra sketch of Turkish girls in Trebinje, 1919. (Neutra lived there for two years.)

Mossehaus (*Berliner Tageblatt* Building, 1923) addition for which Neutra was the project director.

*Berliner Tageblatt* conference room designed by Neutra, 1923.

Wedding day. Dione and Richard Neutra. Hagen, Germany, 1922.

Neutra sketch of Frederick the Great's Sans Souci Palace. Potsdam, 1923.

Neutra's first postcard to Dione from New York.

"Rush City" skyscraper design, conceived in 1923.

Frank Lloyd Wright's Taliesin, Spring Green, Wisconsin, 1924.

Neutra portrait taken in Chicago (1924) and sent to Dione.

Neutras on roof of Taliesin, 1924.

Fireplace corner in Taliesin living room, 1924. *At left*, Frank
Lloyd Wright in a chair; *in front of him*, Sylva Moser with her
baby; Neutra in back of her; *to his right*, Kameki Tsuchiura;
*near the fireplace*, his wife, Nobu; *at right*, Werner Moser
playing the violin, Dione playing the cello.

Frank Lloyd Wright with namesake,
eight-month-old Frank Neutra, on his
lap. Taliesin, 1924.

Dione, Neutra, Frank, and Muetterli at Taliesin, 1924.

Neutra with Frank Lloyd Wright at drafting table.
Taliesin, autumn, 1924.

Erich Mendelsohn, Frank Lloyd Wright, and Neutra at
Taliesin, autumn 1924.

Advertising announcement of Neutra-R. M. Schindler
collaboration, "The Architectural Group for Industry
and Commerce." Los Angeles, 1926.

THE ARCHITECTURAL GROUP FOR INDUSTRY AND COMMERCE
is a working organization giving master service in building matters.
It includes licensed architects as well as engineers and specialists in the
design of storefronts, interiors and landscaping, internationally known
for the progressive character of their work.
All work is handled most practically and with greatest consideration
for business economics.
THE ARCHITECTURAL GROUP FOR INDUSTRY AND COMMERCE
is sustaining its past record of success by making every project yield
outstanding artistic and effective results, thereby securing prestige to
the owner.
Interesting Architecture is the best Advertising.

For information call CRestview 5642·5501
or write to A.G.I.C., 835 Kings Road, Los Angeles

rience only joy when you are with me. Then I would truly rejoice. Oh dear God, what would happen if you were only a little bit disappointed after having pictured me so exaggeratedly? I am sad and angry thinking about it.

Basel, December 1921

I feel as though I'm dreaming. My heart has become still. So often I pictured in my mind how I would visit you alone in Berlin, but that it now should become a reality, I can hardly fathom. If I were a bad girl, I would immediately promise to reform. But as I am always a good girl, I really don't know how I can thank Muetterli enough. And you my darling! I am so moved because you fear I might be disappointed. Was I ever?

Could I not sleep in the attic? I don't want to cause you any inconvenience. Could we go to Luckenwalde? Oh dear me, I am overwhelmed! If only you are not disappointed in me! I would be so glad. I know it will be wonderful, wonderful.

Hagen, December 1921

Richard and I met at the main train station in Berlin, then took the local train to Eichkamp. "Now stand still, I want to blindfold you," commanded Richard. I complied and for about ten minutes Richard guided me. "Do you hear anything?" asked Richard. Suddenly I heard the rustling of treetops that soon grew to a roar. Removing the bandage, I was amazed to find myself in the middle of a pine forest, just ten minutes from the railroad station.

"This is the Grünewald forest, and I live just at the edge of it," said Richard, pleased that he had succeeded so well in surprising me. We were deeply happy to discover each other anew. Richard showed me the beauties of Berlin's surroundings. Whenever the streetcar or the city railway passed through ugly sections of the city, his conversation became so fascinating that I forgot to look out of the window, so now when I remember Berlin in 1921, it is the most beautiful city I had ever seen.

Richard introduced me to his friends Ernst and Lux Freud, Hans Ornstein and his wife, as well as Erich and Luise Mendelsohn.[4] The architect Mendelsohn is a great fancier of Bach's music and listened to me sing the composer's works. He liked especially the songs from Anna Magdalena's note book.

From his wife, Luise, I heard for the first time the name of Hugo Becker who was at that time considered to be the best cello teacher in Europe. "You really should take lessons from him," Mrs. Mendelsohn suggested. I thought how wonderful it would be to have such lessons in Berlin where I could also be together with Richard.

4. Lux Freud, married to Ernst Freud, was a Greek scholar. Hans Ornstein went to high school with Richard and became a lifelong friend.

*Richard to Muetterli*

Yesterday morning, I was in Potsdam and visited the Einstein Tower. We also had the first snow. It lay thickly on the branches of the oak forest surrounding the observatories. There are tree-covered hills on top of which stand the observatories, and among the trees the houses of the professors the sky gazers.

The last and newest one is our Einstein Tower. In its interior, a concrete stairway climbs upward, and through its spiral the refractor lets the rays, captured from the infinite, fall down into a laboratory where they are broken up, and where they are thrown into a subterranean room of great length, three times insulated, absolutely pitch dark and inaccessible. There, the rays pass through a mysterious apparatus which reflects them back to the laboratory. This is all yellow in yellow, while the photochemical basement is red and black. From the cupola, I viewed the snowy silent landscape. The whole building is filled with smoke from the burning coal-fire that is to dry out the interiors. Einstein's assistant is a slender man whom one could describe as nearly beautiful, with an English officer's mustache, who is impatiently waiting to start his work, so he can show these earthlings—what? The stars are waiting too. However, we meanwhile had to paint and build in furniture. Kepler, Copernicus and Galileo are happy in heaven that the work progresses. I also spoke with the gardener, and the greatest nursery man of Germany, Karl Foerster, is going to deliver the plants. I prefer the stately and solemn Cleopatra trees . . . whose roots go deep down while the stems grow towards heaven. To get color, I have chosen the white wonder asters coycoides, the fall heather which keeps on blooming until the first snow falls. It is still here, and one hears the choirs of the spheres from far away. Dear Muetterli, I am so glad that you can sleep again. If one gazes a little at the stars, one can sleep, because why should one not sleep? "Look into the streets and don't forget the stars."

*Mendelsohn involves Richard in challenging projects, especially Mossehaus, headquarters of the prestigious newspaper* Berliner Tageblatt.

*Dione's parents allow her to study for three months in Berlin with famous cello teacher Hugo Becker, but only with the understanding that Richard continue to treat her like a sister.*

*Dione proves capable of coping with Richard's depressions.*

*Despite the catastrophic inflation, Richard and Dione marry in December.*

Hagen, January 1922  *Muetterli to Richard*

I would like to discuss the proposal that Dione study the cello with Hugo Becker. I want you to ponder the following: Do you feel confident and able to hold on to the present status of your relationship, as it seems desirable during the present circumstances despite your living together in such proximity and intimacy? If your answer is yes, I am ready to let Dione have her lessons with Professor Becker in Berlin. Not so much to study the cello, but because your present state of health gives me concern and I think Dione should look after you and improve it. This consideration seems to me much more important than the scruples of outsiders who will be scandalized that we parents allow such a visit.

Hagen, January 1922  *Dione to Richard*

What do you say to Muetterli's letter? I reject Muetterli's statement that feeding and taking care of you is the most important consideration. To study with Becker is the prime consideration. That I can be together with you is also wonderful, but I go to Berlin to study the cello. I beg you to give us clearly your opinion one way or the other. Of course, I know that you, too, would like us to be together, only not perhaps under the present circumstances. If you say no, I would understand it, although with grief. . . .

*Muetterli to Richard*

This morning while the bell tolls and the sun shines, I had had the somewhat painful impression of having forced my daughter on you. Once I have my household again, I shall be able to take care of you. Your thinness pains me. Dione weighs nearly as much as you do.

Now we are very curious to know whether our Berlin plans will be realized. For the time being my husband and myself thank you sincerely that you pursue this matter with such intensity.

I may be permitted to add a few more words and write you a declaration of love. Be glad that Dione is not quite like Muetterli. I am afraid that I would find you too differentiated to suit me, my dear complicated one!

*Richard to Muetterli*

Berlin, January 1922

Muetterli, I sweat that I do not want to flatter you. You write that Dione, fortunately, is not quite like you. She is completely Dione, I know that. But so often, whenever a resemblance to you surfaced, I glowed. Also, I cherished every resemblance to her father, even her grandfather. Surely, you cannot have the suspicion that I want to flatter him too!

*From Dione's Diary*

Hagen, January 1922

What I did not deem possible has become a reality. I shall be allowed to study for three months with Hugo Becker. But most of all, I shall be together with Richard. At first I was supposed to again stay with the Boldins. This made me somewhat apprehensive because it is not natural for two young people who love one another to live in such close proximity and still be unable to live together. A solution has been found. I shall stay with Mrs. Von Truetzschler who lives quite near Richard's office. Thus, we can be together often and still not be so near that each night I have to think: "Now he lies above my room wishing we could be together." I am so glad about this solution, looking with confidence and happiness toward the coming weeks. They will show what we can mean to each other.

*From Dione's Diary*

Berlin, March 1922

Since yesterday I am living in a nice, sunny room with an unusual, vivacious woman, the mother of four children.

This evening Richard said a few words that made me happy, although one could think to the contrary. We took a walk through the forest. Later on, lying on the couch, he begged me to have confidence in him even if he could not be as tender to me as he would like to be. Otherwise it would finish him in three weeks. Did I not realize how he longed for me? Would I under these conditions rather not be together with him? Dear God, I am so glad that I now understand how matters stand. I shall make a real effort not to be tender myself, although this is my real nature. This will be terribly difficult for me when I find him so lovable. I will have to suppress my emotions. But I am glad to discover that my love does not depend so much on physical contact. If it did, everything would be so much easier, because with a kiss one can say more than with ten words.

Berlin, March 1922

It is far from being as easy as I had hoped it would be; and I must not let him notice anything in order not to burden his heart.

Yesterday we were at a musical party until after one in the morning. After we left, I longed so ardently to behave towards him as my heart wanted to and my darling, he just gave me a quick good-bye kiss at the garden door. Also this evening, he worked until seven o'clock, resting on the couch while I sang for him. Then he buried his face into the cushions. I experience so intensely how he feels and what he thinks but must remain silent. Never mind, it is all right as it is. A little struggle cannot harm us, as we have our hope for the mutual future. When I observe his emotional conflict, I long to press him to my heart, but this would make the situation only worse. Two feet distant from each other is the order of the day. What a joke! Thank goodness we can look at the situation with merriment. Despite a great longing in our hearts, we, nevertheless, can be cheerful. . . .

Berlin, March 1922

*Richard to Muetterli*

My mine has exploded. I hasten to give you the good news. Erich Mendelsohn has returned. Everything happens at once. He is enthusiastic about my concept. Today the client from Silesia came again. I was in my element, spoke like a waterfall. For the time being, the client thinks I am his man. He trembles that Mendelsohn might change my design sketches. This, however, he has no intention of doing. On the contrary, he is radiant. I developed the ideas to form a corporation, produced all sorts of proofs to show what income my scheme would produce, proposed ways and means how to advertise his products, and behaved like a wise, gray bearded expert of finance and realestate broker. I gave the impression that financing and setting up a new business have been my lifelong specialties. How much I have contributed to the design of the Mossehaus,[1] you are well aware of. Today, we received the commission under very favorable conditions. Tomorrow, I start to measure, and begin in earnest.

I proved to myself to be a better businessman than Mendelsohn, regarding the contract condition for the project in Silesia. I did this, however, in order to impress him, and not without success. In his joy, he invited Dione and me to accompany him on a planned trip to Vienna.

Berlin, April 1922

*Dione to Her Parents*

Richard left a large roll of plans on which he had worked for many nights in order to have more time for me. While he was gone, I looked

---

1. Mendelsohn won a competition to add two floors to the existing building owned by the prestigious newspaper *Das Berliner Tageblatt*. Richard played a vital part in the planning and design.

thoughtfully at each sheet. As I was coming to the end, I noticed the design of a small house. Typically Mendelsohn, I thought, quite unusual, but I liked it. When Richard later on showed me the sheet, I did not quite dare to utter an opinion. Do you know what I discovered? It was Richard who had made this design for his Silesian client while Mendelsohn was absent. Now Mendelsohn is going to put his name underneath this design, and nobody will ever know that it was another head that invented it.

*From Dione's Diary*                                                                       Berlin, April 1922

Today I am happy. My Richard was full of vigor when he returned, discussing architecture with me. He told me it was not frozen music but a reflection of time and circumstance, that all difficulties with contractors are a part of it and can be detected in the building. He told me also that he is less interested in independent work than in the opportunity to learn and observe as much as possible. Privy counselor architect Koenig from Vienna pitied every man who could build a house before his fortieth birthday. Architects mature late. The greatest architects have done their best work between the ages of seventy to ninety. One has to reach a certain maturity before one can build. Even more so to write a poem or compose a song and learn with what kind of people one has to deal.

*Dione to Muetterli*                                                                      Berlin, April 1922

. . . In the evening we often read books to each other. At the moment it is one by Dostoyevsky, *The Village of Stepanchikovo*, and we are delighted with it. It is a book one has to read slowly and contemplatively. Richard influences my literary taste to the better, which is very necessary. The book is well suited to being read aloud. Characterizations are brilliant. It is exciting and very funny. We take turns in reading. At certain, especially beautiful passages we look at each other radiant with joy. At amusing passages we dance around the room. It is simply pure pleasure. . . .

*From Dione's Diary*                                                                       Berlin, April 1922

. . . Today we spoke at length about man's capacity to adapt to various circumstances. All Richard said is so clear-sighted and true to life that I listen with wide-open eyes and ears. Oh, it is so wonderful how we understand each other. It is getting more beautiful it seems to me. . . .

*Dione to Her Parents*                                                                    Berlin, April 1922
*and Sisters*

I have just experienced a wonderful, wonderful Easter.

Friday at 6:00 A.M. we went to town. There we took a commuter train to Greifswald. Of course, Richard regretted that he could not put me casually in his trouser pocket to retrieve me in Greifswald and then savor my surprise. However, surprise me he did just the same, because we did not stay in Greifswald, crossing it only, then marching for one-and-a-quarter hours to the village Eldena. It was terribly hot. Groaning a little, we dragged our two bags, winter coats, raincoats, and my fur jacket through the avenue of trees, peering longingly towards the blue sliver of ocean that sparkled in the distance beyond the meadows.

We tried to find quarters in Eldena. No success. Crossing the river, we came to Wick, which is a small village situated on a peninsula bordering the ocean. There we found two nice rooms in a comfortable inn with an ocean view, and we were their only guests.

After enjoying coffee and cake, we took a leisurely walk towards a spot where we could see the ocean clearly. There we settled down for five hours. The sea undulated softly and serenely while above it stretched an endless sky filled with beautiful clouds. For the first time in my life I consciously heard the singing of larks; so full of exultation and jubilation that I felt in my heart these first days of spring.

Farther out the seagulls shrieked and circled. The wind moved in gusts, fanning out the sparse grass. Otherwise all was quiet except the little gnats that danced before our eyes. It was intoxicating and unreal, especially after the hubbub of the railway car. Richard sketched the ocean. Afterwards it became still quieter and darker. We returned in silence, stopping occasionally to lift our heads to admire the boundless sky.

The next morning we had a breakfast of coffee and eggs, then walked to the cloister ruins of Hilda which stand quite nearby in a park. Walking through this lofty hall one perceives at first a high brick wall with a huge gothic window. Through an opening one enters the former nave identified by massive, old columns where now one hundred-year-old birch trees grow. There is also a cloister. Taken altogether, it has a dreamlike beauty. Richard sat down and immediately began to sketch while I walked reverently for about an hour through these remnants of a bygone age.

The weather was so sparkling, it was heavenly. We then took a small steamer downstream to Greifswald. There we sauntered through the streets, looked at several old churches and an occasional beautiful old house. Richard again sketched, surrounded by a bevy of children as the sun shone bright and warm. How charming is such an old town! To go to college there for anyone who loves nature, must be enchanting.

Afterwards we returned, took a nap, and then sat on the pier from where we could see the ocean even better. The evening became magical. We sat in silence and gazed and gazed at the sun setting in a reddish glow. The ocean was like a mirror, reflecting the blue sky and the clouds that turned purple once the sun had disappeared beyond the horizon. When they lost color, the stars appeared. Slowly we walked back on the narrow pier.

The next morning I awakened Richard at 5:00 A.M., and we walked in the fresh morning air to Greifswald to get a boat to Stralsund. From there we wanted to go to Hiddensee, a beautiful island near Rugen where we wished to spend the night. But on Sunday there is no boat service, so we dawdled along in search of an inn. It was too funny. The people could absolutely not understand why we wanted two rooms but offered us a room with two beds. Finally we decided to return to Wick. The churches in Stralsund are much bigger and more impressive than those in Greifswald.

When we arrived in Wick, we again sat near the ocean. This time it was even more wonderful. Surely, it would regenerate heart and mind if one could spend several weeks here. The rooms at the inn were comfortable and the innkeeper very nice. There were no other tourists, a real paradise.

*Richard to Muetterli*

Eichkamp, April 1922

I hope you like the garden drawings I sent you. I told the client, "Surely, you will not be indignant because your baby in the crib has no moustache yet?" My mood is somewhat like April weather, probably will always remain so with Erich Mendelsohn.

At the moment, I am in good shape. I have learned to limit my work to a tolerable degree which was, however, only possible because of my former industriousness. The Mossehaus is progressing nicely.

Day before yesterday I visited the sculptor who for 10,000 marks is preparing a model $\frac{1}{20}$ of the corner pieces. It is gigantic and creates such an impression—dimensions like one of the temples in Selinunte,[2] beside which a person seems merely a flea. It will be the highest building in Berlin (except, of course, the churches). No other building addition in Berlin can come up to it, and everywhere one is adding floors. It is half as high as the Votive Church in Vienna. As one is building from the top downward, the effect is that of a new building. It is most worthwhile for me to have such a decisive part in this monumental structure. I am very curious to know how long I shall have a chance to participate. Some very exotic constructions occur, but I could greatly benefit not only on account of the technical and artistic procedures but also by having to deal directly with the clients, the contractors, and subcontractors. I must give Mendelsohn due credit because he always introduces me as his collaborator and not as his underling. Nevertheless, there are many things that are not to my heart's satisfaction. And Dione noticed those right away. Well, lets see how matters develop. Beginning next Monday, a new time schedule has been decided on. We start at seven in the morning, and are usually through in the afternoon.

*Richard to Muetterli*

Eichkamp-Berlin, April 1922

The situation regarding the Mossehaus is again critical. Erich Mendelsohn has paid the building permit; however, the situation is very strained, especially so because the client has become nervous regarding finances. Strike of the typesetters, foreign exchange manipulations. Yesterday it was proposed to leave out the corner solution (to leave everything as is and only add two second floors). If enforced, it would be a catastrophe.

*Richard to Muetterli*

Berlin, April 1922

When I am tired and look miserable, because I have not had a meal for six hours, not being able to get away from the Mosse construction site, then

2. Ancient Greek city in Sicily, noted for its ruins.

tiring myself out by standing in the crowded subway, so that wrinkles remain in my cheeks, I approach Dionerl as if I had committed some crime, just like a sinner. But I press my hand over my heart, and I assure you that I shall try to do everything possible to remain healthy for Dione's sake. I know that health is not ultimate happiness, but it surely is a foundation for it.

Berlin, April 1922

*Dione to Muetterli*

I wrote in one of my last letters that I have not had a clouded hour. I have thought better of it and now believe it is all right to have sad moments if one can be comforted by someone so dear. I would not like to experience bitter or indifferent moments, but sad ones unite the heart.

Today I thought how lucky a child is to have a mother, also, how much we need you. Of course, you are right and I should always be serene and well balanced, but this I first have to learn. When Richard looks so hollow-eyed and exhausted, I immediately feel a weight on my heart. Dear Muetterli, don't you think it is important for Richard to see me not only when I am happy but also when I'm despondent? On the other hand, I see how wonderfully he can comfort me. I almost enjoy weeping because he is then so charming. But usually I laugh. Now, between lunch and supper I cook for him a cereal which I mix with cream. This is surely very nourishing and does not need long cooking. He loves it.

On Monday I had an excellent lesson. Professor Becker prophesied that I would some day play very well. Today, Thursday, he admired my lilac cambric dress and after I had played the first movement of the Eccles sonata, he turned around and said very emphatically that I should come with him to Ober-Bozen, that I had a true feeling and a beautiful tone. I should come at least every year for a month, just like taking a cure. Well, I am, of course, delighted with his good opinion and in any case am learning *very* much during these weeks.

Berlin, April 1922

*From Dione's Diary*

. . . Yesterday was again a difficult day. Richard had a very painful discussion with Mendelsohn about his future. When he returned he was silent and distant towards me. We took a walk and he told me of his discussion. I felt useless and had the oppressing feeling that I should say something to make him see how much I care. . . .

Berlin, May 1922

*Richard to Muetterli*

I beg you to leave Dionerl here until you have room for her in your new apartment. Also, she will have advanced more in a few disciplines. Imagine, Muetterli, Dione did not know where spring comes from or the circumstances that produce it. At the same time, she sings songs about spring so beautifully, especially one by Brahms, where one can feel the setting of the sun so clearly that one notices how cool and damp it is getting and that one had better put on an overcoat, while far far away one hears a nightingale sing in a minor key. Dione also has too little knowledge why the sun is setting, and whom we have to thank for the various seasons. Well, we already have thoroughly discussed the orbit of the intro- and extra-terrestrial planets, the propensity of planet axes and their eclipses; even so, I don't believe that we can bring this discussion to a happy end in the short time remaining to us.

It has made me so happy that you gave so much thought to my well-being. I don't think my state of health is any different at the moment. I had hoped so much to have a few leisurely days with Dione, but Mendelsohn burst into the office, full of vim and vigor after his vacation, and full of furious creative-work drive. To me he shows the most winning (one could almost say calculating) friendship. He is a man of great vitality and has nothing in mind but his own advancement. At the moment, Dione is more important to me, may God forgive me.

I think *continuously* about her. I do my work with only my left hand, and when something important comes along, I can barely squeeze myself into it. My Muetterli says always that a man cannot do or think two things at the same time. Therefore, I must be a man after all, despite my walking on a cloud.

*From Dione's Diary*                                                   Berlin, May 1922

Today Vaterli visited us for a few hours. After we took him to the station and returned, I felt clearly for the first time that my home is now with Richard and no longer with my parents. Oh, how insignificant a momentary upset appears in comparison to such moments when one feels in his innermost fiber that he loves a particular human being. How strange! Here I have lived in my parent's home for twenty years, and such a wonderful home. Then a strange man appears on the scene and in the shortest time I am willing to give up my happy sheltered existence.

*Dione to Muetterli*                                                   Berlin, May 1922

This week was full of external happenings as well as internal ones. As much as I rejoice to be seeing you all again, it is, at the same time, hard on me to be leaving my poor Richard alone. With me gone he will be desolate and forlorn. I am fearful that he will again be working long hours if nothing draws him home. How lucky it is that he at least lives in such nice surroundings. When we are downcast, we tell ourselves we have no right to be, but should remember with thankful hearts the past weeks which we enjoyed together.

*After Dione returns home from her stay with Richard in Berlin, he writes to Muetterli.*

*Richard to Muetterli*                                                 Eichkamp, July 1922

I thank you fervently. Just now Mrs. Boldin gives me your comforting letter which shows me that you can well imagine what goes on inside me, because you write me thus at this time

*I thank you from the bottom of my heart*, and I am happy. Have no sleepless nights. You are absolutely right. I carried a terrible watch inside me while Dione was here (and my actual one was at the watchmaker to be repaired), counting the hours, the minutes, and, really a few times in the office, the seconds as they relentlessy dissolved or did not. I am glad that we were obedient and that Dione reached you at the appointed time, because you deserve our obedience, and not only because you are her mother. I don't have to search my soul very much but am distressed at the thought that Dione should need to nurse me. I am in complete agreement with you regarding my endless labors but good advice is expensive, or perhaps it is cheap but its execution is expensive. I was very healthy and again very ill. (May the devil be held responsible for the war.) I have become sufficiently aware what good health means and *how* poor we become without it, even losing friends. Yes, in the last moment, I saw most people lonely, their health excruciatingly tampered with. Don't believe for a moment that I am lighthearted about it. I have, however, to work, compelled outwardly and by an inner force.

This year I had to change jobs, bosses, and employment conditions four times. You know from my credentials that I was always able in the shortest time to create a real position, and that each change was a useful one. A tremendous effort was always necessary. On top of that, always a change of domicil, providing for all necessities, trying to get accustomed to new surroundings. I had no help from anybody. Should I tell the few people who gave me extra work—no, I have to decline—and thus jeopardize my few connections? No, I simply have to stand it, have stood many more disparate situations. Treasured Muetterli, I am convinced that you understand me. No vacation? O.K.—no vacation. If my constitution is not as good as it was before the war, well, I have to go on nevertheless.

Muetterli, I don't submit my body to any pleasures that could harm it. I go to bed early, I don't drink, I try hard not to work at night, try to nourish myself as well as I can, don't economize, and want to give you every proof to show you how much I am aware what good health means, how worthwhile it is to be healthy. Sometimes I am very downcast about my dark future and uncertain situation.

Hagen, July 1922 *Muetterli to Richard*

Your handwriting was quite small, and you call your future dark. What does this signify? Of course, you cannot know how your future is going to be, but that it is going to be successful in the last analysis, satisfying to yourself, this *I know*, and for this reason you insult me, when you speak of a dark future. When I hear such talk, I say to myself: "This man needs a vacation," come with us to the seaside.

It seems to me that your relationship to Mendelsohn is not very beneficial to you. Does it not help to tell yourself that this is a transition, that something unforeseen will happen or might happen which might change your situation to advantage? Of course, to advantage if one is Richard Neutra. Do not write about "dark future," I react to this with dismay. I cannot imagine a more beautiful future than yours and Dione's. Surely, you will be able to build as you imagine it. Is your rise from Zurich-Luckenwalde-Berlin not rapid enough? Surely, you do not expect to immediately get a commission to build an entire city, or who knows what is in your mind!

*Richard to Muetterli*

Berlin, July 1922

I don't think I wrote you that the new publication of Wright's buildings has appeared in *Wendingen*. It was sent to us as a present by architect Wydeveldt, a pioneer of modern architecture in Holland. It costs 18,000 marks. Wydeveldt was here, and is a very nice person. But the evening with him and Mendelsohn was a failure. Present at the same time were Dr. Behne, Duvinage and his bride, about whom I have yet to tell you.[3] In short: I have seen Wright's new buildings in a professionally poor presentation. No floor plans—it was hardly believable. Also the hotel in Tokyo where I was to participate. Also a kind of housing project in Los Angeles. My stand to this architecture is something I never discussed with Mendelsohn. He is quite aware that Wright is at this moment the greatest living architect.

*Dione to Richard*

Hagen, July 1922

. . . I am in the same quandary as I was after my visit with you last Christmas. I have not yet found a satisfactory relationship to you and thus it is difficult for me to write to you.

I practice diligently but do not feel, by a long shot, as well here as I did in Berlin. This may have something to do with the air here or possibly on account of our separation. My rosy cheeks are gone. I look forward to a letter from which I can gauge your mood. I hope so much that you have accustomed yourself to the fact that your Dionerl is gone and you are again by yourself.

To see verdure again has been unbelievably beneficial for my composure. I realize only now that the absence of nature was a contributing factor to my abominable state of mind in Hagen. To live constantly in the same one room, always a gray wall to look out on, always rain, always bad air and soot, was simply too overwhelming for me. Of course, nobody around me noticed how I felt, but at night and while I tried to practice, I behaved in a way surely not worthy of you. What made it worse was the fact that I clearly realized what was happening inside me, but had no energy or power to change my mood. The present and the future appeared gray and bleak.

*Muetterli to Richard*

Hagen, July 1922

I rejoice, rejoice, rejoice. At last a *binding* promise of a visit from you. As you belong to the few people who build only realizable castles in the air,

3. Dr. Behne was a famous art historian in Berlin. Duvinage worked in Mendelsohn's office.

I indulge in this joy of anticipation of having you with us comparatively without worries. Soon and with great solemnity and raised spirits I shall light the domestic hearth.

Hagen, July 1922

*Dione to Richard*

I find the condition of being a bride not at all agreeable. I cannot remember that I ever felt such unrest, felt so disjointed, felt so dissatisfied. I long so much to find peace and clarity. Did you not notice it during your visit?

Berlin, Summer 1922

*Richard to Dione*

Yesterday, Sunday morning, I went into the forest, laid myself underneath a tree and spent several hours there. I thought, slept, drew a little, and kept on thinking. Then I slowly walked back to Eichkamp, worked, drew some more, and went to bed early.

I could observe the evening sky and was awake for a long time, thinking of Trebinje, where I spent time during my war years. Underneath my window I heard children chattering and heard the neighbors talking with their visitors. I remembered more and more about Trebinje, the landscape around it, and the two years I lived there, from my twenty-second to my twenty-fourth year. Trebinje is surely the most romantic spot in which I ever lived. It is a tiny Turkish fortification, so tiny that one could shout from one end to the other, but unfathomable and full of secrets.

Oh Dionerl, why have I never told you about it? Trebinje is only an empty word for you. But there is so much to tell and it has much to do with my inner life.

There the sunshine became glowing hot, the moon rose above houses that looked like theater sets. There were courtyards and flying buttresses and two minarets above the river. I felt desperate and lonely, but at times also happy. Often I believed that never again in my life would I come back to Europe.

Berlin, Summer 1922

*Richard to Dione*

During the war, I tried to make every hole I had to inhabit, habitable. For instance, in Montenegro, in the city of Nickschitsch, I did not separate myself from my company but lived with them in miserable quarters outside of town. I rented a small room beside a saddlemaker who hammered on his cowhide just like Hans Sachs in the second act of *Die Meistersinger*. I had the room thoroughly washed with soap until it gleamed white. I put up a small stove because it was bitter cold winter and went downtown to borrow from a merchant from whom I bought a rough linen sheet, an iron bedstead with brass fittings, mattress, and blankets. On the now white floor, I put a piece of canvas in lieu of a rug. I managed to find a tablecloth for the rough table, and a petroleum lamp. I had the wall tinted in a pale reddish hue. Now the window panes were clean, I bought some kind of thin cloth, folded it, and hung it as a curtain. I had a fire made in my wood stove, and from my military pack I extracted the second part of Goethe's *Faust*, *The Decline of the Roman Empire* by Montesquieu, the second part of *The Era of Louis XIV* by Voltaire, all paperbacks.

Now you have to imagine that previously I had slept in the snow for fourteen days, without a chance to even wash myself, so you have to feel with me how comfortable I felt in the warm room, looking at the bending trees that stand between me and the city.

Later I took position with my battery, 300 meters above the harbor of Shenjan, Albania. We built four low stone walls so near together that there was just room enough for a few boards that served as a table, and in front a stone bench on which I laid cushions filled with hay. We covered everything with a few boards and scraps of tar paper. We hung a piece of canvas in front of the opening to provide a sunshield, and from here, I could look down for thirty kilometers towards the ocean. Here, I would lie at night, underneath my oak trees, between the low stone walls, filled with crawling scorpions. I heard the immense agglomeration of Albania's insect world chirp away. For two years, I had not been farther north than Rome, had not left this crazy part of the world, had not been home. Sometimes, it took four weeks for mail to reach me, and when it did, it brought me torn pages from paperback books, as one only could send single pages.

It rained night and day, as the rainy season had already started. It was an anxious time, because most of my company was already down with bloody dysentery. Nobody was left to care for my 125 poor horses soaked in the rain, mired in mud, underneath the flimsy roofs of reeds, in this Albanian wilderness. Who should lead them to pasture, who watch over them? Everybody was staggering around like drunk from the fever.

It was a bad time for all of us, and we were so immensely far away from our hearth and home. Then, it got me too, and I started to shiver, my head ached, my strength started to ebb. I shook and shivered the whole night underneath my blankets, while the rain pounded onto my reed roof. Finally, I started to perspire, always more violently, until my sweat trickled into the hay beneath me, and my strength started to ebb away. In the morning, I dragged myself to a wagon, and the company leader Prochaska, who was a good and faithful companion, rode with me through the water that covered all sorts of holes in the ground into which the wagon lurched. It poured onto the roof canvas. Beside me cowered my orderly who also shook with fever.

Finally, we came to the "hospital" which could accommodate three hundred persons, but where two thousand men lay in the mud, without blankets, as those had been taken from them to be deloused, disinfected, or only God knows the reason. Infantry men, trainees, Russian prisoners from the neglected working camps—they all lay in the muck and rain. I crawled from the wagon into the barrack, where I had to give all my personal information such as where my family lived, details, so they could be advised about my probable demise. Then I came into a tiny barrack, started again to shake and sweat into the haysack, on which I was lying, so that in my feverish dreams I believed to be a fox because I smelled like one. It was lucky that no mother had to be anxious about me.

After a week or longer, I staggered one night at 3:00 A.M. to the horse carriage and, together with a priest and others, was stowed away in an open lorry. Thus, we rolled through the dark night while the rain poured over the canvas with which we tried to protect ourselves. The Catholic priest was no philosopher. When the dawn broke, really gray in gray, we were already far away, rolling through the Zadrima flatlands. We, finally, arrived in Skutari. There, we remained for a long time in a Turkish hospital, a widespread building complex. Oh, how I then slowly got over the lake, and by slow steps through Montenegro, and over the mountain to Cattaro in an automobile, and through seventeen hospitals—oh, what an endless story I am starting to tell here.

Berlin, July 1922

Today I worked from 8:00 A.M. to 9:15 P.M. in the office. During the short lunch period, I discussed with my gardener the costs of my newest garden design. At 7:30 P.M. Mr. Mendelsohn gave me a cheese sandwich and a cup of tea. Darling Dione, no doubt you think I must be exhausted. Totally wrong: I walked with great gusto in the rain and thought incessantly: Today is the day when I could prove to you how kind, communicative, sparkling I can be after fruitful work.

Berlin, July 1922

Yesterday I sat on a spot I will describe for you: A stream emanating from a high mountain chain had torn a crevasse into the slope which dried out during the summer. Round blocks of stone lay in the bottom, rotated and deposited there by the once-rushing stream. Now they formed the steps of a cascade. There I sat beside one of these huge blocks, looking up over this luscious watercourse, now filled with rank growth. Between the steps were small, light green patches that had overgrown the river bottom. The side slopes appeared to the eye like swollen cushions, an appearance which fills one's heart with joy when one observes them between high mountain rocks. Behind a few blocks I saw unfurled ferns. Above the full-grown heather, along the hill slopes, blooming profusedly with a marvelous pure force were the mountain roses embedded in their tiny, shiny leaves with their gnarled stems. Above everything was a sunny evening sky behind a slight veil of haze, because only half an hour ago did a slight rain cease to fall. I was, you must know, in the real fabulous fairylike botanical garden of Dahlem, of which I told you during your Berlin visit.

I was, practically, the only visitor after the rain. I really love botanical gardens, even the small one in Vienna where we were last together. One takes a few steps and is suddenly in the Rocky Mountains or in the Andes, or in the Caucasus, or in a German landscape. He really stands on that earth and in front of what it all signifies.

*Richard to Dione*

Berlin, July 1922

It is Sunday forenoon, the middle of July and I write you while I am lying in the forest. Erich Mendelsohn has left for a week to visit his wife. Beaming all over, he made a proposal supposed to make me happy. This proposal would enslave me just like a Versailles treaty. To earn a few thousand more, I would have to promise to abstain from any other work and further promise, in case I leave him, to also leave Berlin for three years so that he could be sure I was not taking clients away from him.

Well, I am not particularly attached to Berlin, nor do I have work there. The saddest thing is that I may never expect anything else from E. M. This I knew from the first moment, but thought of it only intermittently. I would rather resign and live a little longer than to think that this proposal is the one way to a marvelous career.

This is the way to look at the matter: Mendelsohn has a great knowledge of people and what is advantageous for himself. He demands much from his office chief. His proposals show a higher regard for my person than any flattering words he might bestow upon me. That he makes such ridiculously difficult conditions to prevent my becoming his competitor if, as he says, his working capability is diminished, is, of course, also flattering for me. So I have good reason to be in high spirits.

*Dione to Richard*

Hagen, July 1922

I cannot imagine how you can keep on working with Mendelsohn if you refuse his proposition. If you accept it I have the feeling that you will be in his hands and may lose your freedom. That would not be so bad if he were a person with whom you were artistically in full accord and who allowed you ever free initiative, but that is not the case.

*Richard to Dione*

Berlin, August 1922

Today is the first of August, the national Swiss holiday. Three years ago we were together in Stäfa and watched the festive bonfires. If only you remain healthy, my great treasure, and continue to have much patience with me, then I am hopeful that I shall always get back onto the right track.

I know it would be marvelous if we could be together today. I would pour out my whole heart and show you that I am truly a better human being than you picture me in your diary.

My negotiations with Mendelsohn are still not resolved because there has been no time for discussion.

*Richard to Dione*

Berlin, August 1922

I want to ask your advice. It was hard on me to be without news from you for three weeks while I had such difficult and weighty discussions with Mendelsohn.

He offers me a small share of seventy-five percent of his net income, and declares that this is sufficient for me to marry and thus enable me to ask my future wife to share her life with me. He absolutely refuses to discuss a worthwhile minimum wage. Overtime will no longer be paid. For a year I have no possibility to leave. After that period, I insisted on a three-months cancellation period. How mobile I shall be after that, depends very much on your courage.

My boat is coupled, my oar is his oar, is hitched to his. You will have to describe to Muetterli what kind of a person Mendelsohn is. I have not changed my opinion about him. He is an artist who thinks only of his art, and this permeates his personality. As far as form is concerned, his behavior towards me could not be more correct or, according to his character, hardly ever less open and without ulterior motives. Sometimes he is exhausting but hardly ever acutely inconsiderate. In financial matters, he is much my superior, not so much because I lack intelligence, but because of his incessant, imperturbable interest in it. Whoever takes a bet regarding his career is on the right track as far as he is concerned, and his success so far is much greater than any of you can evaluate.

At the present time, it is hardly possible to find better conditions in Germany as an employee than those offered to me.

To go to America now is too costly and too much of an adventure to ask from you. It would be difficult for me to bear your worries or to propose a separation for an undetermined period.

But Dione, it will be *your* present to me if you make it possible for me to go to America while the possibility exists, and it is not yet too late. It will not only be a present for me but, hopefully, also for you, my treasured one. Maybe, you will be glad to be rid of me for a while? Erich Mendelsohn is not a chosen one, it seems to me; Frank Lloyd Wright is.

Perhaps I am wrong in many of my considerations, or perhaps there is no error at all. I don't want to contemplate how my thoughts are influenced thinking of you or about you while I picture this whole situation. I don't even want to think in terms of "you" or "me." It must be "we" if we do not want to be fools and on the other side of human love (like millions of marriages that failed). I ask whether and when you want to become my wife, despite all difficulties and troubles, my *dear* Dione.

Hagen, August 1922

Your letter reached me quite unexpectedly on Saturday afternoon. I put it between the pages of a musical score, as I wanted to read it only at night when I could be by myself. However, Vrene and Doris wanted to go to the beautiful Rankenpark so I took it along to read in the midst of all that greenery. After reading it I hid my face behind my hands and harkened to what my heart told me. Then I walked up and down along the path. In five minutes I was quite clear as to what to do. I reach decisions intuitively and quite fast. To ponder on them for days is unknown to me. Either I know the answer right away or not at all.

*Whether* I want to be your wife I cannot tell you. This question is too surprising for me—has not yet been digested by me. You ask *when*! In the coming spring, dear Richard. Did you think of an earlier date? It is not possible. My parents will not part with me this winter now that we shall again finally have a beautiful apartment with our own furniture, where we all can be together after so long a time and without worries. I believe you will understand these considerations as you know how loathe my parents are to part with me.

I feel like in a dream. I have a strange sensation as though I could soar. But I am afraid you will be disappointed that we cannot marry before spring. As far as I am concerned you surely know I would come right away. Is this not so? Surely you also know that I dare not leave in order not to seem unloving. Also, Vaterli wants me to be twenty-two before I marry. However, these eight months will pass by very quickly and then we have the summer in front of us. Oh my, I rejoice, rejoice! I cannot write anymore and anyway this letter has to be dispatched so that you can answer Mendelsohn. I know you will be patient with me as we shall be with each other.

*Richard to Muetterli*                                         Berlin, September 1922

I am in high spirits. Naturally, not against the gods, but I think a human being has enough elbowroom to be high spirited, without vexing the gods.

Assuming, of course, that these gods have hearts that understand. They *do* have understanding hearts! The world is much more diversified than we assume. And *all* is created by them. A world so unimaginably vast, and here my poor brain has to stick to *one* portal of the Mossehaus. However, there are poorer brains than mine! Thank goodness, because where should one draw one's self-confidence from if all brains were on the same level? By the way, the Mossehaus is slowly emerging from its scaffolding. (I keep my suitcases packed so I can, if need be, leave Berlin during the night to start anew somewhere else.)

*Muetterli to Richard*                                        Hagen, September 1922

Not for a moment do I think with regret it will be sooner than we could possibly have anticipated that you will take our child away. If I examine my feelings truthfully, I must admit that the possibility of your finally having a chance for a comfortable home life fills me with greater joy than the sorrow of loosing Dione so soon. In reality we really have no loss but a gain, because on top of it all we have the joy of having you. This has deep meaning for us parents even if we cannot be together daily. I, at least, can be happy in the knowledge of what I have, no need to see my pride and happiness daily. For the time being you also are not so far away. I am glad that you are pursuing your American plans because it surely will be to your advantage to have been there. Whether you will really find what you are seeking is another matter altogether. . . .

*While visiting some friends in Basel Dione accompanies them to a party where she encounters for the first time Jewish businessmen, whom she sees mainly interested in financial matters, very foreign to her own interests.*

Basel, October 1922          *Dione to Richard*

. . . Your Jewish race strikes me as peculiar and alien. How strange, too, that I always completely forget that you belong to it. I don't know whether I hurt your feelings if I tell you that I feel you do not belong to them. With you one has the impression that you stand above everything and simply are a human being.

Berlin, October 1922          *Richard to Dione*

My soul responds fully to your description of the Jewish milieu you experienced. I do not have the wretched feeling that I am a renegade to be writing thus. A renegade is one who denies his origin, his parentage, as do the Germans in a hundred countries. I don't want to include my parents in this connection, but all the Jewish families I grew up with have no resemblance to the circle you describe. Also among the Hindus, Confucians, and Fire Islanders one can find obnoxious cliques. Jews, Jews, Jews—the cunning one, the grasping one, the dirty one, the good one, the wise one, the enlightened one, the idealistic one, the prophetic one, the talker, the visionary, the supporter of art, the usurer, the Communist, the benefactor, the bourgeois, the broker, the journalist, the educated one, the scholarly one, the bibliophile, the operetta singer, the soldier, and the idealistically striving student. All Jews, a handful in this European world. My father, for instance, was not among those just mentioned. He was first a metal worker, then a master journeyman; a metal pourer, a metal lathehand, a metal fitter.

Berlin, November 1922          *Richard to Dione*

I spent all yesterday evening writing a long letter to Muetterli. She wants me to repudiate my Jewish faith. Probably she and Vaterli have had quite some arguments about it.

However, must I not try to help her, eh? Does she cling to a formality or do I? The gravest operation cannot change me. Who in Hagen has to know this? Who takes any interest in it unless it is unnecessarily pointed out? I am a descendant of my ancestors who were massacred, burnt, and tormented in many ways.

Berlin, November 1922          *Richard to Muetterli*

I want to tell you about my family background. My paternal grandfather was born in Budapest. His name was Wilhelm. He studied medicine in Pest and in Vienna and became the municipal physician in the provincial capital of Beregzasz. There he married my grandmother Therese, daughter of one of the most esteemed families and the best educated among her relatives.

My father, Samuel, surely a name which will have to appear in my papers, had to enter an apprenticeship in a metal foundry after graduating from high school because his father caught typhus from a patient during an epidemic and no money was left for a university career. Surely an unusual fate for a child of intellectual parents. He completed his apprenticeship, worked in various factories, and advanced there, reaching his highest position in the Siegel Locomotive factory in Wiener Neustadt. He devoted a third of his salary to taking private lessons in French, mathematics, geometry, as well as in mechanical drawing. (I remember having seen his exercise books.)

He kept in touch with one of his colleagues during his apprenticeship, Josef Kron, and finally made him his partner when he started a small concern of his own. They manufactured water meters, gas meters, metal hardware, kitchenware, flat irons, and bells. At first Neutra and Kron worked by themselves, and an apprentice made the deliveries with a handcart.

Kron married Josephine Boehm. Neutra married Elisabeth Glaser. Kron, a deeply honest man, was the more passive. He looked up to his partner with great admiration. They sold their business after thirty years, really too early. Oh, if only they had patriotically made hand grenades during the war! During their working years they employed no more than twenty-two people including a coach and watchman. They were known for their quality work and won prizes in different exhibitions from Philipoppel to Dresden. At their twenty-fifth anniversary twenty of their employees put an advertisement notice in *Die Arbeitzeitung* (worker's newspaper) praising their employers and their relationship to them. (At least five of them had started from the beginning as apprentices. I remember them well.) This alone shows that my father had no gifts to head a grand enterprise businesswise. Even I have no gifts in this respect. Ethically, however, I must admit he was superior.

My mother, Betty, suited my father exactly with her industrious, naïve nature. She was the fifth child of Solomon and Regine Glaser from Bisenz and was born in the Hanna, a fertile part of Maehren. Solomon Glaser was an innkeeper and had a cheese store. When the Swiss bought him out, he sold his round cheeses in Vienna. Before 1848, only firstborn boys could marry, as Austria had a law that forbade Jewish marriages. Therefore, my grandfather could marry my grandmother only after they had already had two children. My mother described my grandfather as a childlike, jolly man with little business sense. Once he acquired a new suit he loved it so much that he would also wear it while making cheese. I resemble him a little around the mouth and am as thin as he was. Of his seven children only one is living, Leopold Glaser. who has a foundry in Vienna.

The marriage of my parents has given me from childhood on an unshakable faith that a marriage can be something good and wonderful. During their early years my parents were good-looking and for twenty-five years they hardly had any illnesses. Both marriage partners were industrious. They identified with each other and, as far as I know or could observe, there was no problem regarding faithfulness. This question never even surfaced. Everything which I write here is the truth as far as it is known to me. My parents were deeply devoted to each other without having many outside interests and were highly valued and loved in their circle, both as a couple and individually.

Hagen, November 1922

I must unfortunately conclude that you misunderstand completely my point of view regarding the question of religion. I am pretty free of any prejudices regarding racial questions as long as they don't concern Hottentots or certain Asiatic people. Otherwise, I look only at the inner qualities a man possesses, how he acts, what he achieves. It is true, however, that certain racial character traits could alienate my sympathy even if they were only superficial. This is not the case as far as you are concerned, and as long as we now know each other, everything is in good order.

I assume, however, that your remarks concern the request from my wife to omit the question of religion in the wedding banns. This you apparently misunderstood. The request was made mainly through me and I repeat it here again. Should my letter seem matter-of-fact and dry, I hope nevertheless your fine ear can discern my real feelings.

Hagen, November 1922

I have nothing to say regarding your Jewish religion. I am proud that you are a Jew. In Hagen, as well as in Zurich, it will appear thus in the wedding banns. Muetterli does not want people to turn up their noses without knowing who you are. You will have to settle it with my parents. If I say anything they scornfully reply that I am under your influence. I am *convinced* that you can *personally* change their minds.

Vaterli is really an anti-Semite, only somewhat subdued through Muetterli. Instinctively Muetterli feels the same way, but intellectually she tries to combat it from a feeling of justice. This she will not admit.

Berlin, November 1922

I have only one consolation in this whole matter of religion, namely that you, dear Dione, not even *once* mentioned to me that you see any blemish in me through my parent's religion, rather to the contrary. If you mention this to your parents, "they think scornfully I am under your influence." This you write me.

How would it be if I had friends who shrugged their shoulders not because I was marrying a Gentile girl, but because I played a masquerade with my nature and put my head in the sand? How would you feel if my relatives liked you personally but secretly feared you might bring shame and disgrace on the family?

*Dione to Richard*

Everybody has reason to esteem, if not to admire, you. If the mention of religion cannot be omitted from the wedding banns, which, of course, would be the best solution, then we have to mention it. Don't worry about it. Vaterli will be impressed that you remain firm.

As far as I am concerned, I wish you would do what you consider the right thing. Somehow people will discover the facts anyway and to me personally it is surely a matter of indifference what strangers say about us. Anyone whom we meet personally and who gets to know you will overcome his prejudice, and if by chance they don't, do I not have you? What more do I need?

I also feel that if Vaterli's position is so precarious that such an item could hurt him, then any other matter could also shake him. I understand his reasoning but am so glad that you stick to your guns. You have to affirm your heritage.

I know in my heart that we fit well together, that I wish nothing more ardently than to see you happy and creative. What has that to do with religion? If I were you, I would know that I am a worthy member of my people. If others cannot see it, then it is, of course, sad but unimportant. What is essential, it seems to me, is how *we* look at it. You would have reason to be sad if I felt lukewarm about it, which, however, I do not at all. If I had the choice of getting for Christmas a Richard who was a Gentile rather than a Jew, I would not want him. Probably because I would know that as a Gentile he could never have those qualities which I treasure most in you. Nothing is further from my mind than to endure upturned noses or shrugging shoulders. This will glide off us like oil. I hope you feel the same way.

*Richard to Dione*

Surely nobody can claim that I am dumbstruck, but I *absolutely cannot* find words to express to you, my treasure, my faithful good one, *how* happy every word in your letter has made me. Such a wave of kind and loving resolutions you have been able to raise in my innermost being, bringing them into motion. If you keep on thinking and being as you write you will surely influence me through your nature as I may influence you, my great, great treasure. And from whom do you have this nature, from your parents, from your ancestors? But in the last analysis you are your own self, the Dione who exists only once. Tell this to your parents when they mention again that you are influenced by me. Tell them that you know *how* to direct me and *how* to influence me. Tell them that you intend to try not to forget this knowledge but to deeply intensify it, that you see this as the clearly delineated path which you intend to pursue, that nothing will sway you to the contrary.

My sweet darling, I am so happy! You were for me the focal point in this whole controversy, but I did not want to estrange you from your family and do not intend to do so in the future. If my path in this direction has so far not been the right one, I know no other, I cannot learn another one. My intelligence, my heart cannot grasp another one. Many things I have to tell you, but all this is unimportant because I am so happy about you and how you wrote me.

Of course all this is "incredibly stupid and crack-brained" as you write, but you can now *see* what a weight off my soul it was to recognize that you stand by me. If fate grants it, then your children and my children will be *your* children and my children. But I have no idea how to educate them "confessionally." However, it is my firm resolve to behave in such a way that later on they can acknowledge, without anxious hearts, that I was their father and my parents their grandparents. If your parents were deeply religious, afraid that their grandchildren might lose their souls unless they were baptized, I would probably have to respect their fearful forebodings and perhaps something could be done to alleviate their superstition.

Do you know that everything is failing? The currency debacle is very detrimental and unsettling. There is cessation of building activity, catastrophic unemployment throughout. The financial gain this year is equal to zero. All savings have now vanished. All possibilities look impenetrably black. In normal times, without a much higher salary, I could have easily married and could have covered all initial expenses. That's how the devil fools you.

Berlin, November 1922      *Richard to Dione*

I can foresee that I shall have a very painful financial discussion with Mendelsohn. He will try to avoid honoring the sliding index of my salary. I realize myself that this may be difficult for him, and I don't quite know what counter proposals I could make. Still, I don't want to admit defeat. All the big projects are far progressed, and thus the building costs on which, of course, our salaries are based, are diminished. Times are unbelievably difficult. I beg you, dear Dionerl, to keep these matters to yourself, for the time being. This winter will probably prove to be an obstacle course for me.

Hagen, November 1922      *Dione to Richard*

These are really trying and desperate times and I understand your despondency. I felt the same way when I saw this misfortune approaching ever faster and nearer so that one could only with hesitation look into the future. We will not lose courage.

I was so afraid you would write me that we'd better forget our wedding plans.

Berlin, November 1922      *Richard to Dione*

My dear bride Dione  Today, I have only the choice to either not write at all or write a short letter for Sunday. Yesterday night, I had another discussion with Mendelsohn. This goes for weeks. All anticipated difficulties are here, and I defended you like a wounded leopard—because for myself I need not much. At times, I felt my strength ebbing—I work so hard during the day—and the ground under me gives way.

For instance, when I said I had written to you that Mendelsohn had great confidence in my good business sense and that I would be ashamed to conduct contract negotiations like a fool. You supposedly had answered that in *this* case (conducting contract negotiations foolishly) Mr. Mendelsohn would gladly close an eye. Resounding laughter. I cannot deny, unfortunately, that he has been using the period I asked him to wait, so that I could confer with you, to narrow down many of his proposals and withdraw others silently, but decisively.

*Richard to Frances*
*Toplitz*

Berlin, December 1922

This past year I have lived in complete isolation. Also, my work did not leave any time for happiness, except in my work, and an occasional walk in the forest. I would like to have the happiness to care for someone else, and nevertheless try to remain an artist. We architects are not mimosas like musicians. Anyone who wants to build must learn to *live* with difficulties and worries. All-around life is the school of the architect. In the final realization, the architect is probably a hermit, but he cannot always have been a hermit.

Dione, that is the name of my future wife, is mobile, adaptable, as far as one can see now. I hope to God she will be able to bear with patience all inconveniences and unexpected changes that will confront her, as she wants to be my companion. I cannot help that my path is not quite a bourgeois one.

*Richard to Dione*

Berlin, December 1922

You have been my sweet, heavenly treasure for a long time and are thus today. I was very happy about your letter. I believe you will be able to remain happy during your whole life with or despite all the adventures you must experience with me. We shall mightily strive to become a proper and well-matched couple and remain so. One difficulty which I have and which I cannot help is that my body and soul are terribly intertwined so that bodily irritations visibly accompany emotional variations. But this could be both a fault and a virtue.

This evening I feel sorrowfully threatened because you are supposed to be a mortal creature. Of course, I know that this is not so. The greatest happiness one experiences when young is not fully recognized nor fully savored if one has to be separated prematurely, before the time has arrived to look back to a past shared together. Youth shows no great understanding, chases after different styles of happiness and play. For the future one can always find companions. Those who know the past one should be able to keep. Every event and every emotion is irretrievable, cannot be brought back and separates us from all those who did not share our experiences (no matter what distance separates us), but with those who shared, we are cordially united (wonderful when the heart can feel it thus).

Write me everything that unburdens your heart.

First of all, you know me by now and *know* how I want to treat you and do everything according to your heart's desire. Also, you are neither losing yourself nor your freedom. Only you must always openly tell me what bothers you. If you prefer you can have your own room and I shall keep away from you. . . . I will tell you stories and you will read to me. There will be smooth and rough stretches in life. Surely, it need not be a paradise, but only a true earthly existence. Naturally, we will not forget the stars. Look, my darling, have no care; I must be not only your beloved and your friend but also your girl friend, giving you a chance to complain about the two previously mentioned ones. Be of good cheer and jump! You need not be stouter, nonsense! First *I* decide about your beauty and long afterwards, you. I also know what an architect needs as far as your cello playing is concerned, to savor life. If we can halfway swing it, you must take vocal lessons again. Dear, treasured Dionerl, my Dionerl, keep your peace and may God protect you.

Berlin, December 1922

For years you may have found it amusing to speak about a "bride-groom." No thought is given as to how the poor devil should cope with his solitude. Solitary but independent, that's possible. No sad glance, no responsibility towards anyone for whatever crazy or daring step one contemplates. Or: lonely but in grievous, yearning cohesion with a faithful soul, separated for the time being on account of a life-important idea, a life advancement—that's possible, must be possible.

Children fulfill this need in addition to fulfilling their own need of growing up, even though they may force their progenitors into a thousand worries, a hundred concerns, and five mortal terrors.

The most comfortable situation is to live childless with one's wife, and the man who wants to remain mobile tends very much in this direction. A marriage that starts out with this premise is not much more than a liaison for a time. Children out of wedlock appeared to me always to be the most beautiful and noble ones, even when neither the father nor the mother completely fulfilled their tasks. To have children legitimizes the relation of man to woman. To comfortably "indulge" sexually, to "playfully" learn something great, to manipulate religion in an easy manner, subscribe to a reading circle, what is this? NO—drudgery, effort, painful moments cannot be avoided if being a happy human being is to keep its meaning and greatness.

"Happiness" may result after one is able to overcome certain terrors. Perhaps I am wrong? The shepherd and his shepherdess in their idyllic hut, without danger and without mother's-milk will, in the long run, become like animals. When I hear the term "gratification" used instead of "happiness," I get an upset stomach for a moment. (That's an example of what I wrote you recently, namely, that an emotion immediately manifests itself in me physically.)

When two human beings, hand in hand, and with blissful eyes, finally enter the Garden of Eden, they must together have endured some soul torment, pangs of hunger, separation, disappointments, with regard to human relations and children.

*Dione to Richard*

Hagen, December 1922

We want to say to each other right away, dear Richard, should we have children, we should not expect anything from them. They are only a loan and when they leave the house, we will again be alone as at the start. So many mothers forget this. However, I think they forget and hang on to their children because they are disappointed in their mates.

Oh, how wonderful it would be if we could grow old together! I shall take good care of you. Hopefully, you will not always continue in the same tempo as now with Mendelsohn. Hopefully I shall become ever less centered as time goes on and expect less and less.

*Richard to Dione*

Berlin, December 1922

I am happy in my innermost being to know how you feel with regard to having children. Besides all actual facts, just your feelings about this make me happy. To start out, right from the beginning to play God is not only ugly but perhaps also somewhat of a curse. After all, both parents "receive" a child from *beyond*; only a fool can claim here his *free will*. We will thoroughly reinforce each other and speak our minds.

*Richard to Dione*

Berlin, December 1922

I have my periodic days nearly as regularly as you have them. If not a belly ache, a general emotional and physical depression which I now expect on December 30 or 31. For this reason I would rather not be with you during these days. It is sufficient that I shocked Muetterli around October 2 when I visited you. After a more pronounced depression I sometimes have three especially good weeks, as I had in the following October weeks. It is sometimes very difficult when unavoidable decisions or transactions need to be made on these days.

*Dione to Richard*

Hagen, December 1922

Naturally, I was very interested in what you wrote me concerning your depressed days. However, I was not as surprised as you might imagine. Wille once read to me from a book which described how men, as well as women, have their days of diminished vitality. Muetterli, however, believes that married men are less frequently thus afflicted. I wanted to discuss this in person; that's why I did not write about it. Would it not be wonderful if these depressed periods occurred less frequently or you would completely lose them? However, I rather assume that you will keep them, but perhaps they will be less pronounced.

The letterhead of the paper on which I am writing has been with me since I've been so unhappy, even unhappier than I was in January 1915. But I believed in you, my dear Dione and took up the struggle. During these three years I have taken gigantic steps in my profession.

While I waited at the boat pier in Waedenswil at 7:30 A.M. during a November rain, after I had drawn all afternoon a ridiculous spiral stairway in a housing project, I felt terribly wretched. In yearning excitement I watched the evening train race by. These people are perhaps on their way to Cherbourg, or so I thought. Not even your letters cheered me up. From nowhere, nowhere, nowhere did I find an understanding for my plight. Whoever observed my efforts during these three years, my hard work, my ambition, will surely admit that my friends at that time only *very* partially understood my grief. Many often repeat that I am too modest, but in some very important points they think much more modestly about my gifts, or rather they do not think at all and only the success of my efforts will be decisive for them. No use complaining about that. After all, these are the "others."

If you want to be as one with me, your belief in me must be independent of every success, must be absolute where it touches on what is essential, where it concerns the core, the primeval essence.

Every good wife should thus believe in her husband. She should recognize and love all his good natural tendencies despite the most adverse entanglements and unfavorable circumstances. That other persons should behave in such a way is surely not to be expected. However, the most intimate friend and companion in misfortune must become a more loving, a more cognizant witness of what Providence attempted here, even if she does not fully accomplish her objective. What is an objective? Is it not enough of a goal if there is at least a second human being in this awesome, empty universe who reacts positively this way or that? I sincerely hope that you are capable of echoing each high and worthwhile sound. Don't let it bother you if others call you uncritical for silly reasons. Let others seldom see it.

On account of my adaptability it could have been very possible for me, here I have no doubts at all, to find a wife in circles financially and socially way above mine. My thoughts rise playfully as high as the Duke of Buckingham. You know, my treasure, that this is not idle boasting. Nearly all, or let's quietly say *all*, people I have met and who let me come near them according to their wishes have found me sympathetic. But just because I am able to put myself instinctively in their accustomed field of vision I have hardly ever been able to have anyone take interest in my own work. This is my greatest weakness. It is doubtful whether even concentrated effort could overcome this. It is not only a practical but also a moral failing, even if behind this adaptability lies hidden a true individual substance. However, I hide everything that is worthwhile and sacred to me. I hide it from those who *cannot*, without my arousing their enthusiasm, surmise and feel with me. To become a full success one has to use propaganda to propagate one's ideals, foregoing modest reserve.

On the face of it I could ride magnificently—and how—with a bride who owned millions, could hunt with the hounds on magnificent horses, magnificently done up, without having to unlearn anything. Only I would have to have shirts of the right size with collars that fit. In the same way, I could cook and drink a cup of cocoa in any kind of lodgings with you, my treasure. I truly know that this is so and not only on the face of it. I do not know anyone in my acquaintance to whom I could ascribe a similar ability, namely such a peculiar strangeness with regard to social, societal regulations and at that I am anything but a swindler or quick-change artist.

Undoubtedly I am somewhat of an oddity in a soup kitchen as well as in an aristocratic society, but there or here or anywhere I can, well liked, fit in.

How does it all help? Perhaps not much, but it is a fact. I am neither this nor that, and some believe, instinctively, that I am this or that and that I lead them astray. But towards you, my dear, I have faith that you recognize my true self and that you will help me strengthen and fortify all that is good and worthwhile in my nature. For this reason I have lived such a solitary existence during all these years and have unreservedly remained faithful to you with all my soul which may not be self-evident in a man of my versatile character. I put all my faith in you, my life's treasure.

*Richard to Muetterli*

Berlin, December 1922

My Muetterli, I *understand* that you are again and again concerned with what kind of man I am, not *what* kind of an architect, what kind of a working-day person or Sunday person, but what kind of a nocturnal person of the masculine gender.

My dear, sweet Muetterli, every evening I resolve to become for my beloved Dionerl, my heart's treasure, your child, a good, faithful, sensitive and considerate husband. I am resolved to be at moments (as they happen to come) like a mother to her, as you would be. Should she feel lonely because she does not have an understanding feminine person around her, she must know that she has a loving husband who, however, is yet only a man.

It is my intention to merge myself into her as if I had her body, her soul. If my love is not capable of that then it is not more than selfishness and the best advice falls flat. You know that I am right. My Muetterli, I am not a cool person. My sexual powers have not been wasted. My body has been healthy (only somewhat sensitive through this long period of abstinence). How Dionerl is in this respect I hardly know, do not dare to ask her either as I do not intend to base any decisions on it. However as she loves me so much, also likes to keep my body in her arms, I hope that fate will grant me that she will be permanently happy with me. I don't know how to express myself differently. *If only I never cause her grief or sorrow!*

What happened between us was always as natural as could be expected under the given conditions. I cannot boast about my self-control. If we became more intimate than you would have allowed, then it surely is my fault and not hers, but I truly did not treat her badly and rejoice in this knowledge.

My dear, kind Muetterli, I have this deep-felt request: Don't ask Dionerl how we feel towards each other sexually. For us this should remain a holy secret. We will want to talk about it only when we are much older. Anything factual you want to know, I shall truthfully and gladly tell you.

Berlin, December 1922

Miss Dione Niedermann, I shall now stop writing. We did correspond honestly and nicely, did we not? Well—I am not a letter writer. If I am tired, I don't like to write and if I feel fresh I'd rather take a walk and think or work. But to you I will always like to write because you read my letters with joy and attention, just as I read yours.

When you return to Berlin you will like it much less than when you left it in June's sunshine. Well—we shall try to do our best to forget about Berlin. In my heart there is a piece of Vienna and the lake of Zurich and so there must be in yours. Otherwise we shall think of other regions, think of California, of the California coast and palm trees.

I hope you will become accustomed to my eccentricities sooner than to my virtues. Are you not very much afraid that through habituation I may lose some or all charm? Be not afraid, my great treasure, and face bravely what may even be unattractive to you. What comes toward us from the lap of the gods? We do not wish to know it. We want to be young and good, my sweet Dione.

Berlin, December 1922

My wife shall above all fortify me and unequivocally let me feel that she knows the good which is in me and in my gifts. Nothing romantic—rather something ETERNAL.

In our profession there are only a handful of men who strive with a pure heart, and those are known. There may also be a few unknowns, like my friend Schindler. All else was created in a spirit of speculation, a seeking for originality by any means, or in just imitating and changing examples of former periods. All these people do not have the ethical calling to be architects or teachers. I am modest, not a conceited fool; above all, I know the limits of my gifts or, even more, those of my interest for the daily battle.

Perhaps I am more gifted to be director of an enterprise than to be an entrepreneur on my own account; I am sure I could be one just like anybody else, but my preference is not sufficient. The small tragedy of my life is clearly delineated in soul and body as it is in every human being.

The time will probably come when I will feel that this early period may be the happiest one, even if I should be successful at a later period. Each success has to be bought with a thousand neglects. But you should never feel neglected, as long as I am engaged with my better self and my work. For this is your companion, and this shall be our common work. A man neglects his wife only when he makes love to another woman, when he sits in a club or in a cafe gambling, when he is too much of a businessman or a bibliophile, and in all these endeavors does not integrate his own self while he could have aspired to something greater.

Mendelsohn once said: "If a man can stand marriage, can endure a marriage, and continue with his gifts, then only has he proven himself." I think it shows above all his recklessness. There could be a gifted man who might abstain from certain tasks because he values his family too much. A man with vision, surely would love above all his inner path, because this is the highest he can give his beloved. Otherwise, he has made a present of glittering stones, keeping the real diamonds for himself.

I hope to God—and he has to be our hope in this immense mysterious black universe—O God, may these words not sound high and mighty, flying through the air like Spanish race horses, but sound convincing in this last letter which I write to you, my beloved, as a bachelor. . . .

*Dione to Richard*                                        Hagen, December 1922

I can fully enter into your feelings and thoughts, but am fearful that I may not always be able to do so, or that you may have thoughts and feelings which I may be unable to share with you. But, my beloved friend, I think I can say with a good conscience that you will not find another girl who sees her task as clearly as I see mine.

"To fulfill one's potentials"—this you once told me and I have never forgotten it. That I can keep your love best by keeping this always in mind, by helping you towards this goal or at least never hinder you in it, I am quite aware of. I may perhaps forget it for hours, because every person is a little selfish and I have my share of selfishness. I cannot tell you how inexpressively glad I am that I learned to know you before our marriage, because I might have lost your love or perhaps your confidence if I had understood you so little. You would have become accustomed to settle difficulties within yourself alone, and later on it might have been impossible or very difficult to regain lost confidence—the tragedy of many marriages, I believe. My dear Richard, I am quite aware that our marriage can be a wonderful one, that I am a woman who could be envied if I am able to fulfill the task I see in front of me. But the path leading to this goal is a long one and the devil may have a chance to set many traps. Let's never harbor resentment against each other; let's discuss what seems unclear. Otherwise, there is not much to think about. After all, we love one another and feeling with one another will accomplish more than talking about it. The most important thing is to be clear about one's path and always to find back to it.

You write me that you want to make everything lovely and easy for me, my darling. But do I want that? Oh, no. I want to have the feeling that if you have to work very hard, I also should work very hard so I don't have to be ashamed of myself.

Our wedding ceremony will take place at 9:00 A.M. We shall have breakfast afterwards and then Richard and Dione will take a lovely walk together while the family prepares for the festivities and the wedding feast. Then your Dionerl will don her wedding dress and her Richard a black suit after which the couple will be celebrated by the family. Juchhe! My mother thinks it is absolutely unnecessary that I write you a letter so shortly before our marriage. But it is important for me to write you and while writing become clear myself.

Spinster Dionerl sends her love to her bachelor Richard.

*As a part of the wedding festivities in Hagen on December 23, 1922, sister Vreneli wrote the following puppet show: "A devil and an angel are busily working to put the finishing touches and necessary ingredients into a soul they have fashioned together. Then the devil runs out of material and goes back to hell to fetch some more. 'Now, while he is gone, is my golden opportunity to fashion a perfect soul,' thought the angel. She worked feverishly, reflecting at the last moment, 'If I make this soul too perfect, she will be unhappy on earth.' So she put in a few unimportant foibles like love for coffee, love for chocolate, and love for detective stories. Then she tied the soul that she and the devil had fashioned and the angel's 'perfect' soul together with one of her golden hairs, signifying that these two had to find one another on earth. When the devil returned from hell he discovered the deed and, full of fury, tore the two souls apart, hurling the first one down to earth, exclaiming: 'I will put a hundred years between them so that they cannot find each other.' Then the devil and the angel wrestled with each other. But by the count of nine the angel managed to throw down the second soul." (Richard was nine years older than Dione.)*

*Richard and Dione enjoy married life in Eichkamp.*

*An expected baby in December causes them to appraise their immediate and future plans.*

*Richard redoubles his efforts to get to the United States.*

*Mendelsohn and Richard win a first prize for a harbor development plan for Haifa. With his share of the prize money Richard is able to afford a trip to the U.S., arriving in October.*

*Dione stays with her parents to have their baby and thus not complicate his start in the New World.*

*Richard finds a job with an architectural firm in Brooklyn.*

*1923*

*Richard to Muetterli*

When we took the train from Hagen to Frankfurt Dione had a chance to rest for a while in the compartment. Her dear head lay on her music satchel towards the door, with my handkerchief underneath. Her left arm lay stretched out on the blue-gray cushion. (We were traveling second class like rich folk!) One could readily observe the curve of her elbows. Her right underarm was stretched upward along the wall and the hand, adorned with the wedding ring, lay nicely on the armrest. The smooth arms contrasted flowery white against the black satin and velvet of her dress. Her eyes were closed. I stood outside in the corridor, Muetterli, and I looked at her. Such happiness welled up in my heart every few minutes that I had to turn away and look out the window.

Darling Muetterli, I shall think of you when you say good-bye to our Dione. It is not only up to us to learn to adjust nicely to each other in the coming months, and we shall write you happy letters, but we will be tuned in to each other deeply and most gratefully because we found each other. We will put, so to speak, the "idol" of our domestic bliss between us, we shall nourish it with our virtues, shall carefully consolidate it with our assets, and for its sake keep our vices down and play our weaknesses down. I know that it will be more difficult for Dione, but I hope and trust that she will learn to forgive my shortcomings, that she will understand me.

*Dione to Her Parents*

I want to describe to you how we now live in Berlin. Entering the front door, a straight stairway leads to the first floor of this small house. Straight ahead is the W.C. with a water faucet near the floor. At right is the room which used to be Richard's bachelor quarters and is now our living room.

All four walls, from ceiling to floor, are covered by a soft, light beige material. The floor is covered with wall-to-wall carpeting. Against one wall stands a piano. A couch and a few simple easy chairs complete the room where guests are to be received. Now, however, comes the biggest surprise. After climbing the narrow garret stairs one sees something that looks like a kitchen and therein is a make-believe sink and drainboard. As it was economically not feasible to extend the water pipe to the attic, I have to fetch water from the faucet in the W.C. and carry the bucket of dirty water from underneath the sink back down the steep stairway to be emptied into the toilet. However, the installation looks like a real kitchen. Also the little attic room I remembered has been completely changed. The form of the slanting ceiling made it possible to attach a ceiling-to-floor drape on one end behind which a bed and a washstand are hidden. On the opposite wall stand a couch with a colorful cover, a table and chairs, as well as the famous "Grude" oven on which I do my cooking. Of course, there is no ice chest, not to speak of a refrigerator! Later in the summer when it becomes very hot, I will have to climb down three stairways to the basement where I will fill the bathtub with water and float containers filled with butter, eggs, or leftovers in order to keep them from spoiling.

I have to walk half an hour to do my shopping and usually carry my purchases back in a knapsack. Nevertheless, I am enthusiastic observing how lovingly and ingeniously Richard has managed to transform our surroundings.

*Richard to Muetterli*

Erich Mendelsohn has returned from his trip. I spoke with him this afternoon. In the morning, we celebrated the completion of the rough building phase of the Mossehaus, while the fragrance of Dutch imports wafted into the air. "Oveja blanca," what a strange name for a black cigar! Well—if I compare Mendelsohn to a black sheep that seems out of place among all the white ones, so he seems out of place among the Zionists in Palestine. The planning commissioner of Jerusalem lives with his wife in a small room and draws from dawn to midnight housing plans for which he received a pittance. Mendelsohn had a very peculiar experience with him which seems to characterize Mendelsohn or, at least, his attitude with regard to a common goal or task. In short, there is "no money" at hand in Palestine or "no money" as it would appear to him. Our battle is starting again, and I can already see how he starts manipulating. I am convinced that I shall have to give in. The crisis in the building sector is now very apparent. The funniest thing is that I have done locally for the prospects in Palestine as much as Mendelsohn himself has done in Palestine.

Eichkamp, March 1923

Sunday I went to the office with Richard for a few hours and sewed. I love to look at him while he works and thus I mind it less when he also has to work on Sundays. . . .

. . . We really get along very well, dear Muetterli, but I believe Dione will be less pliable towards you than when she was a bride. I am sure she will want to boss you around as she does me. In this point we now resemble an honest-to-goodness real American couple. . . .

You ask me about your daughter's future. I don't know it! I assume that I shall not always stay with Mendelsohn; however, there are no other heart and soul-filling possibilities in sight. After he returns from Palestine, my relationship with him may change, since the relationship is so unstable.

Eichkamp, April 1923

I am out of sorts at the moment because I have artistic differences with Mendelsohn and have to contend with his envy. I have never stopped being amazed how I was able to hold on to this position, how I could achieve this balancing act and still hold on to my integrity. In order to be married to an architect one has to be endowed with a steady, gay disposition; one sees him as little as if he were a sea captain.

I had a string of successes and could show Mendelsohn effectively my worth and significance, as for instance, during the really interesting competition for a business center in Haifa

It remains a tragedy that my success, once it becomes apparent beyond the confines of our office, is not something he appreciates. Here I can feel with him, can even appreciate it, because he is an artist, but on the other hand, I cannot see a solution.

I say all this without wanting to disparage Mendelsohn in the least who has other excellent qualities. It would be quite wrong to try to stir me up against him, or try to get me to leave him.

As far as my political convictions are concerned, which Dione mentioned, I know that Germany is unhappy, but that nevertheless all other countries believe in its exterior future. I know that a vast number of German people are completely innocent about the present unhappy state of affairs, are sad about it and suffer, although they are innocent. Out of inner necessity, I believe that there must be human beings in all countries who are reasonable and of goodwill, and the only hope for peace is that some of them gain power in the various countries, communicate with each other, and reach an agreement above and beyond the fruitless feelings of revenge and prejudice.

*Dione to Her Parents*

Finally spring has come. The air is filled with the most delicious scents. I am unspeakably happy that we can live in the country and not in the city where it is horrible, where people sit on benches in the park like half-dead flies, and the air is full of dust, where one hardly dares to breathe. However, out here it is wonderful.

We spent three hours in the aquarium on Saturday. I was quite giddy with delight. First we looked at the crocodiles. Some were small, some fat, some tremendous with mouths agape, others half submerged like lifeless logs. They were most uncanny. However, when a piece of meat sailed through the air, a sort of convulsion went through their bodies. Voracious eyes glared, wide-open jaws snapped, tails slapped the water, a most uncomfortable sight.

On Sunday we took the train to Potsdam and Werder. We got off at Potsdam and walked toward the city, then to the small Sans Souci Palace that seems to grow out of the ground and which one approaches over a terraced terrain planted solidly with purple pansies. I looked through the window into Frederick the Great's study and thought of Doris who loves the king more than any of us. Also, the park has most magnificent trees.

Then we walked through the forest in the midst of a stream of people on the way to Werder which is famous for its blooming fruit trees. The houses lie imbedded in white bloom. We tried to get away from the mass of people and miraculously found a little green valley bordered by large orchards. There we spent the whole afternoon, far from all the hubbub. It was rather cool but the sun shone warmly and we savored the blossoms, the scent, and the blue sky. Most of the trees were plum trees, small ones, planted very near each other, so that the effect was completely different from orchards in Switzerland.

In Werder we saw drunk men and women. This is the rule as the fruit wine is very potent. I was thirsty and wanted to try some too. However, this I shall never, never do again. It tasted marvelous but I got very dizzy and it wasn't worth it.

*From Dione's Diary*

Berlin, June 1923

We have difficulties with Mendelsohn. The altercations and discussions are continuous and Richard is down with his nerves. His relationship to Mendelsohn has become so intolerable that Richard is willing to give notice on July 1.

We had a letter from Schindler informing us that Wright[1] was considering to invite Richard to come to Los Angeles. I shall stay with Muetterli as I expect my child in December. I am so thankful that this will happen just at a time when there is a chance for a change . . . I am so gratefully aware how well suited we are to each other, what a good counter balance I am. We still do not know whether Richard will get his entry visa. Dear God, help us . . .

1. Frank Lloyd Wright.

Dione has ever more clearly recognized that my life is not smooth and easy, I agonize about matters that seem far removed from anybody else's thoughts. As yet, nobody can foretell whether my abilities will prove to be a compensation for these vexations. Dione understands my nature thoroughly and loves me nevertheless. I cannot say that this caused me to love her more but it gave me the confidence that we two could venture into matrimony. I am not an egoist who wants to torment anyone with his moods, especially not my wonderful Dione or you.

Just now I have terminated one of the best, perhaps *the* most prestigious and highly paid position for an employed architect. I leave this office whose future looks most promising to me. For a year and a half, I helped it along with all my energy and my perhaps excessive devotion. The disadvantages compared with the present situation are very grave indeed, and the American venture, not being a bird in the hand, will be something to be struggled for.

During your visit, my nerves were frayed, and I was *forced* to act *despite* my condition. To top it all, I am forced to come to grips with my convictions about architecture, and what path I should follow.

*The following letter to Richard is from Henry Menkes, a college friend from Vienna, living in New York City. He was responding to Richard's announcement of his impending move to the United States. It was Menkes with whom Richard first stayed on arriving in New York and who got him a job with the architect C. W. Short.*

Dear Richard Neutra   It is unimaginable what stories one hears regarding the immigration. Ellis Island has become a nightmare, a nocturnal demon. Besides, all the legal obstacles, there is rampant corruption as was discovered lately through various scandals. You are not only "looking for a job" but for something quite different? Possibly "ideas," a "new horizon"? Well, I surely sincerely hope that you will not be disappointed in your search once you have arrived. I hope and believe that you are capable to pierce the surface and find underneath the "something better" and "more worthwhile" you are seeking. I don't presume to doubt the idealism of a people but, really, what are the ideas of the day as they are depicted in the daily papers? Dempsey and Carpenter, prohibition and antiprohibition, "blue laws" and "anti blue laws," bobbed hair and vice versa, and the newest: The slow beginning of Jewbaiting, as they call it here, with Henry Ford, the famous automaker, organizer, philanthrope, and friend of Edison, as its leader! This is the "something quite different" you will first stumble over.

Doesn't Professor Einstein have the right idea when he states: "People here are so utterly bored that they gulp down every new sensation, even one like the 'relativity theory' which most people do not understand." With this criticism he offended many people. Many are deeply hurt.

As far as I am concerned, I am still in a bad fix. As I write this, I do not know where I will get the money for the postage. I can also boast that my record of starving has now reached 3½ days in a row. The unemployment situation is terrible. Whenever the most miserable position is advertised, a queue starts to form at 5:00 A.M. By 6:00 A.M., there are hundreds in line who produce a traffic jam; by 7:00 A.M. the police arrives to disperse the people. It is estimated that we have 500,000 persons without work, and nobody gives a hoot.

Thank you for your good advice to "start as a carpenter, cement worker, or what have you." Have you the faintest idea what kind of a monopoly or tyranny the labor unions exert here, and that a "greenhorn," a foreigner, could rather breach a wall by running with all his force against it than find entrance into a labor union? Do you know what happens to somebody who does not belong to a labor union, the so-called open-shop worker? Everybody tells him impatiently "no help wanted, the position is filled."

However, once you belong to a union, and *if* there is work, the situation is quite nice. A construction worker earns 80 cents an hour—even $1.20, and he can make approximately $8.00 a day.

Well, I shall stop lamenting. Let's speak of something else. I continue this letter after a week's interruption. In the meantime, I have found some work in a shirt factory. Heavy hard work during a nine-hour day. I earn about $18.00 weekly. I have to rise at 6:00 A.M., have to travel for an hour, to be at my place of work by 8:00 A.M.

There, I have to do tedious, hateful hard work for eight hours with three one-quarter-of-an-hour breaks, no shirking is possible. I return dead tired by 7:00 P.M., perspiring in the ovenlike heat in New York.

*Richard to Frances Toplitz*

Berlin, September 1923

My work here is almost completed. I am glad to leave something worthwhile to the Europeans while I float towards the Americans. I am told at the Cunard Line office that the *Laconia* will leave Hamburg October 13, reaching New York on the twenty-third. It appears to me it is high time to leave this district of humanity. During the last days, we lost again, for the hundredth time, half of our savings without being horrified. We have learned to be experienced losers. My Vienna is now a more secure place than this city where a streetcar ticket costs 250 marks. You simply cannot imagine how awful the situation has become. Well, Berlin is neither my nor my wife's hometown, and I cannot help. I understand very little about politics and I have no inclination for it. By the middle of this month, I hope to place my wife with her parents.

*From Dione's Diary*

Hagen, October 1923

. . . Yesterday my Richard left me. We do not know how long we shall be separated. Whenever I think about this separation my heart contracts. However, are we not united even if separated? . . .

Hagen, October 1923

. . . It is 11:00 A.M. and I have just figured out that you must already be in Hamburg or at least nearing it. If only you have good weather! During the night it was simply awful. The wind howled, the rain splashed with such fury against the window panes that I feared they would cave in.

It is so wonderful to feel that we belong to one another. If the baby in me did not move, I could believe that it was all a dream. . . .

Hagen, October 1923

. . . It is Sunday morning and I am trying to imagine what you may be doing at the moment, whether you have already reached Cherbourg, how you have slept, whether you feel well. All questions that will remain unanswered.

This morning I received your letter which made me very glad although I learned from it that you were very tired and had a terrible rush, my poor darling. I am so glad that at least on the ship you may have had a chance to be quiet, although I would not be at all surprised if even there you would manage to see and hear more than the ordinary mortals, my mobile Richard.

New York, October 1923

Dear Dionerl   Today, October 24, I really am in New York! Although I have only been here three and a half hours, I find myself already in a most amusing situation. I don't think it is possible to describe it to you. I sit alone, at a round table in a small apartment where the sunlight is enhanced by a gas flame.

Yesterday, and even the day before, a terrible storm developed. The ship lay more and more on its side, sometimes forty-five degrees. Everything movable crashed noisily against the slippery railing, while the rain poured down horizontally. Huge long and broad breakers moved like a jagged theater decoration one after another into the milky white foggy mist, smoked a thousand white fine sprays of foam skyward with every convulsive upward thrust of air. The water had the appearance of boiling sulphur. The ship tilted frighteningly in this Poseidon-like hubbub. An old lady tried to reach her cabin, fell down, took hold of me and a passing steward. All three of us stumbled into the heap of chairs piled up on the railing. Despite my efforts, the lady fell on her face. Suddenly on the left, a quarter mile away, a tanker loomed above the foaming waves, its course in a right angle towards us. (Even I could determine that it was a tanker, as I recognized the position of its smoke stack.) Due to our slanting position, it seemed as if the other ship, looked at from below, was descending on us, down the turbulent water slope with bulletlike rapidity. Our siren bellowed signals. One could see white vapor pour out of the other ship's foghorn without any sound whatsoever reaching us. Both ships maneuvered against the storm, stopped, honked, staggered against the frenzied horizon. The *Laconia* executed a huge curve, and the dancing tanker disappeared in the fog.

*Richard to Dione*

I continue my account: During the night the boat behaved in a most erratic manner. Finally, I lay down, fully dressed, and slept until midnight. Then, I undressed and slept until the dawn broke. We had already passed the canal between Long Island and Staten Island. The fog was thinner, the sea had quieted down. Now started a counting and maltreatment of passengers, interrupted by breakfast but most annoyingly continued in New York. On account of the fog, we could hardly see anything of the imposing entrance sight of New York. The Statue of Liberty was merely a shadow against the fog. When we arrived at the Cunard pier, we had to pass a lengthy immigration control in the dining room. The unusual cut of my overcoat helped me again to get through easily. Thus one enters a new part of the world in turmoil, hardly even noticing it. Then came a thorough customs control. My roll of drawings evoked an unusual and lengthy inspection.

I continue writing three days later, on Sunday morning, lying in bed. Only three days have passed, it is not to be believed! I wonder how you feel, because it is nearly three weeks that I do not know your state of mind.

Well, I took the streetcar and went as far as Union Square. From there I went on foot to Mr. Cypelman, whom I have quarters with.[2] While walking, my eyes took with pleasure all these huge building shapes. Twenty-first Street, at first glance, looked very shabby to me. Two-, three-, and four-story houses, painted red, occasionally of brick, rather dirty.

However, Gramercy Park immediately took my fancy. It is a small green spot, with a few trees, much smaller than Drescher Park in Vienna, in front of my brother's window. It is surrounded by small, larger, and huge buildings with wildly protruding contour lines, silhouetted against the sky. This tiny spot represents a forgotten peace where one only hears the striking of the huge Metropolitan Life Insurance Building's clocktower in Madison Square where the traffic rushes by. I climbed a steep, rather dilapidated, stairway to the fourth floor, was received and immediately recognized by Mr. Cypelman. To describe this man is the opposite from easy, and his surroundings seem to be made of the same stuff. Beforehand I should mention that Henry Menkes told me later: "Cypelman's soul is made of pure crystal," and I believe him. (If one dares making a comparison between a soul of gelatinelike consistency, or the rigidity of crystals.)

Herewith a floor plan of Cypelman's apartment. The corridor is very dark. Around the round walnut table in the living room are grouped an assortment of well-built, but rather old, leather-covered easy chairs. Dilapidated sliding windows, as seems usual here, seem not very stable. The blue-green oil paint in the breakfast room is peeling off in large patches.

My first impression is one of poverty and neglect without benefit of a housewife. Cypelman greeted me without a collar, in shirt sleeves with peculiarly upturned shoes of old vintage. He is perhaps 1.38 meters in height. He is bald, a tiny man with a long straight nose, underneath a gray moustache; occasionally, and with a rapid flick of the tongue from a mouth

2. Cypelman rented a room to Richard's friend Henry Menkes.

with many missing teeth, he seems to lick it with a peculiar tongue movement. I seemed to recall that he was a tailor. He told me that he came to New York from Kowno in Poland in his seventeenth year. He jumped around me quite gleefully and is very agile, as I soon found out. He gave me a letter from Henry Menkes informing me that Cypelman was going to celebrate in the afternoon his fifty-ninth birthday with his children and would leave the apartment. I rose solemnly and congratulated him on his birthday and on his youthful agility. Compared to him, I felt a clumsy giant. With the quickness of a darting weasel, he started to prepare a lunch for me, as it was by now two o'clock. Meanwhile, I lay down on Henry's clean bed in his small room. Then Cypelman led me to the kitchen table, served me a delicious omelette, some grits, cooked in milk, white bread and butter, tomato sauce in a bottle, and finally excellent grapes.

I was extremely and pleasantly surprised, expressed my feelings on various occasions, which apparently pleased him immensely, although he tried to look nonchalant. During the meal, I asked him about his profession, as he seemed to be such an excellent cook, and I nearly choked when he answered: "Singer"! He mentioned that he was a tenor who sang in vaudeville. In order to quiet my swallowing apparatus I figured with lightening speed that he sang in the chorus, though before I could swallow, I learned, however, that he was a soloist! With great pride, expansive movements, and glances, he led me to his record collection, to the piano opposite a grand piano in gothic style. He showed me a record Henry had given him for his birthday, a Schubert serenade. I fearfully glanced towards the dilapidated brick wall of the light shaft which one could dimly see through the gloomy window panes. Cypelman declared that Henry's record was not to his taste and he intended to exchange it. (Perhaps for "Love Is Just a Flower"—a fox-trot.)

Putting on a white collar, tucking the record under his arm, carefully locking his door, we descended the stairs, and I had to employ a special breathing technique to keep up with this small fifty-nine-year-old as we approached Irving Place at a fast pace. Passing Gramercy Park, he showed me a statue depicting Hamlet (quite good). Around Irving Place, there are modern 12–14-story-high office buildings, between them a row of "ancient" 2½-story-high gloomy houses, standing there perhaps since 70–80 years. Over an exterior stairway one enters into the gloomy interior of such a dwelling. Mrs. Urbahn, the German landlady, is a still young, pregnant woman who led us up on a steep, very dark stairway to the tiny, but very clean, room from which I write you this letter. However, it is light as there are no tall buildings, and the air that enters is quite good. Now we went to the record shop on Fourteenth Street to exchange the record. This Fourteenth Street is going to be my headquarters. In the store Cypelman chose some duets. A young lady brought us to a booth, gave us various new releases to listen to, which Cypelman disdainfully refused. I pleaded for the duet from *Don Giovanni*, "Tendimi la Mano," this product from Salzburg, but Cypelman thought it was not his cup of tea. I started to feel uncomfortably hot in this small space, until Cypelman found something to his liking. "The Shining Window," an Italian folk song, sung by the incomparable

Enrico. Truly an excellent production and my ear slowly became accustomed. The shopkeeper seemed visibly glad that we found something to our liking. Schubert was left behind, and pressing the Caruso record lovingly to his waistcoat, Cypelman sped towards the department store Hearn on Fourteenth Street, meanwhile explaining to me his ideas on physiotherapy, consisting mainly in drinking lots of water like Gil Blas as well as cold water rubs.

Cypelman purchased a marvelous rough yellow bathtowel from the magnificently dolled-up shop girl. Then we drank the right quantity of ice water from the fountain and left. We crossed Madison Square in a fast trot, passed the famous Flatiron Building and returned to Cypelman's apartment. He asked me about my musical taste. He could play *everything* worthwhile for me. I mentioned *Aida*. "What?" he said. "*Aida*," I said. But "What?" he said again. "I have six *Aida* records."

"I don't care," was my reply. He started with the overture. Then followed the tenor solo during the march, played by the brass instruments, finally the farewell death duet. I sat and my weariness slowly changed into a mellow mood. I was not exactly two hours in America. Here I sat, on the fourth floor of a proletarian apartment house, looked out to a sad wildly disorderly light shaft downward, a chimney upward, while I listened to Caruso and another famous Russian singer sing a duet I had not heard for many years, which had so deeply impressed me in Milano, in the Teatro dal Verme. I begged Cypelman to play this record again. The rain had stopped, through the clear transparent sky a bevy of birds was swirling. A late evening sun lay on the crown of the highest chimneys.

I looked out of the window when I heard the entrance bell ring, and who entered? Cypelman's youngest daughter—an elegantly dressed young woman with the here customary wavy bobbed hair. I was introduced. She is a teacher. Then, the son arrived with the here customary horn spectacles. He is a professor at a high school. Finally, the oldest daughter arrived. She had a well-formed intelligent face, surrounded by curly hair. Very soon the two young girls laughingly started to play on the two pianos, as if they were playing tennis or badminton. In the middle of their playing the brother would tear one sister away and laughing uproariously would continue to play himself until the sister would relieve him. Especially the older girl played with great technical skill. Finally, Cypelman made his appearance and put on the newly purchased Caruso record "The Shining Window." Once again I heard the beginning piano accords until Caruso let loose. Cypelman sat on the high piano stool, underneath a glass chandelier in form of a grape whose red light illuminated this temple of music. He sat with his head bowed, with his eyes closed, his short legs dangling without touching the floor. With his hands he followed quite unconsciously the tonal figures. As the sad melody swelled down to its finale, I observed with what deep love and affection his children looked at him, how at the end, they came to him to embrace and kiss him. I noticed how tears ran over his cheeks, because the music affected him so deeply. He hurried to put the record away and to blow his nose. Now these three presented to their father—my face became longer and longer—their birthday present: *The*

*Outline of the History of Mankind* by Wells. Kisses were exchanged, and I had to pull my ear whether I was really experiencing all this. Now, I had been 3½ hours in America. But you and I, we can clearly see that in the future I shall have to be briefer!

Hagen, November 1923

. . . Hurrah, this morning as I was deliberating whether I should get up, Vreneli brought me your letter, which was marvelous. I did not expect to get a letter so soon. I had been thinking: From November 4 on I shall silently hope for one. From November 8 on I shall expect one. That's typical of Dione, is it not, my darling?

The sentence in which you write that you have been thinking about your professional development and that you suddenly see your work from an astoundingly different angle, occupies my mind most. You write you will tell me in person about it. Oh, my mystery monger! I surely cannot come earlier than in four months, especially if the baby does not arrive before the middle of January. Will you really let me hang fire for so long? No. I hope you will sit down at your desk one rainy Sunday and write your Dione what thoughts occupy your mind. Concrete facts are, of course, very important, but they do not hold my interest for longer than the three or four minutes time in which I'm reading them, while thoughts spoken from your heart to mine stay with me always. It is these passages that I continually re-read.

That you will not be with me at the birth now makes me somewhat sad. I hear your voice saying: "But Dionerl, I *am* with you." This you are, but if I remain silent you will never know what thoughts assail me.

New York, November 1923

I am telling you of my first job—pronounced "djab." The situation is as hard as I imagined it, and it is difficult to figure in ⅜ inches. To subtract 9′10″ from 13′8″, for instance, is cumbersome. At the same time, all sorts of technical expressions whirl around my ears, as well as office jargon of regular English words, often incorrectly pronounced (according to the ideas of blue-blooded Americans, too), spoken by many foreigners who make up 70 percent of New York's population. Mrs. Toplitz speaks by far the most cultivated English. On top of all, this Mr. Short is a terrible squabbler.[3] He is very impatient and shouts around. Short's wrathful eruptions are mainly in three-minute intervals, directed towards his two oldest draftsmen who really must be pitied. Nothing is done fast enough. There is no time for even the most crucial explanation. The two commissions we are working on, have not yet been awarded, and so my employment is explicitly temporary. The floor plans of these clubhouses may have advantages (as yet I do not understand enough of American club life), but they look very haphazard to me, thrown together without regard for struc-

3. C. W. Short in Brooklyn, Richard's first employer. See above, "Henry Menkes to Richard."

tural necessities or light influx. Regarding all the above mentioned difficulties, Henry estimated that I would receive a weekly wage of $15.00; thus it was a very agreeable surprise when Short granted me without ado a wage of $30.00. Thus, I have so far earned $35.00 in America! Everything is somewhat easier, as I have no other aim but to prolong my employment from one day to the other and use this opportunity to acquire a little knowledge of technical English. On the other hand, Short's character traits complicate the situation. So far, he treats me with a certain respect, probably because Henry told him how independently I worked in Germany.

Yesterday I took a walk through the East Side where the Jews have settled in unbelievable masses and from where they advance into the highest strata of society. Sometimes, very fast. Above all, they have an unbelievable thirst for knowledge. More than 90 percent of all New York college students are Jews. There is tremendous activity in these quarters and one could imagine that these people are a threat to Anglo-Saxon America.

Then, I saw the metal shops of the Palestinian and Syrian Jews, saw the unbelievable masses of people pouring out of all sorts of evening seminars. One also hears excellent music. Finally, I came to the Chinese in Chinatown. All of this is very strange indeed, my Dionerl. Dionerl, I am just thinking how marvelous it is that every week one pays the same amount for rent, food, etc. No prices are raised, no need to run and hastily make a purchase. People here create their unrest in a different way. I find it strange, for instance, that there is no spot that corresponds to our cafes. Even restaurants are used purely for consuming a meal. In order to be social, one belongs to a club. In a way, it is very funny that some people possess good traits which are stunted in others, nearly atrophied, so that they seem to miss certain advantages. I have to experience each new set of circumstances with tolerance and learn to enjoy what is there.

*Richard to Dione*                                                  New York, November 1923

In many ways I shall not see America as a tourist would. It is simply not in the cards. Even with my iron will, it cannot be done. I do not have the time, the money, and the opportunity to see "everything." But in my own bittersweet way, I shall battle to gain experience, of course not in a stoic manner like the Indians or with an Anglo-Saxon fortitude. They do not show any emotion regarding painful experiences.

. . . It would really be quite interesting to once work for two months in a French architectural office as well as in an English and Dutch one. This would provide a chance to get a real insight into the limitations of our profession. . . .

As far as I am concerned, I have to tunnel through a mountain of difficulties, hardly noticed by those surrounding me. Who really knows who I am? Well—let's see what will happen. In any case, should I ever attain success I will have achieved it not through trickery but by having been lucky, because by being only industrious one does not get to the top, but fate rewards the industrious one, because contrary to the gambler, he expects less and adapts himself to the surrounding circumstances.

New York, November 1923

I visited the Natural History Museum and came into the room of the Pueblo Indians. These are the people who influenced the modern Californian building activity. Whole villages were built in one block on the top of a mountain. These cubes, hardly without any windows, are more than one story, have terraces on front of the setback of the upper stories. It is impossible to comprehend the complexity of this agglomeration of building cubes. Everything in this museum seems unbelievably rich and massive but not very systematic. It caters somewhat to the curiosity seeker. It seems less scientific, is meant more for the general visitors who have a sense of humour, who like to see interesting juxtapositions or read explanations like in a newspaper article.

I am glad when I have to do so much mechanical ink-drawing (although it is hard on my eyes), for it gives me a chance to think of you. With great persistency I have to tunnel my way here through a mountain. It is not only my command or "my will," it is God's will and my nature. You are surely right, my beloved friend, in writing me I am gaining a lot of worthwhile experiences, have not even a choice to avoid them. I am propelled whether I want it or not.

. . . There is not much danger that I ever lose the faith in the future development of life, which cannot be separated from building and constructing. But if I am a creative architect, I hope I shall find, too, the attitude of a philosopher with regard to the part I can contribute to the progress with all my power. The size and quantity of this part are very much dependent on circumstances beyond my power . . .

Now there is no time for reflection but to keep on going and fulfill one's inner calling. Others have an easier time of it, and you are aware of it, my dear one. However, I am not envious of these others, even if all my efforts should bear no fruits, because the toilsome struggle in itself is worthwhile, and thirst the high point before quenching it. Everything is connected with love—everything, everything! Science, art, humanitarian thoughts originating in our brains, branch out into a million new forms, or they may lead to horrible destruction.

Hagen, November 1923

Fate has been kind to me. It has always provided time for periods of reflection. When I first met Richard I was very young and had no understanding of his art which is so intertwined with his personality. Sometimes I find it uncanny that I could have loved him from the start without knowing him at all.

When we could be together in Vienna I experienced my first eye-opener. Afterwards in Niederweningen I had the most wonderful peace and quiet. I could digest all the various impressions and learn slowly that Richard was not only a man who loved me very much, but before all else an artist with inner obligations. Never to forget this was my evening's prayer. I also real-

---

4. Richard's sister in Vienna.

ized that his character was such that he might omit certain decisions vital to his career out of deference for me and never to permit this was my firm resolve. I had to learn to be an efficient housewife, learn to be self-sufficient and not burden him with household chores. I needed time to recognize this and it was my good fortune to be allowed to do so. Also, my initiation from girlhood to wifehood was so gradual that it will remain a blessing throughout our whole lives.

During our three months together in Berlin I had a chance to see whether I was capable of enduring Richard's periods of depression as well as the ups and downs of his profession, whether I possessed the necessary counterbalance and cheerful disposition required. Afterwards I again had a whole summer in which to become clear about the future I would face as Richard's wife. Don't think that this was then so clear in my mind. I see it only now.

Presently I again have time to digest the experiences of my first year of marriage and to think how I can improve; also to realize what it will mean to be a mother. With one child it will not be so hard, but with several children it would be difficult not to lose oneself in household chores. I must always keep in mind that first and foremost I am Richard's wife and counselor, as he calls me to my great pride, and that I shall be alone with him in the end—just as we were alone when we started.

*Dione to Richard*

Hagen, November 1923

During the day I am not so conscious of it, but in bed at night, left to my own thoughts, I am full of longing. It is such a marvelous feeling to know that we belong to each other, supplement and understand each other.

I don't want to keep it from you that occasionally silly notions assail me—that I die after the birth. Then I start to cry because it would be so terrible to die just when we start to live. That I carry your child is always a comforting thought.

*Richard to Dione*

New York, November 1923

. . . It is annoying that I come home so late, secondly that I have no home. My little chamber cannot be heated, has no table, has only a gas burner. My room in Berlin, in contrast, was an elegant bachelor's abode, not to speak of No. 12 in Stäfa. Therefore, from where can I write you, my dear Dione?

*Dione to Richard*

Hagen, November 1923

. . . Is your room really so poor that it does not even have a table? Dear me, written communications are terribly inadequate.

Poor Richard—you fall out of the frying pan into the fire! How does your stomach react to all this pressure? Well, I will not anticipate but wait to see what happens. However, I do long for a letter filled less with concrete facts and more with heartfelt expressions. What you think in New York does not help me here, poor, poor Dione, because I cannot picture it.

How do you savor your bachelorhood? The Sundays in Eichkamp when we lay on the couch and read books to each other must now seem like a dream. By the time you receive this letter you may already have written one to me containing expressions nourishing to my soul and everything I write here may be redundant and tiresome.

New York, December 1923

. . . Oh my Dionerl, how wonderful was Eichkamp! It was really a miracle that we could find such a thing during those terrible times. In many critical instances I cannot imagine how two young people in love could have lived more wonderfully and at such a distance from the everyday world of the nearby metropolis. That we froze quite a bit during the winter months and suffered great heat for some days in the summer is really inconsequential when compared to all advantages. Our isolation, the good air, the little nest we had built for ourselves, the view into and the nearness of the endless green forest, the knowledge that we had all this, *especially* near a city like Berlin, made it a near miracle.

May God stand by you. I do not know how to convey to you how I admire and esteem you. At the same time you are a gay child and not two-faced, changing colors like a soap bubble. Thinking of you is like remembering a rosy dream. I see you working in our miniature household. I see you playing the cello for me, singing for me. I recall how you read for me, how we sat opposite each other on a Sunday morning, our hands touching across the breakfast table. We lay on the couch together looking with pleasure at some of the copper utensils, the flowers in the irridescent vase. We delighted in the rays of the sun that shone through our small attic window. Oh, dear God, it was wonderful. However, my Dione, you will join me again, won't you?

Hagen, December 1923

I am so pleased with your letter. Finally you have found the right style in which to write to me—sentences from which my heart can draw warmth. You know, my dearest, I hope you will always love me more than the child, and I, also, will always love you most. Still for me it is something different than it is for you. I could never understand how a father could love his child more than a mother does, although there are enough examples of this. It is *I* who feel the child growing inside me, observe all changes, also those in my heart. I shall have pain when I bring it forth into the world, therefore, I should naturally be more involved than you. Still, I love it primarily because it comes from you. Apparently, I do not possess real motherly love. This Vreneli and Regula seem to have to a much greater degree. However, I shall wait and report to you all I feel once the baby has arrived.

Hagen, December 1923

I am very well. The reason, I believe, is that my Dionchen is here. I am always so delighted with her. First of all because she is my treasure and secondly because she is still such a sight for sore eyes. She looks marvelously well and blooming. If your child does not turn out to be a model specimen, I cannot imagine who else could bring one forth into this world.

*Dione to Richard*                                                    Hagen, December 1923

How do you like the name we came up with? We had so much fun. Please answer whether you do not prefer Frank to Angelus. To call him after Frank Lloyd Wright would really be lovely in certain ways. In the first place you consider him to be the greatest architect, and secondly, he is the reason for your wanting to go to America.

*Richard to Dione*                                                   New York, December 1923

Your accomplishment of giving birth is much less questionable and much more wonderful than what I do. What you will have to show me cannot bear comparison with what I could possibly show you, that's for sure. Both of us would be badly off if we could not show patience.

*Dione to Richard*                                                    Hagen, December 1923

Sunday I read many of the old letters you wrote to Muetterli. You have changed quite a bit too, since we met, have become surer of yourself, have gained more self-confidence. We have helped each other to develop, don't you think so beloved?

I am filled with a marvelous inner peace and expectation. Perhaps you will be glad if I let you go far away as a matter of course without burdening your field of action when we have more children. Something is already gained if we think about one another every week. It would be so wonderful if we could think the same after having been married for twenty years; if we could, in addition, admire and revere each other even more because we, hopefully, will then have weathered all vicissitudes honorably. If I had to sacrifice my cello playing to achieve this goal, I would do it without hesitancy. Could there possibly be a greater happiness for me than to live for you and my children? Oh dear God, I hope I shall never think differently. It is very interesting for me to see that I start loving my child so much. It is unbelievably more beautiful to be a mother than to be a young girl.

*Richard to Dione*                                                   New York, December 1923

New York is such an artistic city, filled with wild accidental beauty. In contrast to this, whatever was planned looks woefully inadequate. However, I surely do not know any other city that is so picturesque, not even Vienna, Hilbersheim, or Prague. For decades, this city has been, *is* in constant motion, changing its profile. Out of the growing mass the inner core rises always higher, floods gigantically along the river front into the open countryside. With frantic speed, the express subway trains take 2½ hours to cross the city, stopping only at every fourth or fifth station.

Yesterday, I was at 241th Street, in the farthest northeast corner of the city, near the lovely suburb of Pelham on the east bank of the river. Now I am on Twenty-first Street, and from here it takes an hour's walk to the south end of Manhattan. There, one sees the wide bay, and the sky over the ocean behind the outer islands. However, the city continues again behind the East River, with settlements like Brooklyn, Flatbush, Coney Island, Brighton, and Jamaica.

During the summer, in order to receive the North Atlantic breeze, two and a half million people keep their windows open. Elevated trains pass for hours between these houses. On the west side of the river, behind the Hudson, lies New Jersey with Hoboken, Elizabeth, and Newark, with a million inhabitants. Summer and winter, half of them, after getting dressed and having breakfasted, cross in a huge ferry boat, through the Hudson Tunnel, underneath the river, to reach their jobs that feed and clothe them. Not many of them are aware that New York is a beautiful city, but they are convinced of it. The weather is equally full of picturesque changes of audacious variety, just like the city itself. Not so long ago, this teeming Manhattan Island was a silent nature scene like the Hudson and the Catskill Mountains. That scenery is as beautiful as the Rhine Valley, lacking only its old human settlements. I think you and I will congratulate ourselves of having witnessed the phenomenon which is New York. At the same time, it would be wrong to believe that these masses of humanity are not human. They are more so than, for instance, the Berliners. Of course, they do not possess much philosophical insight. The question is whether this does not make them more human. Men and women strike me often as childlike. This is surely a tremendous recommendation!

Every day, in the morning, I had to walk from the Flatiron Building upward on Fifth Avenue to Thirty-fifth Street, and downwards in the evening. Today, there was yet a lot of daylight towards six o'clock, and the million lights appeared anemic against the clear evening sky. The snowy light appeared to be the whitest between the grass surfaces and the black tree skeletons of Madison Square. This square is so full of life and movement that it is difficult to describe it. But God willing, you will be soon able to see it for yourself.

The highest house there is considerably higher than St. Steven's Cathedral in Vienna, and then there are the wildest gradations down to blocks of one-story houses. Some buildings are like square colossuses, others slimmer than a tower, others are steep and sharp like a ship's bow. Behind the lower buildings, there are higher ones, towering against the southern sky, with elevator tracts, fire escapes, water reservoirs and radio masts. The square is broad, and the landscaping surely lovely in spring. In summer, it must be awfully hot, I think.

Late Sunday night, I tramped down Irving Place with a bundle of laundry under my arm. There too are these huge skyscrapers and very elegant, beautiful old houses with uncomfortable but fashionable apartments inside. Especially at the end of Irving Place—which in reality is a not too wide street—around Gramercy Park, which is a diminutive quadrangle with all the adventures of Madison Square partaking of the Metropolitan Life Insurance Tower. The little park with benches is surrounded by an aristocratic high fence, and only the inhabitants of the old-fashioned, distinguished houses have a key to this small green spot that boasts two figures on stone pedestals. Here, they promenade their aristocratic small babies in their carriages up and down the straight path behind the fence, and the lady wanders along the house front that show occasional skyscrapers and spaces between them like gaps in the teeth, and she throws fantastic shadows over this beautiful square.

As I was early this morning, The Metropolitan Life Insurance Tower clock showed only twenty minutes after eight, I circled the park gate three times, having cold ears in the newly fallen snow which reflected the enchanting sunrays. On the north side, a lot of people, coming from the east, crossed over to the west to get to their places of work. The other four sides were quiet, were not yet awake. I used to pass by here earlier, or in darkness; the first time, in an autumn rain, and I liked it immediately.

That New York is such a hurly-burly town is fortunate, otherwise it would be difficult to move on. Everything has its advantages. Whether I shall be able to hold out in my new position where I started today, is questionable. Here the situation is very different. I have daylight until 4:00 P.M. Often, I am alone in the office, located in a large office building with many windows. I overlook rooftops, and my glance skirts a few smaller skyscrapers until it rests on the steel skeleton of—I believe—the Williamsburg Bridge.

In my present situation, I have often pondered, how great my gifts are which I have to offer. I know how they burden my life and that of my dear Dione who wants to share her life with me. These gifts drive me around the world, not as a flighty adventurer, but a frequenter of soup kitchens, alcohol-free restaurants in Switzerland, vegetarian ones in Berlin, and armchair lunchrooms with black fellows in New York. Of all mentioned, the lunchrooms are the best.

*Dione to Richard*

Hagen, December 1923

You call New York an insane city? Then, my dearest, do not stay any longer than you deem absolutely necessary. Whether you are four days farther away really cannot play a role. If anything should happen—God forbid—you could not come back to me anyway.

With the prevailing tempo in New York, one-and-a-half months may suffice you to shed the role of greenhorn, and hopefully, you will find Los Angeles less of a treadmill.

I imagine that you must already be in Los Angeles and, therefore, send my letter there because by the middle of January when the letter arrives, you absolutely should be there. You cannot imagine how I burn to receive news from you. If only the weather is somewhat agreeable and you get a chance to see Wright's house in Chicago! I am sure we will not need ten years to realize that it was worthwhile for you to take this step. Where will you be for Christmas? Surely in California.

New York, December 1923

I am so overburdened with work that I hardly find the time to breathe and hardly the time to sleep. Now I am also desperate that I cannot find a moment to write to you. However, I hope this will change. In my heart I am completely with my dear wife. You write that you expect me to be in Los Angeles already. I cannot stand the thought, at this moment, of being without news from you, and judging from your letters, you feel the same way.

I believe it will be best if I rise a little earlier in order to write you because my eyes are so tired in the evening. Also, I don't want you to see my whole existence here through tired eyes. I do not have a harder time than I had pictured.

Hagen, December 1923

The misery around us is deplorable. There is great unemployment and starvation. Twice a week we feed two children. One now comes every day and we try to help as far as it is in our power. A friend mentioned that the situation in Berlin is even more deplorable. In an apartment underneath his parent's apartment a whole family is on the point of dying of starvation. They live from what his mother can spare. One child has already died, another one is near death. It is simply awful. Vaterli's attempts within his company seem to flounder and we shall have to depend on his fixed salary of 50,000 marks. This we can comfortably do except that my parents cannot save anything.

I relish my peace and quiet. I don't feel need for diversion or stimulation but listen only to what my heart tells me. I don't think I have ever felt so fulfilled except in Niederweningen.

I also speculate about old age. I ask myself why there do not seem to be wise old men around who, transfigured by having lived a full and useful life, can smilingly observe the young with tolerant understanding and without hurting their feelings. It seems to me there are more old women who are intelligent and wise. Altogether in the circle of our acquaintants I know more worthwhile women than men.

I believe you will become a venerable, uplifting old man who will always understand young people, letting them commit whatever unorthodox behavior they want to indulge in without telling them afterwards, smiling sarcastically: "I could have told you so!" To be old should include unending understanding. One should be able to attain a state of mind where one does not expect anything anymore. Hopefully, you will always understand young people.

I don't know what kind of an old woman I am going to be. Perhaps you can better tell because you know me better than I know myself. However, when I see how I look forward to my child, how important it is for me to become a good mother and a good wife, I believe I may also hope to become a lovable old woman. Do you think my children and grandchildren will look down on me because they consider themselves more clever than their grandmother?

*Dione to Richard*

Hagen, December 1923

Today I start my Christmas letter to you. Can you remember how last year we watched the dying out of the flickering Christmas tree candles on New Year's Eve, speculating where we would be a year hence? That we would be separated surely was not in our minds.

And now to your request that I should ignore it when you are not attentive. Oh my Richard, why did you go to America? Surely not with the idea of how you could please your wife? No, that's not my way. Where should my thoughts seek you out? In Chicago, in Los Angeles? In the December rain or in sunshine? I am so sorry that I do not know where you will be on Christmas, but your heart is with me and thus it does not matter so much. . . .

*Richard to Dione*

New York, Christmas 1923

There is nothing to tell about my Christmas. It is a wonderfully clear, moonlit, cold winter night holding nothing festive for me. I already lie in bed at 10:00 P.M. I imagine that soon my Dionerl will awaken. The evening twilight has no meaning for me because I know that with you it would be midnight.

What am I doing here? Did I marry you a year ago in a Westphalien town? Am I from Vienna and the child of my mother? The only thing which is clear and certain is my heartfelt attachment to my young Dionewife and Dione-mother. When will you again sing for me, play Bach, Porpora, Eccles?

The paper on which I am writing is the last sheet of what I bought in Hagen. Everything passes so quickly.

I am on the long desired road to California. Thank goodness not for myself and not alone for my ideas, but especially for you two, no, especially first of all for you, my treasure, loaned to me from Heaven.

*Dione bears a son, Frank. Complications arise and she is hospitalized and nearly dies.*

*Richard leaves New York for Chicago where he finds a job with Holabird and Roche, one of the largest architectural firms in the city, involved at the time with the design of the New Palmer House hotel.*

*During his early months in Chicago, Richard meets both Louis Sullivan and Frank Lloyd Wright, who invites Richard to visit Taliesin, once Dione has joined him in June.*

*Leaving Frank in Muetterli's care, Dione arrives in New York where she is interned at Ellis Island until Richard can "rescue" her.*

*After a short stay with Frances Toplitz in New York, they visit Frank Lloyd Wright, who offers Richard a job at Taliesin.*

*In October Muetterli brings Frank to them at Taliesin.*

Hagen, January 1924

New Year, wonderful sunshine, but the child still floats in darkness. Now there is not the slightest chance that it could be born in the old year.

Richard, my dear, I am sorry for your sake that it takes so long and that you have to continue waiting anxiously. I was able to overcome it and be-have as if no child was to be expected, otherwise I could not stand it.

New York, January 1924

I have as yet not made any roots. I am not, am not at all, determined to stay in this country. The idea to come here was a good one, it seems to me and I have had many worthwhile experiences. Because a lot is going on here, one can learn many practical things. As long as there is no crisis one surely can earn more here. If my Dione is willing to shoulder continuous travel exertions, escaping thus perhaps some German housekeeping wor-ries, she also may experience a lot of interesting happenings. That's the reason she wants to come, is that not so? And because she does not want to keep her husband, who is so full of longing, in the lurch.

New York, January 1924

As my fantasy is not vivid enough to imagine your present situation, I could picture to myself that our Dione is lying down and the prognosis is good, that you find the time to read to her a letter from her husband. Of course, she was always very poor in arithmetic and thus she did not excel in figuring out the date of her delivery.

*Richard to Dione*

New York, January 1924

Dear, dear Dione  Just now I visited Cypelman and found your radiogram. God be praised that everything is behind you, my poor darling. Surely you must have suffered very much because it was your first delivery and you are sensitive to pain. I rushed to the telegraph office to give you a sign that I am in the picture, that I know the long wait is over and you can rest on your laurels. If only you have a healing childbed and everything progresses well, my dearest Dione.

*Muetterli to Richard*

Hagen, January 1924

When we wanted to telegraph "happily" we thought at 8:00 P.M. that we could telegraph "happilissimo." However, first the facts. Splendid specimen of a boy—8 pounds, 56 cm long, head size, 35 cm. Labor pains started at 1:00 A.M. At 2:00 A.M. Dione came to me. As the contractions came in ten-minute intervals we phoned the midwife at 7:00 A.M. Small opening in the uterus. We had a relaxing Sunday breakfast and the midwife left to return at 5:00 P.M. The contractions continued every ten minutes. . . Dione would ask, "Is this now a contraction?" At 8:00 P.M. the same condition. The midwife ordered a warm bath and Dione went to bed after she had walked all day in her warm coat through the warm rooms. The midwife found it necessary to squeeze the water bag in order to hasten the contractions and they increased in intensity. We could see the head sticking out, but despite Dione's brave and heroic efforts the head did not advance. When she started to agonize that she was at the end of her strength, we telephoned the doctor. Ten minutes before 11:00 P.M. he was there. He gave her a light anesthesia of chloroform and ether, applied the forceps, and said he would have to make small cuts to free the baby's head. After that another pull and he exclaimed, "Blast it, what a magnificent specimen." Because the navel cord was around the baby's head there could not be any forward movement. Also, the head was very large.

The physician cut the cord, put the baby, wrapped in a diaper, on a chair to take care of the mother first. He had to do some repair work. Then we heard Dione's soft voice ask, "Is it a boy?" She heard the baby cry as she lay quite fresh and happy. At 11:20 P.M. everything was over. The physician waited for the afterbirth as we brought the baby into the big room so Dione could have peace and quiet. But she slept little on account of the usual afterpains. Vrene and I, of course, could not sleep either on account of all the excitement.

These, surely, were the most difficult hours of my life—9:30 to 10:30. I am so glad that you were not present. Had the head been smaller, had it not been encircled by the navel cord, she would have borne the baby without much pain. The midwife exclaimed, "A real gypsy!"

Hagen, January 1924

God be praised that you did not have to participate in the event. Muetterli and Vreneli helped me a lot. I am so sorry that I was not able to give the final push because I simply had no strength left. I shall never forget that moment. I was so relieved to get the anesthesia and to wake up when I heard the boy cry. Such a big baby. Who could ever have imagined that considering my slender appearance? I am proud! Now the Neutra name succession is signed and sealed. It is so comical to look at this red face. As yet I have no motherly feelings at all. It seems very strange to me that this should be our son and that he has caused me such pain.

New York, January 1924

. . . I really admire your mother. How friendly and dispassionately she describes the birth which, after all, necessitated forceps. But she admits that the whole procedure was hard on her. I surely can feel with her. I hope you will describe to me how you felt the few hours before and after the birth when you have regained your strength. As far as I am concerned, I felt unexpectedly very low towards the evening of that particular Sunday.

On the Sunday when you bore our child, the weather was unbelievably clear and cold. Mrs. Toplitz and I had agreed to travel together to the small town of Yonkers near the Hudson River. We took a streetcar and an autobus which traveled on a marvelous street. We passed large estates and saw huge trees, caught glimpses of the Hudson River glittering in the sun with lovely hills on the opposite shore. I continuously thought of you and how this view would please you. I also mentioned it to Mrs. Toplitz. Suddenly the street curved and over a rise I perceived the Hudson as an enlarged, sunlit expanse of water framed by a mountain landscape. It was about 4:30 P.M., just the moment when you were given the chloroform. Later on we left the bus in Tarrytown and walked towards the old cemetery of Sleepy Hollow.

I am so happy that my Dionerl has no fever and that the child looks normal. With his big head he will be a good mathematician and chess player. In your haste you forgot to mention the eye color. I suppose blue? Oh my Dionerl, just now I have taken a deep breath. If only you continue to remain in good health. I am annoyed at myself that I rejoice that you yourself wrote me, defying all advice to take it easy, my dear, dear Dione who was sent to me by Heaven. . . .

New York, January 1924

I could imagine that it is possible to communicate with a newborn baby although it is completely outside any verbal exchange. One could watch how his soft palate reacts, how quickly the iris in his eye reacts to stimuli and how the opening retracts when the eye is turned towards the light. You can see how fortunate it is that I am not present to start experimenting before I can start to play with him. I would be greatly surprised if his eyes were not blue. Is this not mostly the case with American children?

I like your attitude regarding America and how you expressed it in your letter to my sister, namely "We do not know how long we are going to stay in America." It is all right with me if you state it thus. The two of us must explore everything.

*Richard to Dione and*
*Muetterli*

New York, January 1924

Just at this moment I have received your first letters. All morning I have been thinking about you, Muetterli. Not only do I admire you and have my many reasons for it, but I love you without any reason and suddenly I felt quite miserable when I realized that I might not see you again for a long time. I could be more explicit, but this goes far enough.

*Richard to Dione*

New York, February 1924

I come slowly to the realization that other people often do not have the pressing, I could say painful necessity to be alone and find their inner self, having the leisure to develop ideas.

In any case, it will become ever clearer to you that my whole life is not following an external dependable path. Although I am capable to adapt myself to varying circumstances, the tasks and possibilities that would challenge me and make me quieter are so rare. Occasionally, I am hard-pressed not to complain about it, but that makes no sense. This is my nature, and whatever virtues I possess that give you and me pleasure, they are intertwined with an uncomfortable streak of tragedy. Usually, I am not despairing, not moody, and for my own person agreeably frugal. This I hope will make it possible for you not to fear the future. There is only one thing: You *must not* be too ambitious for me. The best in me looks upon success with a question mark, and laughs good-naturedly about the diligence of my efforts.

There is not much danger that I ever lose faith in the future development of life, which cannot be separated from building and constructing. I am so in love with the idea to experience something new that I am even capable of acknowledging a negative experience as a forward step. I am convinced that this is so. Good experience or *only* such, might often be disastrous.

Today, I have started to work with five other draftsmen in the office of architect Courland.[1] I hope that this will be my last New York employment. I must start to be a provider until the child has reached the age of eighteen.

*Dione's breasts became infected and she had to be rushed to a hospital, suffering from very high fever.*

*Richard to Dione*

New York, February 1924

Now a letter from you is overdue and my thoughts are black concerning you. Dionerl, my treasure, it surely is sinful of me to think of anything else

---

1. Maurice Courland, Richard's second employer in New York.

but you. I feel so despondent that I cannot concentrate on anything else but your illness and that I cannot be with you. I am also in no mood to tell you about myself and my plans. I would need your advice presently. My dear Dione, as you now suffer and are ill, it has at least this consequence, that I realize with exceeding awareness how much I love you. When I imagine that you wept because you thought the end was near, I feel quite paralyzed, and still I know I can help you best by steadily progressing in my work. If I have to assume, however, that you do not tell me the full truth, everything in me is in revolt. I do not know how to write to you because your answer would be a month late. I cannot write about myself.

That you do not love the child as yet should not concern you. I know a very good reason for it. One loves such a tiny baby on account of its helplessness and especially if one is responsible for it. But this baby is surrounded by a lot of loving admirers and the real mother, for the time being, cannot care for him. What other feelings can she have but one of separation since he has left her body. Thus, you are again alone with me while you are lying there and having time to think and reflect. I shall never, never forget that you are my most sacred human treasure, that you have been lent to me, this in addition to our common parental duties and pleasures. Should it be a comfort to you to know that I am all yours, body and soul, then you surely can have this comfort, my Dionerl. I do not feel separated from you, but am with you. This is not an answer but a timeless statement. You are aware of it, but it comforts me to reiterate it. I am not going to follow Schindler's advice, but go first to Chicago. We cannot make any further plans. I am sorry that I cannot write you anything definite, but such matters do not follow the accustomed pattern.

New York, February 1924

*Richard to Dione*

Now it is evening and no letter of yours has arrived. I can well imagine that you do not like to write bad news and thus you wait from day to day. Perhaps you have already been operated on. I do not know whether you are without fever. I do not know anything.

Surely my longing for you is still more understandable when you consider how alone I am here while you are with your family and our child. I am sorry that the situation here will not be completely comfortable for you. But I hope you are not afraid.

In reality I like a life of leisure without any risks. Already as a child I loved to sit behind the stove and watch all the cooking preparations. Money matters little to me. I am hardly ambitious in the ordinary sense of the word. The praise of outsiders mostly surprises me. However, I will tolerate all sorts of mischances that may befall me while I try to pursue my own ideas.

Here in New York among the architects, I have encountered provincial stick-in-the-muds. I had thought the people here would be innovative, more on the move. That was a wrong assumption.

*Dione to Richard*

Today, in the operating room, the doctor told me he had had no idea that his patient was famous. Was I not a cello virtuoso and had even appeared in public? By the way, Feuermann[2] played the C-Major Suite by Bach, here. Vaterli told me, to my great joy, that I play it with more intense feeling. Feuermann's greatest accomplishments, surely, lie anyway in the higher registers. I heard him before Christmas and was deeply disappointed and embittered. If one possesses such marvelous gifts, one has an obligation to live up to them. Instead of that he is frivolous. I see it always more clearly that it is not the technique, not the sweet tone that signifies an artist, but an inner glow, a holy flame which the listener perceives.

*Richard to Dione*

Hull House, Chicago, March 1924

I am now in Chicago. My life in Hull House is very interesting. Maybe I will start a drawing class (in white and black) in the children's art school. However, I may not be able to stay here, because I live in the room of a gentleman who is traveling at the moment. Therefore, my situation is uncertain. However, as I am only here since a week, nothing else can be expected. When your grandfather was born, this city was as big as Stäfa. Now it tops Paris, even with regard to the number of inhabitants. Only an idiot could expect that it could also have the same cultural importance and strength of Paris, instead of keeping his mouth shut and being overcome with awe by this phenomenal development. When your grandparents were children in Mannheim, all capitals in Europe were world capitals, while this city was a small country town. Perhaps they heard belatedly something of the 1848 revolution. Twice a week, a perspiring rider on horseback came around the south end of Lake Michigan, carrying two mail bags, the eastern mail from Detroit; where now, during lunchtime, half a million automobiles confront each other, cows used to graze. It's the truth! An evil smelling cover of gasoline fumes hovers over this land. The automobiles are much worse than the skyscrapers and the phonographs. One must observe this evil to learn how to cope with it. May the devil snatch away the benefactor of the people—Ford. His agents accept a downpayment of $100. Gasoline is a passing childhood disease.

Here, in Chicago, horrible nude figures and tasteless obscenities are on posters on every corner and wall. However, of greatest importance are the murders. Two, no three girl slayers are on the daily agenda. The horrified mothers are besieged by reporters who snatch baby pictures out of their hands. It must be very sad to be the mother of a girl slayer, especially in Chicago. The murderers are being photographed from all sides. They either lie about their involvement or commit suicide. Mrs. Toplitz told me that most crimes are committed by first-generation Americans born here. They appear to be the worst. Also, workmen or small children are killed by cars every day. Automobiles and newspapers are the greatest scourge in this young country that changes by the hour.

I have so far climbed 7,000 feet if I add up all the elevator rides in all

2. Emanuel Feuermann was a famous cello virtuoso.

the office buildings. Naturally, I am already acquainted with the prominent people here, but as yet I do not have a job. I really do not enjoy the prospect of slaving, but a newly arrived one has no other choice.

Chicago, April 1924

Today, my life's treasure, I am moving to Highland Park. Again a new experiment. Nothing but experiments. This one should give me some rest, a chance to come to terms with myself. Rest in the train for three quarters of an hour, one way. Repose during two to three evening hours. However, who knows whether I will not have to chase around in the city following up leads, having nothing but getting up at 6:00 A.M.! It is amazing how adaptable human beings are, I can see it in my own person which I mistreat so atrociously.

Don't believe for one moment that anything worthwhile in this world can be produced without pain and anxiety. Everything has to be paid for. That's how it is and it cannot be changed.

I always told you that life with me would be adventurous. As you were able to discern certain virtues in my nature, I hope this will make it possible for you to see the future not too darkly. Also, do not believe for a moment that other men do not have their drawbacks! Surely, I have some advantages, and you will have to learn to enjoy them. In any case, you will have to expect a few exploratory years and *nobody can predict the outcome*. Most importantly, you must not be too ambitious for me and in the back of your mind imagine that you can lead a comfortable life with me. However, I am convinced that you *know everything better* than I do. I have such confidence in your marvelous sagacity which quite instinctively helps and advises me. I must have some virtues, how else can one explain that so many persons have taken an interest in me and my doings.

Hagen, March 1924

We were married for such a little while that our life together looks like a dream. Now I am again the eldest Niedermann daughter. Still, life with you was the real thing and thus my feelings are mixed up and strange, as though I had lost something and was curious as to whether I would find it again. I do not often think of getting together with you because I could not bear it. Everything seems so unreal to me. When I hold my boy in my arms I do not the feeling that he had anything to do with us two. Altogether I feel so young and immature that I cannot imagine myself being a mother. Still I love the baby very much. . . . But I believe the love for a child cannot be compared to that of a husband and wife. Surely only women who are not fulfilled in their love, love their children more. . . .

Hagen, March 1924

Dear Richard, for heavens sake, I have the impression that you are afraid of what my mood might be and keep forgetting what is uppermost in my mind, namely, that before all else, you are an artist and because you are so kind and considerate you make it difficult for me and yourself to remember this. How I *feel* surely cannot become the most important consideration. You went to America because you made many unsuccessful attempts to get there for many years. I am happy about your decision. What kind of a woman would I be, how unworthy of the high esteem in which you hold me, should I pout, hang my head in despair like any ordinary female if situations prove difficult and disagreeable? I think you are too lenient with me because you were so anxious about my health. Scold me, or even better, remind me in your loving way should I ever forget my bridal resolutions. . . . I constantly marvel at how well we understand each other. Think how dreadful it would be if I proved to be stubborn and in some matters caused repeated occasions for strife. Women, I think, are more stubborn than men. I surely hope I will always be able to understand you as I do now, which I don't find at all difficult. I cannot comprehend why others find you enigmatic, misunderstand your decisions, or don't understand you altogether. . . .

Just now I tried to play the cello. Oh my Richard, it was awful. I have not touched the cello for seven months and now it feels as if I never played it at all. My fingers hurt me. All the calluses have disappeared. I have forgotten the Bach suite and my bowing hand is clumsy. I hope I will regain what was lost when I again start to practice. My singing goes much better. Every day I do some vocalizing and although I have lost my long breath, the tones come through, even the high ones. . . .

I find the photograph of you excellent. You must not, however, conclude that I am thus satisfied. This, no doubt, is my fault. I slowly start to discover that I shall probably never be satisfied with a photograph of you.

*Richard to Dione*                                        Highland Park, April 1924

My life here is without joy if I cannot find the time to concentrate and think of you. Nobody can easily parallel my lonely life, rootless as it is, unless he has practice in it as I have.

Now you, my dear one, will join me.

One thing occupies my mind continuously. It is not the fact that one has "two souls," but that one's inner workings take place on two planes. In some periods one lives as a solitary (stupidly, I wanted to avoid the word "individual") whose circumscribed "persona" is connected to those around him and to the ordinary world. Then again, he is like a wave on the endless waters of human destiny feeling marvelously open to the dark, mysterious universe. His innermost being in such periods only an interesting mold filled with an unfathomable eternal substance. The individual is only a vessel through which the creative spirit has passed for hundreds of thousands of years, a very special vessel through which it flows, then becomes constricted in its own peculiar way. However, there are days when the passage nearing the vessel is slightly inhibited so that the flowing movement is impeded. Then this vessel is particularly empty, unfruitful, commonplace, of a pointless peculiarity. In such periods a woman is only externally a mother and not really a loving being. The man is like a seedless blossom.

Many of our irritable fellow citizens, male and female, are perpetually in such a frame of mind. None of us, however, is free from this and it is *un-natural* to be distressed about it. You should not be distressed with yourself if at times you do not love me as much as you would like to, my treasure. After everything is again open to this eternal flow, one breathes marvelously free again. Impatience can only disturb the flow. Do you believe I was able to describe how it is with us earthlings?

Highland Park, April 1924

Dear friend, you speak about a revolutionary movement in architecture. I don't believe in it, I don't believe that a revolution in art matters is possible, analogous to politics or social conditions. Art is, in the last analysis, and in its effect, a true community affair. It is created by individuals, not at all democratically. In France, five people have created Impressionism, and *have* solved this question. Coming centuries will ignore the 100,000 imitators.

Art, architecture grow out of the community, from mankind, grow up in single hearts.

Revolution? Against what? There are no common rules or laws how to compose a new symphony? Tradition is like a lightening rod through which the comet of an individual movement has passed, turning paler and paler over the centuries. It always was a group of decisive men, responsive to their own sensitive time-spirit, with focus on time-consciousness, displacing the far bigger mass of businessmen who worked comfortably in the tradition. Tradition may linger on for a time, then die, but the single art object is comparatively eternal.

Oh, please excuse my railway car style of philosophy. At the moment, I do not know how to express myself differently, and we are just arriving in Chicago.

Highland Park, April 1924

I visited Sullivan in the Warner Hotel on Cottage Grove Avenue.[3] I brought him violets and wallflowers because I believe he has a tender heart and not many friends. L. H. Sullivan is not as significant as Otto Wagner[4] is, but for this part of the world, he was for a long time the keenest and most enterprising architect. Now he is worn out and hopeless. He is lying a little when he writes hopeful articles about the future.

"In Chicago they all tell me that the new architecture is dying out. Where on this globe can I find a place without defeatists?" The Warner Hotel lies in the south of town, in a part that is in transition. The windows are hardly clean, and from the upholstery in the lobby the stuffing shows through the miserably torn fabric. I had sent my flowers to his room, and was a little afraid that he might be embarrassed because an American al-

3. Louis Henry Sullivan, a pioneer architect, employer and teacher of Frank Lloyd Wright.
4. Architect and founder and leader of the modern movement in European architecture.

ways likes to appear well-to-do and would prefer to receive a guest in splendid surroundings. After a quarter of an hour, he came down fully dressed, ready for going out, the poor old man. He invited me to have dinner with him at the Cliff Dwellers Club. I did not accept but drove with him in the taxicab. Groaning a little, he smoked several cigarettes. His heart, and God knows what other ailments, seemed to torment him. If the weather improves, the doctor told him, he might make it, but the weather has become much worse.

"What is happening here? Who is working for the future? I have no hope," he said. I told him: "You did not only work for Chicago, for the Middle West, or for America, and the results of your endeavours may not be known to you, Mr. Sullivan. Look here, I came from Vienna to visit you." "Oh, well," he said, "perhaps in Sweden or Germany, but not here." Holabird and Roche impress him. Once they were equal to Sullivan and Adler. Now Sullivan is a poor fellow, remembered only in the world history of architecture. The firm of Holabird and Roche, however, is intimately connected with all the fat banks, building a hundred skyscrapers with "petit Trianons" in the twenty-fifth floor to house the ventilators.

Sullivan looks pale and dried out. On Michigan Boulevard he asked the driver to close the window. In front of Orchestra Hall, I took my leave, that's where the Cliff Dwellers Club is located.

*Richard to Dione*                                        Highland Park, April 1924

I have seen some of Wright's work. Country houses, a Jewish club, also a dance hall in the south. All in all, it was no disillusion. However, the people who live in these houses were rather awful. I had always hoped that this new architecture would produce a different human being. I am sorry to be proved wrong.

*Richard to Dione*                                        Highland Park, April 1924

I am not sure whether your mother is right in her statement that life is not worth living without love letters. After all, love letters are only attempts to express what cannot be expressed. A life without love, however, is quite another matter. A life without love letters need not yet be a dark one. But I am full of joy when you write me love letters, darling. The devil knows that reality and theory never quite coincide.

Yesterday I worked until midnight and continue working this morning. Now my brain starts to become lame. I will go to eat something in Mrs. Tiptoe's home restaurant. I shall ask the waitress with protruding upper teeth to make me two sandwiches for my evening meal. Then I will walk for an hour, probably towards the lake. Afterwards I will continue working. If only I wasn't such a sluggard! What I would like best is to walk all day or commune with my Dionerl.

I think of you so lovingly. I reflect how natural, kind, and wonderful you are, high-spirited and compassionate. How well you lead me, how sagacious you are, and how things happen as you envisage and anticipate. I must have a name for all these traits that are combined in one undivided human being. In reality I am married to a whole harem.

This letter may sound infatuated, but my feelings go much deeper, Dionerl, because I love you with my innermost soul and what I owe you cannot be expressed by flattery and beautiful phrases. I kiss your hands and thank heaven that you are alive. As you are not immortal, my life could be destroyed any day. Of this I have been aware these past four weeks and never again will I be presumptuous. I know that I shall never be able to fully thank you for wanting to join me and participate in my difficult life, even shouldering most of the hardships. Then please forgive me. Be forbearing and patient. I am not a bigger fool than most, but perhaps a less common variety.

A bird rasps in the neighbor's tree nearly like a grasshopper. Small clouds sail underneath in the sunshine. I feel my critical day approaching because my soul is so expansive. All sorts of things cross my mind and I perceive them with clarity and power.

Chicago, April 1924

At noon, if I have time, I run during my lunch hour for twenty minutes—(today there is no charge)—to the art museum to throw a few pleasant glances on 500-year-old German, 300-year-old Dutch, and 400-year-old French paintings. Then, to the Glen Inn, and back to the eleventh floor, and the lobby plan of the Palmer House ½" x 1' x 0". There, I draw neatly the riveted steel columns, the tile walls and marble fascias, the ventilation shafts and the registers while I enjoy a peppermint "Lifesaver" which I put into my mouth. I can also get ice water in a Dixie paper cup.

Chicago, April 1924

It is deplorable that the day has only twenty-four hours. Nine hours downtown without any time for myself. Three hours in transit. (At the moment I am sitting in a railway car, where I can write a letter which I am doing right now, or I study the "steel construction" by Burt, which I usually do. I usually reach my room at 10:00 P.M.—unless I have to work overtime.) Then I work without interruption on designs for Mr. Sonderling's Northshore Temple until I go to bed.

Naturally, and as I predicted, without any remuneration. However, I simply must have work for my heart and brain in order to keep my capacity for serious design problems. I cannot tell the clients every week that I have no time if I do not want to appear ridiculous. Also, I have no time to go to a department store to buy Arrow collars and socks. I persuade myself that this is a funny situation. But that's how it is. People who can do their work during office hours, have a free evening. I don't see when I shall be one of them. But I shall not be impatient. So far I have had wonderful luck in this country. In five months, I could lay my hands on two clubhouses, several one- and two-family homes, two synagogues, one apartment house, and the two biggest hotels in the world, (as they are advertised now on the front page of the Chicago papers, namely, the start of the "New Palmer House" construction which is described in lengthy editorials).

*Richard to Dione*

Highland Park, May 1924

Poor Sullivan is dead. I wrote you two weeks ago that I had the good idea to visit him "at home." Oh my, Graceland Cemetery is a more suitable place than the Warner Hotel. I am sure it is not boasting when I tell you that I am probably the only person in Chicago who daily enjoys his buildings. He was not an achiever, never became as radical as the old Otto Wagner, but he surely was one of the most significant Americans. Correspondingly, his funeral was sad. He told me, trying to get his breath and quite desolate: "What is left of all my endeavors? Nothing. What are the young people doing? Oh my!"

I met Wright at Sullivan's funeral and gave him my condolences. He started to apologize that he had not gotten in touch with me, because he was not yet settled, etc. It does not look promising to me that I can work for him. Wright has the head of a lion resting on a rather well proportioned body. He looks about fifty-six, is truly a child, but not a well-behaved one. God only knows. He is one in a million.

I am meeting more and more people who believe they know Frank Lloyd Wright. Whomever I start mentioning the modern movement to starts quickly to regale me with scandal stories about him. They must be known all over town, and must be juicy morsels for the newspapers. The headlines were a foot high and people tell me other details of Wright's lack of character. He supposedly left a wife with many children, he seduced another woman with many children; and after he left them in Spring Green, she, her children, and a Negro cook (!) were murdered.

*Dione to Richard*

Hagen, April 1924

It is marvelous how you can evade a question when I want to know something. Very gently you manage to shift the theme onto another plane and suddenly I discover that I am again far removed, failing to learn something about you that I wanted to know.

Do you know that I have nearly forgotten what it means to be married? I already wrote you once that I feel like a bride who is traveling to her bridegroom. Only the fact that Frank is present proves to me that I must have been married after all. Yes, you may laugh! . . .

I think I am right to have contempt for architects. Most of them have commercial souls, are imitators who, without much thinking, do the same thing, regardless of what it might be. One like you can, perhaps, be found in ten thousand and for this reason you have success, although it does not easily fall in your lap. But you have it and will not lose it. You will never end up being a poor old man like Sullivan.

Highland Park, May 1924

So far I have slept only in six American beds. Not yet many, but on the whole they are very good.

My opinion regarding American circumstances changes on the average of twice daily. It may have something to do with how full my stomach is. The newspapers here are frightful. There is no need to buy one as every neighbor has one in his hands and one can read the two-inch-high head-lines that propagate every falsehood. . . .

I can feel with you that to separate, to say "good-bye" is hard and op-pressing. I wish I could weep with you. However, one thing takes prece-dence, do you believe that Dione can feel happy with me in the long run? How do you advise me after you have pondered the matter to your best knowledge? After all, as you managed to captivate Vaterli up in Dalmatia, you are aware what motivates a female, which I, unfortunately, do *not* know.

And now my dear, don't feel sad when your loved one steps onto the boat. You will be a part of what she experiences. The distance between is not so great as far as emotions are concerned. Only letters are a little older when they are finally read.

Highland Park, May 1924

It is wonderful that you are alive and healthy and will soon join me. My worries we shall discuss in the dark of the night.

No one is this world is protected or out of danger except for moments, and for that there is no time clock. No one is safe from supernatural violent storms, but it is possible for the soul to harbor a deep happiness. Oh my Dione, how wonderful that you are alive.

Let's have our child take lessons from a fakir to prepare him for the fu-ture. One thing worries me, shall I have time for the boy? If not, it will be my loss. If one is observant one can learn much from one's child. No one can educate you more significantly, it seems to me, than a child.

Hagen, June 1924

Oh my Richard, I was devastated when I was told, picking up the ticket, that Frank could not come with me. All my arguments were in vain. He is born in Germany and the German quota is closed. Only if you were an American citizen could I take him along before July 1, but then my visa as a professional musician would have expired and I would have to start all proceedings from scratch. When I pleaded with the clerk at the North Ger-man Lloyd to let me take Frank, trying my luck with the immigration offi-cials in New York, he told me that just recently a mother with four children was sent back after waiting four weeks.

*Muetterli to Richard*

I was so happy with your letter. It arrived just at the right time because today we had to overcome a reversal. Dione wrote you what the authorities have decreed, namely that they will not issue a visa for Frank. Taken altogether, it is not a misfortune for you. So many times I have experienced that providence is much wiser than we. This is especially true in moments of disappointment and anguish when trying to adjust to new circumstances beyond your imagination.

*Dione to Richard*

Hagen, June 1924

I have been thinking about the last days and nights in Hagen before you departed. I then had the feeling that we had just started to grow together. For this reason our long separation is deplorable because in many respects we have to start from scratch. But before all we are not alone anymore. Have you enough imagination to visualize how constrained we shall be and that in all our decisions we will have to consider the child?

I shall leave alone on June 10 and we shall try from the USA to get Frank to come, or have Muetterli visit us and bring Frank. It was very hard for me to leave the child behind, but you are my main consideration and the boy is in such good hands with Muetterli. He is still so small that he will not miss me. I am determined not to wait any longer. . . . I hope you do not think I am a harsh mother, abandoning my child. However, when I contemplate who needs me more, you or the baby, I must admit it is you, it is me, it is us. Our separation was long enough.

*Dione to Her Parents*

Ellis Island, June 1924

Yesterday evening we, the unhappy ones who had to stay onboard, watched the skyline of New York with its electric advertising signs. Then I took a walk on deck with one of the officers who told me revolting stories about the immorality and shamelessness of women and girls. He has lost his belief that decent women still exist. What he has seen and experienced during his many years at sea begs description. I heard that we shall sleep twenty in one room on Ellis Island, and there are prisoners (one cannot leave the building) who have been there since December. The first instance of decision is a court on Ellis Island. If the court decides negatively, the case goes to Washington. There the final decision is made. I really am somewhat apprehensive, but hope to get out all right.

Mrs. Toplitz was very nice but I could hardly understand her. I will try to give this letter to someone so you will have news from me. I am so thankful that Frank is not with me. . . .

8:00 P.M.—What a blatant contrast! At the moment I sit with several hundred persons in a dining hall. The food looks so unappetizing that I subsist on coffee and bread. We spend our time in a huge two-story-high hall filled with nationals from all over the world. Most of them, however, are Italian with a lot of children who scream, run about, and plague their poor mothers. The men, it appears, have to sleep on wooden benches. I do not yet know where we shall sleep. I have tried to play my cello but shall be unable to practice here. The whole atmosphere is laden with discouragement. Ravishingly beautiful Italian women stare with hollow eyes into the void, wearily repulsing their children. One of them has a two-month-old baby which she carries upright, a pitiful sight. Just now I was handed a note saying that Mrs. Toplitz is here but is not allowed to see me. Richard will come on Sunday. I am so relieved. If anybody can get me out, it will be Richard. However, the court deliberates only on Monday.

Saturday morning—After a horrible night I sit again on a bench watching the sunshine through the windows. I just asked one of the servants whether I could help her make up the beds (we get new sheets every day), but this is not permitted. Yesterday at 7:00 P.M. fourteen of us were shut into our room which has adjacent toilet facilities. There were seven double-decker beds. Others sleep seventy to one hundred in a big hall. All of this would have been bearable if one of the children who, apparently, was hungry had not screamed until 2:00 A.M. To be continuously awakened from sleep is irritating and soon everyone was filled with anger. If only it had been a nice child, but it was a fat, ugly, blond Swabian child. The mother knew no English, only Swabian. An older child was very dirty but a real baroque little angel. The woman's husband won't be in New York until July 27 and thus she has to wait for him. She is a very commonplace woman whom I, nevertheless, pity. If only her children were not so abominably brought up. She is quite apathetic and weeps a lot. We also have mice. At 5:30 A.M. we were awakened. What sense does that make? I am so glad that Frank is not with me. There is also a nice Italian girl who has been here ten days with her two-year-old child who was not born in the USA. I am really fed up.

Sunday afternoon—We were allowed to be in the fresh air for two hours. I now sit behind bars near the water looking onto the beautiful view of New York's skyscrapers. If I want to be just, I must admit that the people here are the worst. They fill the atmosphere with their hopelessness. Poor people, like the food, they enjoy not having to work. Twice now we were served ice-cold milk, always in new paper cups. Our guards must be civil, otherwise they are dismissed. Yesterday we were even allowed to make some music, as there is a piano here.

*Richard came from Chicago to the court hearing at Ellis Island and convinced the immigration judges that he could support his wife. After a few days with Frances Toplitz Richard and Dione left to visit Frank Lloyd Wright in Spring Green, Wisconsin, at his estate, Taliesin.*

Highland Park, July 1924      *Dione to Her Parents*

Thursday morning we started from New York, arriving in Spring Green Friday evening. Moser awaited us at the station with his car.[5] He is tall and slender, has brown eyes and sharply cut features. To walk to Wright would

---

5. Werner Moser, son of Professor Karl Moser in Zurich.

take an hour on an impossible road. We passed a wonderful lakelike river, ascended a curve and suddenly there we were without noticing the house. It is a one-story house, quite low, winding around a hill like a snake, becoming higher only on top of the hill. It is impossible to describe the first impression. Immense astonishment is paramount. Then one becomes somewhat anxious at the thought to be soon in the presence of a genius, to meet him at any moment. But first Mrs. Moser came to greet us. She expects her baby today and will have to drive to Madison which is as far as Basel is from Zurich. Can one imagine any woman in Europe driving two hours in this condition? But she was in fine shape. She is tall, slender, has fine features, brown eyes and could easily be his sister. A very enjoyable couple.

Today the air in Taliesin (that's the name of the estate) was charged with electricity. A big industrialist with wife, daughter, and son-in-law were houseguests, and it was to be decided whether Wright would be commissioned to build a skyscraper. All his hopes were based on this. For weeks all had been prepared for this visit. The office had been enlarged, an annex added for twenty draftsmen.

Now Wright came to greet us. He is well built, elegant, of middle height, has an expressive head which could, perhaps, best be compared to that of Liszt, if one cares to make any comparison.

Then Mrs. Moser showed us our room which was rather primitive, having been completed only the day before. Moser had painted it himself. Then we climbed on a flagstone path underneath old trees. A grassy hill bordered by flowering shrubs covering a stone wall led up to the house which, at that point, has several stories. One enters through the kitchen into the dining room which is very simple, like a farmhouse. The walls are whitewashed. There is no tablecloth, benches all around. Milk, cream, fruit, eggs, as much as one wanted. After dinner we were introduced to the young Japanese architect and his wife who is also an architect and is as small and thin as a ten-year-old girl. Both are very charming, children of professors in Tokyo. Richard's black hair looks chestnut brown beside their blackness. We also met a Canadian who is seven years with him, as well as a German who has an eight-months-old child in Los Angeles; lost his wife. He had been all over the world. All these young people have a charming relationship with each other. In reality, they are alone in this world because there are no neighbors, only meadows, forests, sky, and Wright. A great admiration for him unites them all, but a certain state of hate had to be overcome, we were told. He, too, exploits his employees, although in quite another manner than Mendelsohn. Often they have to work nine hours, although there is hardly any work. He doesn't like it if they do work on their own. If I imagine the house winding around the hill like a snake, the head being up there, then the part where he lives is in the tail. There, first of all, is his living room which is quite wonderful. Very low with a beautiful fireplace-corner and, above all, an indescribably magnificent view. The landscape is so untouched and lonely that it open one's heart. All doors and windows are screened.

After our dinner—the guests were served separately—Wright called us to come in as we were standing in a group outside, not knowing if the master wished us to be with him. We were introduced. Mr. Johnson[6] is an elderly, harmless, benevolent, little, dull-looking man. One would never suspect him to be a millionaire. His very amiable, gracious wife seems to be very superficial, their adopted daughter, a powdered, pallid, dull-looking female with a doll-like beauty. Her husband had black hair, laughed, and smiled, and looked like a nincompoop. Wright sat in an easy chair. It was somewhat painful for us to see such an outstanding man humbling himself by being amiable, offering hospitality in order to get a commission.

I was asked to sing. The Steinway grand was completely out of tune and did not impress me. Imagine me thus sitting at the piano singing Bach, Italian arias, after each song anxiously watching the words whirling around me, smiling friendly when spoken to, although I did not understand a word. If it was a question, I looked imploringly at Richard who translated it for me. My singing pleased very much. Then I accompanied Moser to a Handel sonata for violin and piano. He plays very well and praised my accompaniment very much, which really went quite well considering that I did not practice. But the main thing was that we helped Wright out of a great embarrassment because even the best entertainer finds it difficult to entertain these society people in the long run.

As to the room itself, I don't know what more to say. It is so immensely many-sided and different, by no means highly modern compared to Taut[7] but more beautiful than anything I have seen before. Then we went into the studio where Wright fetched miraculous items from his Japanese treasure trove. There were magnificently painted screens in gold and silver on which were painted either colored flowers or clouds with birds or dark green fir boughs. He also showed us magnificent embroideries, marvelously colored fabrics, etc.

Our room is on the first floor. The whole house is on one level as I mentioned before, with exception of the house on the hill. In the morning we were awakened by the chirping of birds. There are magnificently colored birds here, also, supposedly, a lot of snakes. The sun shone. It was a glorious day which seemed fabulously unreal. When we came to the grassy hill, walking over the flagstone path past blooming bushes, we looked over the shrubs, then over a flowering meadow and, finally, into the distant woods.

After breakfast Moser showed us parts of the house which had been built in many periods and has innumerable corners. We came to a basement piled high with books. Imagine now that his magnificent, gigantic edition by Wasmuth rots and molds here in hundreds of copies he bought up to prevent too many people imitating him, we were told. I was quite beside myself and very sorry not to own such a copy. We climbed over the roofs which are covered with wooden shingles, only slightly sloped. We sat on the ridge under a roof of leaves, enjoying a magnificent view while Moser told us about their life here and about Los Angeles.

In the afternoon Wright drove us around the country in his car. The first

6. Albert Johnson, who was at Taliesin to discuss the commission for a Chicago skyscraper to headquarter his insurance empire.

7. Bruno Taut was a highly respected avant-garde architect in Berlin.

thing that strikes you are the barns which are all red. Here, as well as in Highland Park, there are small wooden houses, all built in good taste, without many decorations. We passed through a luscious forest with oak trees totally unknown to me, their leaves wildly serrated. All very lovely and pristine. This estate is like a fairyland. Wright speaks in a winning, agreeably self-conscious manner. One feels that he loves this, his native country, very deeply. All his ancestors lived around here on farms. All moved into the city, died, perished. He is the only one who came out again. We were told that on Sundays hoards of strangers come, go through all the rooms, sniff around everywhere, leave this famous house astonished. Long caravans of cars are standing on the street, even in the courtyard. According to his mood, Wright serves as guide, or is angered by them.

After the drive we three sat in his room and when we asked, he showed us his drawings. Moser had told us beforehand that he loses his drawings due to his disorderliness and carelessness, but supposes, nevertheless, that everybody robs him, so he is full of distrust. In fact, he began to search, became excited, rummaged in all drawers, and said helplessly: "Everything is gone." Eventually, we got something to look at and we saw with deep devotion and great admiration how God's spirit and soul are mirrored in this man, with all the mystery of what is beyond understanding.

His buildings in Los Angeles are quite marvelous. And this man has nothing to do! Richard said rightly, what a tragedy that is. He has a magnificent office in the most marvelous surroundings, room for twenty people, all the requirements for the execution of commissions which go to those who can't lick his boots. Of course, one could say it's his own fault. He quarrels with his clients, his buildings are too expensive, etc. Still, he is a genius and later on he will be as famous as the Italian architects. What about his buildings? His marvelous country houses in Chicago are already surrounded by the city and may, perhaps, soon be torn down to make room for skyscrapers. A great part of his drawings have vanished. The Wasmuth edition is rotting in the basement. He sits without work on his wonderful estate, carrying innumerable construction ideas in his mind; probably too beautiful to fit into our world.

In the evening we lay on the grass while the stars glittered above us. The fireflies sparkled through the night, little kittens wrestled, and a beautiful long-haired dog lay down beside me. Wright spoke much but I scarcely understood what he said. In spite of the many scandal stories that are spread, his heart certainly seems pure. He can't be measured with the yardstick of the ordinary citizen. Those who condemn him are incapable of understanding his art. Those who understand and admire him try to comprehend everything. This is my impression of two days. I don't know, of course, how much it would change after having known him better. Sunday we took another fragrant walk through his forest where we found shining red lilies. After our return Wright asked me to sing in place of a religious service. He liked especially the Bach songs, and you certainly can imagine how wonderful it was to sing in such surroundings. We departed at noon, reaching Highland Park at 1:00 A.M.

Highland Park, August 1924

Last news is that Wright called me up, invited us for dinner at the Congress Hotel and asked me to work with him in Spring Green. Yesterday I wrote him my answer and my conditions.

It looks to me that his present situation is such that he cannot afford more than offer us room and board. It is a tragedy that this man may die without having been able to achieve what he is capable of accomplishing.

Taliesin, September 1924

My dear Richard Neutra    $160.00 per month and your board is what I had in mind. Although in excess of my practice in such matters, I believe you will be able to earn it under the coming circumstances. We'll try it for a while and if you like it and I like you and all goes well we will discuss a contract. I am going to Los Angeles after I return from New York. So you would better come at once to get instructions before I leave Saturday—so you can accomplish something while I am gone . . .

Highland Park, September 1924

On September 27 we received a telegram which we had despaired of receiving, saying that Muetterli and Frank would be taking a boat on the third of October from Bremen. I am beside myself with joy, only hoping all goes well during the trip. Here, everything is practically packed and Sunday we are leaving, somewhat sadly, this little attic room in which we've been so happy, leaving as well the beautiful lake. How we shall fare at Taliesin is doubtful in our minds, but full of courage we embark on the new adventure.

*In late November Muetterli leaves Taliesin to return home to Hagen.*

Taliesin, November 1924

Today it is a week since Wright left Taliesin for Los Angeles. Sunday, Dione sang Bach for me in the living room. I lay on the couch near the fireplace. It is really marvelous to make music in this room. Since I am here my admiration for this man has grown even more. He is the greatest living genius, as far as I am aware of. . . .

When you experience Wright, you may have an inkling of Bernini. However, a hundred Berninis cannot help you to comprehend *one* modern, suffering genius filled with pregnant ideas for the future. He told me once, with sad reference to himself, the story of a monkey caught and roped on his porch by a planter, and how the monkey bit off the rope and the screen cloth during a long night and went back to the jungle. There he was torn limb from limb because he was different. He had a rope around his belly which no other monkey had.

In twenty minutes it will be 6:00 P.M. The air is filled with the smell of kerosene lamps and I write this letter on top of the ground-floor plan for Mr. Johnson's house in the desert. No doubt, you recall that this skyscraper client also commissioned a desert mansion on the sandy hills of Colorado. Wright desires that his building should look like a sprouting cactus.

Where shall all of us be when Johnson drives up in his Cadillac to move in? Will his skyscraper be photographed and so become part of our cultural history? All those immense reflecting glass surfaces! How long can the U.S.A. remain so rich?

It is quite possible that after a swell of interest, America will be out of fashion in Europe in two years. This, however, does not change the fact that there are some individual elements of progress here that seem to be more important than most of the personal individual experiments made in Europe.

*Richard to Frances Toplitz*

Taliesin, November 1924

Five Christmas trees are lying on the pavement of the outer court signifying that Mr. Wright intends a celebration, wants to keep us here, wants us to forget that everybody has to follow his own path.

Did I report anything to you regarding Mendelsohn's visit here? I suppose Muetterli told you everything about Taliesin. She did not like Mendelsohn, and I am afraid you would not like him either. However, he has some good qualities although he is apparently not on the side of a true effective building art. Wright was rather against him, but surely received an exuberant impression of Mendelsohn's creative vitality.

*R. M. Schindler to Richard*

Los Angeles, December 1924

Do you have a clear picture of the West, or is it, as it is for so many, a nostalgic urge? In any case, here you can make a living as well as in Chicago and, for a foreigner there are better prospects for a future and an agreeable way of life. I would be very pleased to receive you here and help you over the initial difficulties, as far as it is in my power. We shall not starve.

*Richard to Muetterli*

Taliesin, December 1924

I talked once more with Wright, told him of our intention to leave in February. Our talk was cordially open and he was, on his part, most amiable. He agreed to let me go although he would have liked to keep me and could not understand my motive completely. It appears to me that he will try to postpone my departure on account of office matters, but he could not be friendlier or more cordial. Also, with regard to money matters he is very fine. That he does not want to stay alone in Taliesin is understandable.

I hope one gets accustomed to traveling, learns how to make it comfortable. I have no talent in that respect. Besides, I have a sentimental attachment to any place where I spend more than two weeks. I shall always think back with admiration, with what ease you managed to get here and leave again.

Yesterday I experienced something pleasant. G. A. Reinhardt, the chief draftsman of Holabird and Roche, wrote me a heartwarming letter which ended with the words, "God's blessing for you and your family," adding an excellent reference letter from his firm. As it is the oldest and largest architectural firm in America, it must be considered a success and might prove useful. I am now a member of the American Institute of Architects, thus a legitimate personality.

Taliesin, January 1925

We are just about ready to leave for California. Richard spoke about it with Wright who was very friendly. However, now he acts as if no discussion had taken place, gives Richard some of his writings for translation, pays no attention to the project Richard is working on and should complete before his departure. How we, therefore, can leave in good grace is a mystery.

I guess we shall leave here February 1. If only Wright would be less difficult. I always try to interject some remarks to remind him of our leaving. When I showed him how Frank has learned to walk, he remarked how he would miss such a baby.

*Richard and Dione leave Taliesin and seek their fortune in California—their ultimate goal.*

*They rent an apartment in R. M. and Pauline Schindler's West Los Angeles home. To work in downtown Los Angeles is a daily two-hour commute for Richard.*

*Richard works with Schindler on numerous projects while also free-lancing for other architects to supplement his income.*

*Richard begins work on his first book,* How America Builds.

*Dione tries to help financially by singing in clubs and over the radio.*

*1925*

Our stay in Taliesin will probably be over in several days. How is it with Mr. Wright? He is very satisfied with my work and he told Dione: "Richard would always find work with me whenever he likes to come again. I don't see why he has to leave. Anybody can leave, but only a few are allowed to stay. So why leave and not enjoy this place and this situation?" Dione answered: "To be happy and to be comfortable was not the single aim we had in mind in coming to this country." He said: "Getting more mature, I have found out that being happy IS the single aim we have to have in mind and no time is lost when spent on this purpose. Fame and money helps only a little. I admit," he added, "anybody should have a little of that too, to feel secure." "As much as I know, my husband is not very eager to achieve fame and money, but he feels an urge to follow an inner calling, and he always profited a lot in wandering and looking around while working in different places."

Taliesin, January 1925

*Richard to Muetterli*

. . . Mary, dear Muetterli, whom you liked so much is a WEAK female. Unfaithful to the Armenian poet, she can be considered as Wright's present sweetheart. He met her yesterday in Madison to bring her in the newly washed Cadillac with a new chauffeur, who proudly wore a special fur cap to Taliesin, where he remained invisible . . .

The Cadillac which raced towards Taliesin, drove over the head of poor Tatters—you remember the funny puppy—and thus ended all further fun for him. She had not sufficiently taught him not to jump around automobiles. Now poor Nelly is again alone, has no one to frolic with in the snow. Quite lonely, she walks with me into the moonlit night. The others are with Wright and the kerosene lamps. I saw them through the window. I pass the hill with the windmill motor. I crawl through the barbed wire fence. I wade with my torn yellow low shoes through the deep snow, raising the collar of my father's overcoat. The sky glistens over the deep green-blue horizon. Orion stands so high. Other stars seem only the width of a hand separated from the towering moon, and underneath are the Sirius stars. I trudge through deepest snow towards the big tree trunk on the high hill behind the cone-shaped, motor windmill. Do you remember, Muetterli? The huge, black, dried mulleins are still there. They are standing like sticks in the moonlit snow. It is so light that I can clearly see the dog's footprints as he runs ahead of me, as if he soon would run back with the dead Tatters. Occasionally, I rub her head and say: "Juhuhu—Nelly, Nelly, Nelly, Nelly.

The naked tree trunks on the slope throw fine, ramified shadows onto the whiteness, the few distant pine trees are like a black hole in this picture. I think what nonsense it is to speculate about the future. Shall we later ever again be so happy? Our Frankli will once say: "My father was with me somewhere in Wisconsin when I was small. My mother showed me beautiful photographs, but I remember nothing. There was a photograph where a Japanese held a cake with one candle on it while I stood in a box with a new wool shawl around me, trying to grasp the cake and the candle. That was photographed on my first year's birthday." These months and the last twelve years I have learned great things of this great master and I am very glad to show my gratitude in having carefully prepared (besides the other work) those two extensive publications which are going to appear in Amsterdam and Berlin. Holabird and Roche have sent me a wonderful reference. We shall hope that good luck does not desert us at the Pacific.

*Dione to Frances Toplitz*

Los Angeles, February 1925

We are settled and are really in Los Angeles. We have had innumerable impressions and the transition from fiercest cold to agreeable warmth took place painlessly. We really had a wonderful trip. In order to make things easier for me, my thoughtful Richard had taken a compartment which proved to be very advantageous.

Schindler awaited us in Los Angeles and brought us to his strange house in Hollywood, which has its own beauty considering how little money he has. We live in the guest apartment, have a large room with kitchen and bath, a separate entrance. Mrs. Schindler is extraordinarily helpful and both of them show great friendship and help us a lot. . . .

Schindler told Richard that he feels a sentimental attachment to him and considers our two families as a "unit." Whether they shall later collaborate remains to be seen. . . .

Unfortunately, Schindler has only very small commissions. . . . When Schindler moved here, three years ago, there was no house to be seen, now he is already surrounded. The weather is ideal, very warm and clear outside, but not hot and always a slight breeze. The interior of the house is cool as it has cement floors and walls.

Los Angeles, March 1925 *Richard to Muetterli*

We have no ink. My fountain pen is on the blink, as unfortunately is our typewriter. I have damned little time for myself. Everything has to settle down. My evening meal is again good, as Dionerl is cooking it. At noon I grab lunch downtown. I sit for two hours in the Pacific Railway car. My new boss is an Englishman, very decent. He treats me excellently. His commissions are executed in early Florentine Renaissance style. Los Angeles is beautiful. The central part of the city reminds me of New York's Fifth Avenue. Naturally, money is more abundant there than it is here. However, without question, this city has a future, a hasty past. Schindler's projects appear excellent to me. However, he does not possess the American know-how to put up a front. Whether any material success for me will bloom here lies yet in deep darkness. I shall have every opportunity to exercise my training in patience.

I shall begin again to write you little notes on scraps of paper, trying your patience, but I intend to write!

We are with all our hearts with you in Germany and only our intellect dwells among this American population. As I have no talent for exclusive nationalistic feelings and thoughts, I have no overheated ambitions to irrevocably sink my roots here. In reality, the whole world is my home and perhaps only Vienna, through childhood memories, is accentuated. To state it quite categorically, I am sick and tired of national pride across oceans, rivers, and mountains. It is my firm belief that it depends rather on the steadiness and competence of people to produce a culture than on their proprietary relation to any piece of earth. . . .

I really prefer to be known as one of the first in our profession, so overgrown with historical considerations, who recognized that fame is a fossil that dates back to the Renaissance where every muck from Perugia to Bergamo was claimed to be built by a "famous" individual. I love Italy and especially Bergamo and the Italian Renaissance too, but today we cannot imitate it. We cannot with a good conscience believe that we are original geniuses, who, like Leonardo, conjured out of an indifferent plateau skyhigh "inventions," as, for instance, airplanes that could not fly at all.

Baden, March 1925 *Muetterli to Richard*

Hardly anyone among our contemporaries has a secure old age. This is something our generation has to cope with, but it is not easy to admit that willy-nilly we must always step down lower to find any kind of job. I am not one who tries to foresee the future, anticipating that a brick will fall on us from the roof. Such worries are idle. All in all, old age is unattractive if one cannot give pleasure to others. America is not a Dorado because you have to hustle there just as you do in Berlin. Nevertheless, these times of utmost exertion are happiest in retrospect. When haste is unnecessary, one sleeps as long as one wants and nothing is missed during the whole day. This, of course, is different with you as you are a creative individual. What a challenge it must be for Dione to give you peace of mind by being successful with her musical endeavors. . . .

About us: When I think of old age, I see myself surrounded by children and grandchildren. Any other life makes no sense to me. Our present unsettled situation, naturally contributes to my disgust with life. . . .

*Richard to Muetterli*                                    Los Angeles, March 1925

. . . When a person who is as beloved as you are speaks of being tired of life, of feeling superfluous, I feel a cold shudder running down my spine, fearing evil will befall you as punishment. Please banish such thoughts from your mind. They are really sinful. You show no trace of *old age* and you must not count on my treating you with reverence for this supposed old age. I only wish that when I am old I can find as many people to love me as you have. On account of this devotion you are probably spoiled and do not know how lonesome some people are who deserve better.

*Dione to Her Parents*                                    Los Angeles, March 1925

. . . Muetterli, your letter, as well as the photograph, has a strange effect on me. You, as always, look young, but you, Vaterli, look much older with your shaven head. All this, together with your depressing words and the rainy weather, which here makes one doubly melancholy, makes me suddenly realize that you will not live as long as we shall and that is awful. The comforting realization is always alive in me that somewhere in Germany two human beings exist who will always welcome me, who will always help me. I know, dear Muetterli, that there is no remedy for such melancholia, but perhaps sometimes it is a comfort to you to know how much I love you.

Pauline does not love her mother at all. She always tells me that her mother's education was terrible, the reason for many of her inhibitions. She is unhappy when she is in her house. In short, she is her "complex."

*Frank Lloyd Wright*                                    Taliesin, March 1925
*to Dione*

I have been worse than graceless to respond to your two charming letters so late. But you know the awful laws of procrastination, that is my destiny—work—all the time. I appreciated more than I can say your sympathy and my conscience smites me regarding that letter. I enclose one picture, but it won't do much good, although I wish it could. I hope to see you all again before you leave the country for "home," or is the USA beginning to look like home?

All is quiet here. Am doing a little drawing and writing. Here my affectionate regards to you and your son and Richard. The telegraphed replies to send back the drawings, the nominations for corresponding member of the Austrian Architects came with Richard's kind notation and I liked it all very much.

Taliesin has not been just the same since its songbird flew away to softer climes—but Taliesin is destined to pain and grief as the shadow of its great joy.

Here to you all from us here.

Los Angeles, April 1925     *Richard to Muetterli*

I am working on a garden for a Schindler house near Griffith Park and for Miss Barnsdall on Olive Hill.[1] I rise at 5:00 A.M. in order to have two hours for my own work. I like to be in bed by 10:00 P.M., which is conspicuous because Schindler's friends usually go to bed around 2:00 A.M. That for sure is not for me. A night spent in cigarette fumes has less attraction for me than a clear head in the morning.

Los Angeles, April 1925     *Dione to Muetterli*

Schindler very often takes a meal with us. I always count him in whether he comes or does not come. Before I did that, he would show up ten minutes before mealtime and then Richard wanted him to stay. Often I had only leftovers that were just enough for the two of us. These two have the most interesting discussions together, which gives me great pleasure. Otherwise Schindler is a very difficult character, very noncommunicative, hiding his true feelings behind a smiling face. One thing however, I like very much. He has such an infectious laugh, especially when Richard makes a joke, which prompts one to tell some more.

Los Angeles, July 1925     *Dione to Frances Toplitz*

At the end of the week I shall sing again in the Hollywood Art Association. This time one hundred people will listen and I am singing some songs accompanying myself on the cello, which did not exist when I was in New York, as I learned them only in Highland Park. Some days later I shall sing again in the League of Garment Workers, very poor Jewish people who showed such an interest; they were so eager to listen that it was a real pleasure to play for them. . . .

Los Angeles, July 1925     *Dione to Muetterli*

Yesterday I had again a tremendous success with the garment workers. There were about eighty of them, worn-out and needy-looking but with interested eyes. It seems that the general economic situation is rather desperate. There are 100,000 people out of work and last week twenty-five

---

1. Aline Barnsdall, prominent Los Angeles citizen and a client of Frank Lloyd Wright.

restaurants had to close. Many houses and stores stand empty. This is not surprising considering the rapid increase in population. If I heard right— 100,000 newcomers since the New Year. Industry simply cannot cope with this situation.

At the start of my program I explained the contents of Schubert's "Erl-koenig," which I played on a horrible piano with no pedals, but Richard said I nevertheless played well and the audience was enthusiastic.

Then I sang Schubert's "Der Tod und das Maedchen" and "Traum duch die Daemmerung." My Swiss cello songs evoked a storm of applause and it is enchanting to perform for these interested faces so full of joyful hope. It is very important to explain the content of a song and I think I have now the knack of it.

While I speak, I look at all the people, smile at them, and they seem to relish it. Plotkin (manager) just told Pauline on the telephone that only once before me an entertainer was able to captivate this audience and keep them enthralled. After I left, they stood in groups and talked about me for twenty minutes.

*Dione to Her Parents*

Los Angeles, July 1925

. . . My twenty-year-old manager, Hodell, is very resourceful. Last week I auditioned at the best radio station. He told me afterwards that everybody rose when I started to sing. I have an engagement for August 6 and, for the second time, will be paid twenty dollars, with the chance of singing a program once a week. . . .

I sang twice last week on different radio stations. Some clippings are enclosed. At the KFI station I sang five Swiss songs, two Bergerettes, accompanying myself on the piano. Richard listened at a neighbor's house and thought it sounded beautiful. . . .

*Muetterli to Dione*

Baden, July 1925

Dear Dione, I am so glad you have some activity besides caring for husband and child. Don't let your talents atrophy. A resourceful woman can accomplish a variety of tasks simultaneously. I approve of how you have arranged your time so that you do not have too much housework. You can leave polishing silver twice a day to those who have nothing more worthwhile to do. . . .

To speak about Frank: Is it not necessary for a growing child to become accustomed to authority at an early age? Must it not learn to be patient, obedient, and cooperative? Believe in your natural instincts. You must accept inconveniences. You cannot have children without assuming a certain amount of responsibility, but they should not be permitted to make a slave of you. . . .

*Richard to Muetterli*

Los Angeles, August 1925

. . . My idea to have the publisher write an introduction to my book *How America Builds* was caused by the consideration that I dislike the idea to enter the book field without being introduced by a professional writer. After all, I am an architect, not a writer. My articles are not literature but a factual compilation based on practical facts and ideas. As many of them are of a technical nature, I am afraid that publishers of literature will shake their heads and miss the point.

One of the greatest stumbling blocks may be the fact that I do not use easily understood or brilliant slogans, which is expected from the literary arbiter of an art magazine so that the reader will feel enlightened and informed in short order. I rather illuminate the problems that were created by unclear questions than give solutions and recipes which cannot flow from one single brain but from an all encompassing mentality. Even so, I try to give solutions in various sectors—traffic solutions, solutions for skyscrapers, for small dwellings. All of them are unusually instructive and interesting. This, and the formulation of existing problems, give this book its value. Another drawing card is its forty to fifty illustrations which may delight the eye of anyone hungry for beauty. The rest is more informative than beautiful. I know presently several hundred architects and those interested in architecture who, without a doubt, would read these articles.

Los Angeles, August 1925

*Dione to Vreneli*

. . . Schindler told me the other day he cannot believe I am one and the same person he first met in New York because I have changed completely. I am sure he is wrong. The truth, however, is that I am very different in comparison with women here. I attract attention because I wear no makeup. I find it makes no sense to try to compete. The extravagance of dresses here is indescribable. . . .

Los Angeles, August 1925

*Dione to Muetterli*

The climate here suits me just fine! I cannot remember when I felt so well anywhere else. I wish I could say the same for Richard. But it is difficult to pinpoint why this is not so. Fortunately, this does not affect our relationship. Occasionally at parties I am introduced as one who claims to be happy, apparently an unknown phenomenon here. In Germany I never heard so much talk about broken marriages and nervous breakdowns. . . .

Los Angeles, August 1925

*Dione to Frances Toplitz*

I know that Richard does not want me to tell this to anybody, not even you, dearest Frances, but I know you love him and wish him the best. I will send you this letter secretly. You better not mention it when writing to him. I shall tell you why Richard is so downhearted. I don't know if you will understand, but you can perhaps imagine how a very creative mind, full of new ideas, must suffer when he has to work the whole day on uninteresting jobs, tiring himself out for other people, never having time for himself. He rises at 5:00 A.M. in the morning to snatch one hour, but you know, ideas cannot be commanded, they come when it pleases them. They come during office hours, say, but one, two, three days pass and the time never comes to carry them out.

*Richard to Frances
Toplitz*

Los Angeles, August 1925

I have just read Dione's letter to you. I find it a little lachrymose. Don't assume for a moment that we are not happy or that we are not successful here. *We have success in America!* True, it is not yet fully satisfactory because I have to dissemble my real ideas and behave as if I had none, although I am known as a first-class designer in Los Angeles. However, in the last month I had an occasion to produce something of substance; besides, it was well paid. Having no connections whatsoever, nobody can expect that I should get independent commissions. One has to be patient, that's all, and I don't complain.

*Dione to Muetterli*

Los Angeles, August 1925

Neither Schindler nor Pauline shows the slightest understanding for Richard which, really, is beyond my comprehension. Schindler does not want to take any risks, desires that everything develop slowly. Richard is filled with good ideas, but what can he do? During the next half year a solution must be found. The situation slowly develops into a crisis. Both are very compatible, which is surely rare among experts, but as I mentioned before, something will have to give.

Richard's health will not improve until either his book is published and is a success, or what is even more important, when he can see the end of his office work based on the whim of his employers. Many complicated considerations regarding Schindler are intertwined and too difficult to describe. I save wherever possible, but some purchases for the child are necessary. The upkeep of the car costs a lot.

If only there were any possibilities to meet bankers or businessmen! It is amazing how difficult it is to break out of the class to which all our friends belong.

The future of Los Angeles seems immense, and surely there will be a lot of building activity.

I shall have completed the typing of Richard's book by the end of the week. Richard has only the early morning hours from 5:30 to 7:00 for his work, and new ideas do not make an appearance on command. . . .

*Richard to Muetterli*

Los Angeles, August 1925

In the midst of my work I think lovingly of you. During our walks and whenever we find ourselves on a beautiful observation point, we exclaim: "Here we will take Muetterli!" But when, oh when? When shall we again be together? When I decided to come here, I had not made up my mind for how long I would remain and so far nothing has occured for or against our staying here. Whether I like it or not, I must willy-nilly be prepared for a slow development of our situation. I am not accustomed to this, although it is the usual thing. The American jobs I have held were in all ways *above my head*, starting with Chicago. By this I mean they were too well paid in comparison to my knowledge of American customs and technical know-how. This has provided me with an unexpectedly rich experience. However, one cannot expect that I should be able to compete with people who have grown up in this business, who do not know anything else, are not interested in anything else but the work they were taught to do since decades. In the last few months I have again drawn a comparatively high salary. For instance, architect Brandner, the American who had to give up his office for lack of work, is less paid than I at the moment, although he is much more experienced, knows all the big firms here, and is a graduate of a Chicago university. I am not sure whether it is clear to you that it takes a few years to grow into such a new situation. For the time being, I was looking for a job with an architect who has a small practice and little experience and where I would be the only draftsman. Such people usually have small commissions, pay little, and are exploiters. By chance, I found a man who knows nothing, but has a first-class commission and, therefore, pays unusually well. This is the reason why I left my first job. Everything developed as anticipated. I was able to conceive and execute the twenty sheets of technical drawings all by myself, after the twenty preliminary drawings had been accepted by the client. Even the construction I figured out in part and two perspective drawings of mine were published in the Los Angeles Times. Since two weeks there are no funds. The client has left for the East Coast, but my employer expects a check momentarily. Suddenly, he discovered that my designs have a similarity to those of Wright. (I wish they had.) In reality, they are tame compromises. . . .

I thought you might be interested to hear what occupies my time and life. I omit the needless word "unfortunately."

Los Angeles, September 1925

I simply cannot find any free time to work for myself, or I have to battle for every 15 minutes of free time. Nobody here except my Dionerl can understand this. This state of affairs is definitely more humorous than tragic. Occasionally I can produce even an inner laugh. My brain really works constantly at full capacity. The country with all its shortcomings provides an unbelievable wealth of learning material for anyone who wants to understand the present world situation.

I have finally completed all the drawings for my school. It is an anomaly if one considers that one single man did it all alone, thirteen large sheets filled with ink drawings. Surely, I never had a chance in Germany to complete plans of such complexity, nor have I seen others do it. As yet I do not know whether I will have to look for new work in a few days, or in a few weeks. . . .

*Although Richard could find so few moments to devote time to what interested him, he managed to use every free hour not only to work on his manuscript but also to write articles about various aspects of American technology—articles that he also illustrated.*

Los Angeles, September 1925

. . . We begin to hear from various sources that Richard's articles are read with great interest. Very soon one of them will be published in a technical magazine. Be sure he works in his spare time—oh my, sometimes we have only two free evenings a week—on his book which will contain several articles about the Palmer House, about Schindler's houses in La Jolla, about American railway terminals, traffic conditions. It will be the first publication that deals rationally with the American building situation. It will have about a hundred illustrations.

We are slowly drawn into the whirl of social activities, although we are only starting to make acquaintances. . .

Los Angeles, December 1925

. . . Our situation here is so uncertain that we cannot make any plans. Schindler is terribly vacillating, neither flesh nor fowl, but Richard thinks he is by far the most interesting of all people here. His architecture is really unique. He is very practical, knows how to build cheaply. He and Richard like to work together, yet he cannot come to any decision. It is really not understandable.

Meanwhile, all sorts of things have happened. Richard did finally lose his job as he had anticipated for weeks. He and Schindler deliberate back and forth how they could build up an association. Richard is full of excellent ideas, but Schindler cannot make any decisions. That is his greatest shortcoming.

Los Angeles, December 1925

Our situation at the moment is without promise, unfortunately, and I am not able to push through the two residences I have been working on for so many months. There is nobody among our acquaintances who shows any inclination to build, and so there is nothing left but work without remuneration in the sweat of my brow on projects whose realization is most uncertain, without a penny. If I write you about such difficulties *please keep them to yourselves*. They are not fit to be broadcast. Somehow I must wiggle myself out of this situation. I am tired of doing all this unpaid work, as you can imagine, and I do not have the peace of mind to take a vacation. In reality it is funny that one should have such a difficult time when one is known as a conscientious worker. But after all we have five million unemployed and among them are probably many capable men. I am enclosing two short articles so that the publicity campaign is not going to sleep. . . . Keep in mind that presently Walter Gropius, Sigfried Giedion, and *Das Neue Frankfurt* are the ones that publish the most sincere and progressive magazines with higher repute than any other. In any case, there are now so many fellow travelers, who try to make a profit in this new architectural movement, that one must try to keep one's reputation unblemished.

*Richard and Schindler form a collaboration, Architectural Group for Industry and Commerce.*

*One of Richard's free-lance projects is to design a clubhouse for the California Lambs Club in Hollywood.*

*Richard and Dione enjoy their first vacation together—a trip to San Francisco.*

*Muetterli persuades Richard to participate in the international design competition for the League of Nations Palace in Geneva. Richard persuades Schindler to join him.*

*Dione's sister Doris joins the family.*

*In October a second son, Dion, is born.*

Los Angeles, April 1926

I write you on the letterhead of our firm in the hope that you abandon all misgivings about our future. Writing on it, I wish it had the same effect on me . . .

Today I have started a new job as principal designer for the Fidelity Construction Company. The outfit consists of a mixture of Gentiles and Jews. All together, they are a crazy bunch and I cannot see how they can succeed in the business world! However, they have 250 times more commissions than we have, thus my evaluation must be faulty. They have exerted quite some effort to obtain my services. (I already seem to have quite a name in Los Angeles as a designer.) Today, on my first day here, they were in ecstasy about a design for a new clubhouse I presented them with. Let's hope the job will last for six weeks.

Los Angeles, April 1926

. . . My situation is still unclear. Despite my being involved in many tasks, I have in fact no work. Every moment someone drops in looking for work. All of them ask for a much smaller salary than I received.

I do not write this to cause you any worries and I myself would love to have a week's respite. That you see my future in a rosy light pleases me immensely. I have no intention to throw in the sponge, although occasionally it irks me that everybody I know seems to have a much easier time than I have. True. I have read in mythological biographies that various

147

gentlemen have started their careers as newspaper vendors, for instance: Edison, Keppler, or Alexander the Great. But those I am acquainted with have had less difficulties. Everything has it advantages and disadvantages. The gifts I undoubtedly have are such that they make it hard for me to fit in everywhere. Less exceptional attributes, less handicaps and smoother sailing. As I wrote you before, in order to acquire connections, one has to have a different financial basis than I have, at least a well-tailored suit, a middle-class automobile, be a member of a fashionable club, participate in dinner and stag parties. This is desirable in order to meet people who give you a chance. In Berlin it is possible to be a poor wretch and a star at the same time. I must employ all my talents to save money, to reach a somewhat modest independence from all this time-consuming work for others. I would have to be pitied if I had to continue the present path. So far, thank goodness, we all have been healthy and had money to spend. What I tell you here has really nothing to do with money matters or even a comfortable life, which I owe to my Dionerl. An ascetic should not marry! But I am none. All I have is an obligation to further my talents in architecture to such a point that they have a chance to flower. At the present moment in history I really can make a contribution. I do not speak at all of eternal values. It is wonderful how Dione has comprehended this. However, I believe that anybody who brings a sacrifice in helping me has not wasted a shot in the air. Here is a chance among my friends and relatives who are interested in anybody who produces art to offer a helping hand. I think of my brothers who have a peculiarly stiff attitude towards my endeavors. How is it possible that not even the best recommendation has ever furthered my work, while there are persons, even qualified ones, who based their whole careers on such assistance. You, dear Muetterli, write me, for instance, that I do not need this. All my friends think likewise. Perhaps you all are right. There must be a reason for such a typical experience. . . .

*Richard to Frances*
*Toplitz*

Los Angeles, April 1926

. . . As far as I am concerned, I find that America is indeed a very strange country when observed from a civilizatory, evolutionary, psychological, technical-managerial viewpoint. I told everybody who gave me advice, everybody I asked for an affidavit—compare my work in the Friends Mission in Vienna—what it was that I hoped to find in America. Within two years I have actually found it. America is full of newly arrived intellectuals who are disparaging and bemoan their lot here. (This could even happen to me as I had not intended to prolong my study trip beyond two years.) For heaven sake, what could anyone find in Pittsburgh unless he is looking for something specific. He will find something worthwhile in the midst of smoke and soot, if he looks for a special coke-burning furnace. He may discover there more interesting variations than anywhere else. *One has to search* for something, knowledge, horizons, also negative experiences. In Naples there is no need to search for anything. Anybody can tell you where to enjoy the Vesuvius above the pine trees, unless one prefers to simply meander along, savoring a thousand glances. This is very different in Pittsburgh or any other American metropolis. After studying the *Bae-decker*, one looks up perturbed, learns that the main post office is built in English Gothic. This is written the same way as in an Italian *Baedecker* where San Giorgio Maggiore is mentioned. The American *Baedecker* has the same soft binding as the European one, but no map is correct, nothing is correct. This is the country of constant flux. It has the majesty of a building site, the majesty of possibilities, at most, if you want to make an attempt to juxtapose their majesty with historical Europe. Europe has possibilities too, but here there is nothing else if one looks sharply . . .

Los Angeles, April 1926     *Dione to Muetterli*

I wrote you a letter yesterday which I am now absolutely unable to find because I have no desk, unfortunately. It can hardly be expected in a Schindler house. His residences are not designed for children, as he does not think about them, and not for people who write, because he hardly ever writes himself. Richard has a kind of a workroom which is, however, filled with his own stuff, thus there is no vacant shelf for me. . . .

Zurich, April 1926     *Muetterli to Dione*

. . . Mendelsohn delivered a very interesting lecture to the Association of Architects and Engineers of Zurich. He gave a brilliant talk. Whether he was able to convince the Swiss listeners is another matter. As usual, they smiled half ironically or made a sour face. I quote a few of his sentences: "Politics, commerce, art evolved through the juxtaposition of the vertical to the horizontal." Or: "It is human beings who lived in the Middle Ages, who needed as a contrast to their lives geared to the horizontal, the verticalism of a dome. And modern man who lives among the piled-up verticals, needs as a release, the horizontal." In his slides he showed familiar objects like the Mosse Building, the business section of Haifa, his fantastic sketch of a car-body factory, all in sketches. All his other building fantasies he prudently omitted. He did not mention the names of other architects while showing interesting buildings of others like the Jahrhunderthalle (Hall of the Century) in Breslau. The chairman mentioned that they had heard of Mendelsohn's visit to their city and had prevailed on him to give this talk. Mendelsohn excused himself at the start that he was not prepared and had only a few slides. However, his whole presentation seemed carefully prepared, had no ad hoc character. My impression was that one of his forebears must have been a politician, a mystic, or a philosopher, because his talk was brilliant, much superior to the one I had heard in Berlin.

Los Angeles, April 1926     *Dione to Muetterli*

In November you will again become a grandmother. (Now Muetterli, I see you put the letter down and say with a sigh, "Oh my!") There is much more against it than for it. However, if we wait too long, the little Verena Elizabeth (I hope it will be a girl) will arrive too late to be a playmate for

Frank and he needs one so desperately. Even if our present situation were an excellent one, everything might be changed half a year from now. It will be a great additional burden for Richard and a lot of work for me, but later on we shall probably be as happy as we are now to have Frank.

I do know that I have always felt deeply sorry for single children and do not want to inflict this on my child. Surely Frank's development would have been very different had he not been an only child. Oh, well, we shall see.

Once the child is born and it is feasible to leave it, and if we have a car, I shall again make an attempt to approach women's clubs with my music. Unfortunately, they pay much less than I would get from other sources and working for them entails a lot of running around. Naturally, I am quite downhearted that my dreams of disemburdening Richard have evaporated, but what can I do?

I always enjoy Sunday morning. Unfortunately, we awake very early, but this gives us a few quiet moments in which to exchange thoughts. Then Richard gets up because the early morning hours are the most precious for him. I stay in bed a bit longer. Then I shower (on Sundays I omit my daily gymnastics), wash dishes, tidy the room, make breakfast, assisted by Doris,[1] pick up Frank, feed him before our breakfast, trying to contain him while we eat by giving him dry toast. We breakfast in the glassed-in corner of the living room where the sun enters wonderfully. Afterwards we make music for two hours starting with a Beethoven symphony written for four hands. Today I am full of good resolutions. I only hope I can keep them, because I have been very slovenly lately. This is especially annoying because our living room, which also functions as bedroom and kitchen, is only beautiful when kept immaculate, which is really difficult under the circumstances. However, with my firm intention to clear up immediately, I should be able to achieve my goal. Also, I have not been dressing attractively, with the thought that Richard would not notice as he is so occupied. But, apparently, he *does* notice!!

*During the early years in Los Angeles, Richard and Dione bought all their clothes in secondhand stores, and when Muetterli occasionally sent a clothing package they were delighted, as seen below.*

*Richard to Muetterli*

Los Angeles, April 1926.

The suit is here. It has arrived! It's unreal, at least improbable!! I stand on a small stool and see myself in the mirror above our washbasin from the shoulder down to the middle of my calf. In this position I remain during the greater part of the day, trying to turn this way or that way, I want you to know, in order to enlarge the circle of what is visible inch by inch. Just like the astronomers who twist their telescopes in order to catch a glimpse of the other side of the moon. How can I manage it to see how I look from the rear? However, I have trustworthy accounts. Dione stands admiringly

1. Dione's third sister.

around me. Her judgment of course may be dazzled by this novel outward appearance; however it is *so* comforting to be overestimated in one's own circle. The suit sits on my skeleton as tight as if designed to a sixteenth of an inch exact. Our imagination is intrigued and baffled as to its origin. Who designed this masterpiece? Does he lie beneath the grass? Did he end his life because he lost on the stock exchange and therefore his wife and relatives left him and men with heavy treads came to deprive him of his Rolls Royce because two monthly payments were overdue? Oh, monthly overdue payments! The wheel of fortune occasionally turns to its optimum significance.

All in all my wardrobe contains many interesting pieces. Here is one that belonged to a Spanish-Swiss tycoon of industry. Here is one that belonged to the son of the founder of psychoanalysis. Here are two: A light one and a heavier one that belonged to a pioneer of the battle for nature-cures. Here is the overcoat of a leading executive of Sweets Catalogue, here the felt hat of an architect who nowadays walks around without one.

Dear Muetterli, picture to yourself a young girl who is accustomed to powder her nose with two quick manipulations a few seconds before ensnaring someone. Picture to yourself that this girl somehow suddenly receives the gift of a naturally mat skin. She has to change over completely. Now you see! That's how it is with me to whom it had become second nature to darken the knees of his pants with spittle to make them appear the same in color as the rest of the suit, seconds before meeting an important personage. . . .

Dione to Her Parents

Los Angeles, May 1926

I would like to describe to you our trip to San Francisco. At first I knew nothing of Richard's plans. I am full of inner joy at the prospect of having my dearest husband all to myself.

First San Francisco. What does one do at night in a strange city, knowing no one? Naturally one goes to a movie. After walking along the street, reading titles like *Let's Get Married, The Splendid Crime, The Nervous Wreck, The Prince of Pilsen,* etc., we opted for a Wild West film with Tom Mix and his famous horse and dog. A lot of shooting, a burning forest, bad and good guys, all very transparent and still this stupid Dione sits with a beating heart and knees trembling so visibly that Richard wants to leave right then and there.

In Carmel we met some very nice people. I sang some Schumann songs to a very attentive audience.

Around nine o'clock we started to discuss where we should spend the night; Virginia, one of the girls, started to tell us how much she would like to offer us her "cabin," however, it was so primitive that she did not dare. I told her of my early youth, how I slept in the barn of peasants, etc. When Richard heard that our acceptance would mean dislodging the girls, he decided that we should go back to the village and find a hotel. There was only one vacant room in the hotel and it was expensive, so we decided to try to find a private room. While the girls were driving, they started to whisper together and suddenly left the tree-shaded street. The car drove through high grass which was sharply illuminated by its headlights. All around was darkness. Only a few conifers were visible. Without warning among the grass and a few bushes stood a wooden garage. We disembarked. Virginia went ahead. We followed, our eyes slowly adjusting to the dark. We came to a wooden cabin. A few steps led us into a large room where kerosene lamps burned. We saw two large, low windows braced from the outside and underneath two small couches. Everything charming and comfortable despite its primitiveness.

Utter silence around us, only the murmuring of the distant sea. I felt marvelously at peace after noisy San Francisco and the typical rented room in which we had slept. Virginia tried to persuade us to stay. I withdrew discreetly so as not to show how much I wanted to stay and let Richard do the negotiating that finally led to our acceptance. Because I had seen Richard so little my heart was filled with delight. How wonderful not to have a program or duties! Suddenly I remembered with remorse my little Frank whom I had completely forgotten.

We arose late and took a walk to the poet's tower. The poet, whose name is Robinson Jeffers, seems to be well known. He built the tower all by himself from sea rocks. It has a winding stairway and a small room with two Gothic windows. His wife with her head of heavy tresses wore white leather boots, which seemed to fit her surroundings well. Below, her two little boys played with a huge dog. The poet was watering two small conifers. Although we passed by very near and his eyes looked friendly and inviting, his wife did not introduce us. She keeps all visitors at a distance and, as she no doubt knows what is best for him, we showed no surprise. . . .

*Richard to Frances*
*Toplitz*

Los Angeles, May 1926

. . . Now we have been to San Francisco! It certainly is magnificently located! I can understand why you are sometimes homesick for it. The Bay reminded me somehow of Cattaro and her bays, although the mountains there are steeper and wilder. We sailed up on an old-fashioned boat, getting pretty seasick and sunburned. It took us nearly forty-eight hours. We passed the Golden Gate in clear sunshine. My arrival was more favorable than in New York. There is a skyline, too, in San Francisco! Huge apartment houses are indiscriminately built on these beautiful hills. Not knowing where else to go, we registered in a downtown hotel and had noisy nights until we found a private room around the corner of Jones and Sacramento, right above the Fairmont. We walked around in this distinguished shopping district.

The next morning I had an instinctive urge to visit Mill Valley and Muir Woods. Quite by myself I decided that, and we had a wonderful day there. Also we liked the people we met there hiking. They seemed very European to our Los Angeles eyes. This was our very first view of a redwood grove. We were perfectly happy in those beautiful surroundings, managing to climb to the wildest peak through the thickest brush. Besides the landscape and the view, we enjoyed the Hawaiian fishes in the Aquarium and the lovely Japanese garden in Golden Gate Park.

Los Angeles, May 1926

When you ask me how long I intend to stay in Los Angeles, your thought surely is when we shall see each other again. I think about it not less often than you do, although in the beginning I had to create a starting point. However, we must keep in mind that after all we want to live with you and not without you or at least in such proximity that long and repeated visits are possible. For the time being I cannot see how I can manage it, especially if the book matter does not bring results. Taking the present situation in Europe, how could I venture forth with my whole family? I guess I have to stick it out here, also it is difficult for me to be vacillating in my intentions. Success on one line allows perhaps other combinations. I was never in any doubt that my soul gravitates towards Europe. . . .

This envelope will contain a lot about our life here. It was very eventful during the last month. I passed my examination with flying colors and with this certificate have associated myself with Schindler, who was incapable of obtaining such a license. I guess I am the only foreigner here who was able to do it. Schindler surely had all the qualifications to do it too.

I have since the last three years spent my most valuable time on my manuscript, which is in your hands,[2] and I have no other worthwhile results of my labors than what is put down in it.

To tell the truth, literary endeavors are not a by-product, but the full expression and study-results of my American stay here as a European. Everything depends now on finding a publisher. If I cannot create a link between Europe and America with this maximum effort, I would have to try to become Americanized.

Los Angeles, June 1926

So far, the main reason for my happiness was that I am surrounded by well-wishers and no one has as yet attacked me. Up until now, emotionally I have lived without analyzing what is happening to me. This state of affairs continued until I moved into the Schindler house where I found human beings with a very different set of values than mine. They make fun of me, laugh about matters that are sacred to me. I, on my part, make the mistake of speaking too openly about topics of no concern to them. But most importantly, I suddenly realize that I *do* make mistakes of which, quite innocently, I was previously unaware.

I ponder over criticism for days. Perhaps it is desirable that I do more reflecting. Certainly it could have been my lot to come into contact with a person other than Pauline who might have uttered her critical remarks in a friendlier manner instead of treating my every new idea with contempt, being appalled at my "stupidity" and "narrowness." It has taken me quite a while to recognize that Pauline herself is an unstable, mixed-up, unhappy human being. She is certainly unhappy in her relationship to R. M. S. Many of their differences have surfaced. Perhaps you have enough imagination to understand our involvement with the Schindlers, considering how inter-

---

2. Richard had sent the completed manuscript of *How America Builds* to Dione's parents and had put them in charge of finding a European publisher.

twined our lives are. Conditions are improving, but I no longer have an unbiased opinion of Pauline. When I meditate about it, I realize how much I have changed, recognizing that I am beginning to shed my childlike attitude. Everybody thinks I am thirty!

You may ask yourself, "Why does she continue to live there?" There are so many good reasons, but they are too difficult for me to explain to you who are on the outside. Truth is, neither do I want to run away like a coward in order to avoid an uncomfortable situation. I still hope to rise completely above it. An aggravation is that the apartment is so impractical and it will be even more so when our second child arrives. If we had money we could, of course, do a lot, but we have no savings.

This afternoon I tried to visualize what I would need to lighten my work load, enabling me to handle the children without help and still have some time for my music. I suddenly realized that any plan I might conceive would be costly and as we have no money to spare and Richard is already having a difficult time meeting our expenses, I would not want to burden him further. Richard is now trying to work only half a day in a commercial office, helping R. M. S. the other half. All these external pressures quite naturally influence our relationship. Richard treats me wonderfully, but when evening comes I am, especially in my condition, so exhausted that I am not much good and evening is the only time we have a chance to be together. Luckily, we had our marvelous outing, a time when I again was able to see that all is well with us, that our hearts beat in unison.

*Richard to Muetterli*                                          Los Angeles, July 1926

Dione is a wonderful human being. Although others may value her qualities, nobody, strangely enough, has the slightest inkling of our relationship. Her intelligence is far removed from any dialectic and to outsiders it seems ununderstandable that I do not have the slightest wish for clever talky-talky. Dione never puts up a hypothesis just to test it, as little as a walnut tree would try as a test to simulate wisteria blossoms. She does not twaddle and she does not wrap herself into mysterious taciturnity. I do not blame her for her weakness to admire me, the less so, as it is not my external success she admires. In many cases she is often correct when she assumes that in many instances I have shown my good judgment. Surely, she is a splendid daughter of yours, dear Muetterli.

*Muetterli to Dione*                                              Zurich, July 1926

I hope that the League of Nations program has arrived. I was so delighted that Richard has decided to compete. I can only reiterate, don't become impatient. Do what has to be done and don't expect more than is possible from the difficult times we live in.

*Dione to Muetterli*                                        Los Angeles, August 1926

We have many worries, and this year will be crucial for us. Most important is the fate of the manuscript. The long delay, the possibility of not finding a publisher would be something that Richard could hardly bear and I, too, for that matter, because you cannot possibly know how many blows from behind occurred, so that it nearly appears as if ill fortune was pursuing us. I tell Richard all the time, "We cannot see at present whether all these delays are not beneficial." But they are difficult to bear.

Los Angeles, August 1926 *Dione to Muetterli*

The League of Nations Palace competition material has arrived. It will require an immense effort of at least six months' work. I am filled with family pride that you handled this matter so promptly. Richard hopes to be able to persuade Schindler to participate in this competition which means that for several months there will be no income. Could the wives help out in some way? Pauline has a teaching certificate and vaguely mentioned yesterday that she might try to find a position as a teacher. I am, unfortunately, out of the running for the next few months as I am expecting a second child. However, today I have figured out that if I take care of the Schindler household too, by that I mean, clean, cook, shop for groceries, I shall have contributed something on my part. Naturally, no time will be left to make music. For the time being I cannot imagine how I will manage as I am so tired taking care of my own household, but everything will fall into place, I am convinced. In any case, the two men should try to work on it. . . .

Richard is home all day, runs about the house clad only in bathing trunks, even lies in the sun occasionally, and already looks ever so much better. We are not yet sure whether he will be able to work on the competition. We still do not know whether Schindler intends to participate. Slowly he seems to warm up, and for the time being, Richard works alone having already conceived an extraordinarily interesting floor plan and, as I observed today, a marvelous elevation. Instead of having the prescribed parking place for twenty-five cars, he has one for five hundred cars as well as provisions to land airplanes on the water, handle arrivals by motor boats, the blending of lake and building, marvelous toilet facilities common here but, apparently, not yet known in Geneva. . . .

Los Angeles, September 1926 *Dione to Muetterli*

The competition is still a source of excitement. Schindler's participation is minimal. When I have a chance to speak with Richard at 2:00 A.M. he tells me again: "Schindler participated only for a while," or "He did not show up at all," or "He again changed everything," or "It is very doubtful how we can reach a satisfactory solution." I feel as if someone had hit me over the head. Richard, fortunately, can take it with humor must of the time. In reality, he is delighted to have this chance, sitting daily for seventeen hours at a task from which he learns so much.

Yesterday, while we shared our supper with the Schindlers, I mentioned that it would be very desirable to have not only several draftsmen who could share the excitement but also several wives. Pauline asked, surprised: "Why are you so concerned?" Richard replied: "You take it with a cold shoulder," whereupon she replied: "I do not know a thing about the competition." Sometimes I feel sorry for her because she is married to a man who does not let her participate in anything, who makes fun of all she undertakes, who believes she is all wrong in her ideas about education and everything else. . . .

*Dione to Vreneli*

Los Angeles, September 1926

I wonder how you could stand to see Ruben really only at mealtime. Richard works all the time, also in the evening, as well as all Sunday. Occasionally he manages a two-hour rest in the afternoon. Many times he cannot go to sleep before 2:00 A.M. because this is the only hour of the night Schindler can perhaps devote some time.

He now works at home in bathing trunks, and I can see him for seconds. It is not the length of time that counts but the intensity of feelings. I consider it great good fortune that Richard lets me participate in everything.

It looks as if now, at such a late date, Schindler has decided to participate in the competition, although now we shall have to break our necks, even if we hire a draftsman. At the moment Richard is nothing but a workhorse, twelve to fourteen hours a day. It will be necessary to endure it until spring.

*Dione to Muetterli*

Los Angeles, September 1926

. . . Within the next year it should really become apparent whether Richard and Schindler can collaborate and are able to get commissions. At the moment they have excellent rapport and it is such a joy for me to see them harmoniously sitting together on a bench, only their heads in shadow, deliberating. I am so delighted to see the League of Nations Building taking shape. I think it will be a beautiful building. However, it is still doubtful whether they can enter the competition because the drafting work alone would require the labor of one single man for three and one-half months to fill the eighteen two-meter long and one and one-half meter-wide boards. At that, they would have to earn some money at the same time because Schindler has no savings and does not have such a thrifty wife as Richard has. However, I am so happy that Richard managed to get Schindler so far as to deliberate together until 2:00 A.M. Is it not wonderful that two such worthwhile architects can understand one another so excellently? I am very fond of Schindler and he is fond of me. However, he is such a difficult character and so many matters distract him that I should thank God every day that I have such a loving husband who lets me participate in everything that concerns him.

Pauline is jealous, and she has every right to feel so. Schindler has the kind of erotic makeup you always thought Richard had. He perplexes American women who are not accustomed to this, while Richard, exactly like Vaterli, would have to be persuaded to court other women, considering it immoral. Both of us dislike flirting.

*At the beginning of September Richard received a telegram from his father-in-law: "Contract with Hoffman in the mail"—that is, the contract for Richard's first book,* How America Builds.

Los Angeles, October 1926

Schindlers gave a party for the dancer John Bovingdon.[3] Richard and I participated. It was a lovely sight. Against the sky, forming the background, different sounding gongs in various sizes hung from twelve poles. The dancer, clad only in a loin cloth made out of batik, sounded these gongs in ten-minute intervals, gracefully and in slow motion, moving between them. Then he started to dance, portraying primitive man before he was walking upright or could use his hands; first writhing on the ground, then in an ecstasy of joy, discovering that he could walk erect. All this without music. It was very gripping in the open landscape. He lives in the guest house which we occupied at first. I am really curious to see what will develop here. He is a nature-worshiper, very erotic, and nearly all females he meets fall in love with him, except myself. It is very interesting for me to observe how untouched I am by all homage and how indifferent to other men. . . .

. . . You must picture to yourself how strange it is for me to read of Vreneli's dissatisfaction regarding luxuries and her too many fancy dresses. I still wear the same old green coat and shall keep on wearing it this winter, as I weigh every penny asking myself when contemplating a purchase, "Is this really necessary?" Richard wants me to look elegant. To achieve this, however, without spending money is really a problem. Naturally, I do not let it bother me. Luckily, among our acquaintances originality ranks high because most of them are also short of cash. However, we want to know well-to-do people, and should know them. . . .

. . . Yesterday I had my second "party" with forty invited guests. Can you picture your Dionchen as a successful hostess? If I had not met Pauline, this would have been unthinkable. I imitated her and Richard says I even surpassed her. Come to think of it, I really can be proud that all went so smoothly and with no help whatsoever, especially considering the fact that Doris and I were the entertainers. Our program consisted of the first two movements of the G Minor Beethoven Sonata, which only now I really start to appreciate. I think we played it well. Then I sang two songs by Gellert, "Vom Tode" Op. 48 and No. 3, which I find marvelous and which fit my voice excellently. My voice sounds quite powerful and not strained, so Richard and Doris tell me. This will be the last time I will sing because it has become a colossal strain on me. It is unbelievable how the breath presses on the unborn. We ended with the Fourth Beethoven Trio. I wish you could have seen how entrancing everything looked. . . .

I find it quite a challenge to spend as little money as possible. All the plans to rearrange the kitchen, create a room for the coming baby, a drafting room on the roof for Richard, which would have to cost several hun-

---

3. Colorful personality and tenant in the Schindler house.

dred dollars, have been given up. My kitchen consists of two boards covered with oilcloth, supported by two wood blocks. It is primitive but suffices. During the day I shall handle the child in Richard's tiny drafting room and on cold nights he will also sleep there. While Richard draws the Geneva project, the baby will be bathed.

*Richard to Frances*
*Toplitz*

Los Angeles, October 1926

Three representatives of the male sex now surround one female in this family. We have a second son, as yet unnamed. He weighed seven pounds and nine ounces at birth. Dione behaved excellently, without histrionics, although she had to endure a lot of pain. She bore it wonderfully during the last hour and at the moment of delivery I gave her ether when it was necessary to take a few stitches. She blithely discussed the possibility of the boys having a sister to keep them company in the not too distant future. . . .

*Richard to Vreneli*
*and Ruben*

Los Angeles, December 1926

Today we have our second autumn rainfall. Three gas stoves are in operation as I sit here working at my drafting table. The roof leaks quite badly in two places. Rain falls through the fireplace which thus becomes a waterplace. The boys are restricted to playing in their small playroom. They annoy their mother by inventing all sorts of active and boisterous games stemming from their lively dispositions. Both of our sons are admirable. When the Greek hero Heracles was still a baby in his crib, in self-defense with his baby hands he strangled two enormous snakes that had been sent by the goddess Hera to destroy him. Little Dion, who begins to sit up, yesterday managed to smash a two-dollar baking dish which shattered on the cement floor. Such is the power of our young hero and not even in self-defense.

Frank is very imaginative. Just now I observed how he spit into the palm of his hand and in joyful contemplation observed the light reflected from the pale rainy sky mirrored in the spittle.

It is difficult for me to tell you how I try to suppress the happy vanity in my bosom that comes from being the father of two such sons; this in order not to commit a sin in my exuberance while I watch such goings-on.

Yesterday evening we left our sons alone to go to a movie to hear the Vitaphone. Do you know what it is? It is a new device that produces sound and picture at the same time. In this manner we heard a few Italian operatic arias, seeing at the same time the stars from the Metropolitan Opera. It sounds marvelous. Coming home after midnight, we were very excited contemplating the repercussions this new invention might produce.

*Muetterli reports periodically to Richard on the progress of the League of Nations competition.*

*Richard's first book,* How America Builds, *is published by Julius Hoffmann, Stuttgart.*

*He begins work on a second book,* America: New Building in the World.

*He receives a commission to design Lovell Health House, the residence destined to establish his reputation.*

By now you must have received the photographs of the competition. I would be pleased if you like them. I am not at all sure whether I should not become a nature doctor or a minister in order to be a better provider for my family. Dione thinks I am an excellent "salesman," but I have nothing to show for it. Also, my energy is ebbing away. I should, though, increase it dramatically to combat my sluggish tendency—an embittered battle, slowly showing signs of defeat, a spectacle painful to observe for wife, children, and in-laws. . . .

*By the end of April Richard and Dione were wondering why they had heard nothing on the League of Nations competition. Dione wrote Muetterli: "Richard believes that we did not get a prize, because you did not send a telegram which surely you would have done when you heard about the results?"*

Zurich, May 1927     *Muetterli to Dione*

Our attitude regarding our problems is more important than the problem itself, and your steadfast belief in Richard must compensate him for his effort and toil. I hope that the disappointment regarding the outcome of the competition has not hit you too hard. I was really ill for twenty-four hours. Nausea and a migraine headache promptly assailed me. Even today I feel miserable. Your disappointments hit me harder than my own. I know how important a success now would have been for you and how much you

161

deserve it. I feel descending on me the disappointment of three hundred other mothers and I believe that this radiant, sunny Sunday will be one of gloom in many households.

Nobody is satisfied. Among the jurors were mummies who built the Louvre. I have made an appointment with the young Moser so that Vaterli can hear some details. Meyer and Gantner (two editors of magazines) are outraged and are going to voice this in their publications. Gantner was enthusiastic about your project and intends to publish it yet in his May issue.[1]

*Shortly thereafter Muetterli wrote again and gave an interesting glimpse of what happened during the jury deliberations.*

*Muetterli to Richard and Dione*

Zurich, May 1927

Vaterli visited Moser today, showed him photographs of your project, whereupon Moser said: "That must be the project which the jurors labeled 'The Airplane Project.' I gleaned this from my father's notebook. This project was considered by a hair's breadth to receive a prize. As far as I know the jurors could not understand the meaning of the overhanging balconies."

Moser intends to send the photos with your description to his father, asking him to write you. Moser had a very difficult stand. As was well known, of the nine jurors five were very conservative. Among the other four, only Moser and Berlage, decisively modern. Moser declared that had he had the chairmanship, the whole matter would have been decided in fourteen days, but the Belgian chairman was not able to show any authority. At first they tried to eliminate all projects that in any way did not adhere to the program. In this way only the most mediocre and staid projects remained, so that four of the jurors threatened to resign unless some of the rejected projects would be reintroduced. Finally, they could hardly bear the sight of each other and were furious until they devised a scheme to establish the 3 x 9 category where each juror had the right to nominate one prize winner for each category. That so many of them were Italian can be explained by the fact that most were under the impression that they were French. (Thus the French have this advantage of their mistake.)

The competition anonymity was well preserved. None of the jurors showed any signs of favoritism. Corbusier had sent each juror a photograph of the only house he has ever built in hideous beaux art style, built for Lemaresquier on the Boulevard Sebastopol. Old Mr. Moser declared that the Corbusier project really was a good one and he had to declare himself for it, as far as he could understand it from photographs. However, the palace would, of course, be built by a Frenchman. The competition contained a lot of crazy drawings. One submission, for instance, looked like an egg! The exhibition will take place at the end of June.

1. *Das Neue Frankfurt.*

*Muetterli wrote on July 8 that Giedion had told her that from the four hundred project drawings, the ones by Le Corbusier, Richard, and Hannes Meyer (Basel) had been chosen to be displayed in Stuttgart. Richard was beside himself when he started to notice that Muetterli and Vaterli spoke only of the "Neutra project" without mentioning Schindler's name. He finally sent two telegrams in order to establish the fact that the architects of the competition were to be designated in all publications as R. M. Schindler and Richard Neutra.*

Los Angeles, August 1927      *Dione to Her Parents*

. . . We cannot understand that you always speak in your letters of the "Neutra project" despite Richard's telegrams where he clearly requested that it be labeled the "Neutra-Schindler project." How can Richard justify this mistake in front of Schindler who will simply not believe him, although Richard sent you two telegrams. . . .

Zurich, August 1927      *Vaterli to Dione*

. . . Unfortunately, I overlooked that Schindler should be mentioned and I shall take immediate steps to rectify this mistake. (Personally, I am so convinced that you carried the lion's share in this competition, that the mention of Schindler's name is out of propriety, that I, too, overlooked your request.)

Los Angeles, March 1927      *Richard to Muetterli*

In order to be fair I think it desirable to make, every few months, an inventory of happiness, make in all humility a confession to a friend instead of always complaining in letters while later boring young visitors with the "good old times" long gone.

Here and now is the moment to state honestly, without a trace of self-complacency, that God, or the great powers, have treated you quite decently.

As quite often on a Sunday morning I was awakened by a song coming from a far distance, entering my consciousness, still shrouded in the fog of waking up; I hear the loveliest soprano voice, which occasionally turns into a true alto. The voice becomes distinct as I become aware that this is Dionerl's voice and that this sticky sweet style of song is by Brahms. I don't mean to be deprecatory, but I thank her creator that Dione most often dips into Bach's *St. Matthew Passion* and chooses arias and recitatives from it as well as from seventy-one Bach spirituals. She is able to put so much humanness into this sweet Brahms style that one is happily fulfilled to picture one's life companion sitting down there at the piano singing, while I gaze into this Sunday morning. I want to become aware of such a happiness while I experience it and not after it might have perished and disappeared. Now she sings "Guten Abend, gute Nacht." Every child can be congratulated to have such a sterling and clear-cut human mother. "A fong, a fong" little Frank says in his high-pitched voice and asks endlessly for one more.

While my limbs are still in a somnambulant state I glance from my sleeping porch into the green spring greenery. It has rained yesterday and this night. The leaves of our trumpet vine glisten with raindrops. The huge bamboo stalks—together with a contingent of birds, who, with their twittering, apply the colorful background music to Dione's songs, sway gently in the breeze. Now my gaze focuses on the feathery foliage of a young pepper tree that peeps over the roof and a reddish climbing rose whips gently near Dion's chimney. Dione makes a change. She starts to abandon Brahms. I always had the feeling that Brahms represented too much the epoch of his times. A time when Strindberg and Mahler were young fellows, where Gottfried Keller, as an old man, saw his first bicycle in Selwyla,[2] where women wore puffed sleeves, were enthusiastic about Bayreuth, the love lyrics of the second romantic period, and in a few instances were interested in women's rights. All brewed together in one period of time.

The tops of twenty Eucalyptus trees that block our view west, pierce a compact gray-white wall of clouds that cover this Sunday morning sky, which becomes lighter where the sun rays want to push through. From across the street, from the far distant live oak trees, from the wild rose hedge, the scent of orange blossoms waft through the air of the roof porch. Beginning with the "Litanei," Dione has switched to Schubert. Apparently it is to be a romantic Sunday morning.

On other Sunday mornings it is Handel or bel canto songs from Scarlatti to Pergolesi or hundred percent Bach. I get up, descend the humid rainy stairway towards the bathroom. How long will my soul remain in this peaceful mood? Never mind, for half an hour this day it remained thus. After breakfast Dione and I will take a short walk around the block and gaze at the richness of wisteria vines, yellow blooming acacias, and many more blooming bushes all immigrants from Australia, as we are immigrants from Vienna and Zurich. Now it is 10:30; my Sunday has ended and I start to work.

*Dione to Muetterli*

Los Angeles, March 1927

My dear Richard wrote you a beautiful letter today. It is wonderful when two people find themselves in the same mood. Occasionally one sees everything clear and luminous. That's how we felt today during our short walk, while Dion remained alone in his playroom. (He emptied my forgotten sewing basket, unwinding all the bobbins.) During our walk everything looked ravishing. We have had little rain this year, making the change in greenery very apparent.

As I rise every morning at the sound of an alarm clock, even if I go to bed at 1:00, I allow myself to sleep a little longer on Sundays. When I awake at 7:00, parting my curtain, I see little Dion, who has the patience

---

2. Selwyla is a fictional city in Switzerland—the invention of the famous Swiss author, Gottfried Keller, and figures prominently in many of his novels.

of an angel, sitting in his bed looking out into the garden. This is especially fascinating when raindrops fall from the roof. My heart is moved as I creep silently away to light the gas stove and get Dion a glass of orange juice. As soon as he hears me his face beams with joy. He hops up and down cooing and making other baby sounds. Patiently he waits for me to put down the glass, close the sliding doors, and light his gas stove.

I take a shower and dress while he sits on his potty, usually with no results. Then he gets a bath and is dressed. I make breakfast. Lately he has it with us because he no longer sleeps at 10:00 A.M. but at noon and now has only three meals. Afterwards, on weekdays, I practice the cello for an hour and a half while little Dion is put in his playroom where he immediately runs to his beloved rocking horse. I blow him a kiss, barricade the exit (there is no door), and, because today is Sunday, sit down to my piano. While I sing I think of home and our Sundays, imagining that I am visiting you. Then I think of my dear Richard who has such a difficult time but who is such a wonderful human being and father with his deep understanding and lack of prejudice. It is easy to live with him, probably because we are so well suited to each other. I only hope we continue to develop together. It is a terrible thought to contemplate what can happen to make a person unhappy!

Zurich, March 1927

*Muetterli to Dione*

. . . Your loving letter shows me again how much you accomplish, dear Dione. That you get so little sleep will, however, leave its mark when you approach your thirtieth year. You will age more rapidly. If Vaterli gets the job with the travel agency and we send you travel expenses, can you and the boys visit us for half a year, Richard following in case he cannot stay away for any length of time? It would make me so happy to let you have a vacation. You could again take cello and vocal lessons. My dear Dione, I try to picture to myself in what manner your life would be altered should you become financially secure. Then, surely, a trip to Europe would materialize, although Richard would probably be unable to get away with you.

Zurich, June 1927

*Vaterli to Dione*
*and Doris*

Dear Angels[3]   I appreciate very much knowing you would like to get more letters from me. I am little accustomed to having anyone want anything from me or enjoying hearing from me except hearing me play. Nobody ever seems to mention me, not even indirectly, because everything worthwhile in your makeup comes to you only through Muetterli. It is a fact that nothing is more interesting and stimulating than her letters, especially considering how uneventful our lives are which are filled with vexations and trivia. . . .

---

3. Derived from Los Angeles.

Los Angeles, June 1927

My day must have a certain rhythm, be filled with accomplishments. Housework is boring unless one treats it as a sport looking for enjoyment in whatever else one can do.

Every day I thank God for my boy Frank. You cannot imagine how delightful it is to observe him in his uninhibited lust for life and song. To see his daily enjoyment and merriment is so unbelievably comforting. Yesterday he lay beside me drumming a rhythm on his naked belly, beaming with joy when a part of my song especially pleased him. Very apparent is his complete indifference towards children and grown-ups. Our friend Mrs. Peck mentioned again yesterday that she considers him to be a baby genius. His pranks are innocent enough, but often they cause me a lot of work. Yesterday, for instance, I expected dinner guests and had put branches of a castor-bean bush into a vase. When I returned to the room a few minutes later, he had stripped off all the big leaves because he wanted only the stems.

Doris helped me finish a charming dress which I made over from a white frock Vreneli sent me. I designed lovely sleeves from a silky material. I adore being dressed beautifully and trifles evoke feelings of happiness in me—a sunset while I drive, Richard's face during a discussion, observing little Dion convulsed with laughter as he tries out his four new teeth on an aluminum cup, or watching Frank pursue whatever he undertakes with such intensity. Please, dear Muetterli, do not lose courage. Surely, we will again be together.

Los Angeles, July 1927

Richard is continuously overloaded with work. Sometimes I am so anxious observing how life slips away. All of a sudden we shall be old and then may not enjoy being together. Last week, at least, we had a few days' vacation. But these were also filled with haste. Damn it!

We left Friday noon letting Dion have his nap on the back seat of the car, while we drove at a speed of 45 miles per hour over the concrete road along the ocean. Sometimes we rose 60 meters above the ocean. It took us five hours to reach Wright's house. Such a drive is, of course, no recreation. Every hour we changed seats. Although one carries on a conversation, it is necessary to watch the road, and on top of that, Dion, who has become quicksilver, is restless. At one elevated spot the road winds its way through a magnificent grove of pine trees which grow only at that particular location. We had no difficulty finding Wright's house on South Coast Boulevard in La Jolla.

We entered through a patio with a fountain in the middle which aroused Dion's enthusiasm. Wright, who was in, greeted us warmly. The house is, of course, rented, but it is most pleasant. It has flagstone in the foreground and faces the ocean.

Wright immediately fixed Dion's bed with the mattress we had brought along. Pretty soon Olgivanna came in with Iovanna who has brown eyes and golden locks.[4] She is not as well developed as Dion, although one and a half years his senior. A completely self-sufficient child, she has her own strong will. When Dion tried to touch the cutlery on the table, she whispered, "Don't touch, Daddy makes spanky, spanky." She demonstrated it by giving Dion a few smacks.

After supper Wright read us various articles. The following morning we all bathed together. Wright swam far out and I enjoyed, for the first time in my life, a swim in the ocean. The breakers buffeted me around quite a bit, but it was marvelously refreshing. After lunch I sang a few songs then, unfortunately, it was time to go because we had to visit the Lovells on the way home.

I sent you photographs of Schindler's beach house. It is beautiful in itself, but not in its surroundings. It stands amidst small, cheap houses, a main traffic boulevard in the rear and in front a wide stretch of beach. The three children come and go creating a great feeling of unrest combined with the tension sensed between the couple. It is not comforting.

Los Angeles, July 1927

Today, July 14, Dione drove with Frankli to the Child Guidance Clinic to elicit some advice regarding his tardy speech development. She has been waiting for two months to get this appointment.

Everybody is now enchanted with Dion. He is definitely a friendly, quiet child. It appears as though he will develop towards the contemplative, social side of life. In contrast, Frank is uninhibited, an emotional self-expressionist. He is good-natured but unable to make contact with others, which will cause difficulties in later years.

Los Angeles, August 1927

Finally I have time to write again. These last weeks were too exciting. Pauline has left. She packed her belongings and I did not even see her go. Everything had to be done in secrecy to avoid a confrontation between the couple. I think it is awful when outsiders take matters into their hand and those most affected have to dance like puppets.

Zurich, August 1927

How deplorable is this whole Schindler affair! Has now a separation occurred? That still seems to be the best way out of an untenable situation if the principals have so little understanding for each other. Left to her own devices Pauline will try to find her own way. Does she love him? Too bad when people are unable to communciate with each other. I am also sorry for you, that you had to suffer from this uncomfortable situation.

---

4. Olgivanna, Frank Lloyd Wright's eventual wife; Iovanna, their daughter.

1927

*Richard wrote Dione this important letter while she was on a short vacation with Frank and Dion in Ojai.*

*Richard to Dione*

Los Angeles, August 1927

. . . Now I want to tell you a few facts about myself. I had a good talk with Lovell[5] and proposed quite successfully an agreement with him which he has, however, not yet signed. He wants to retype it with a few changes. He gave me in any case an adequate downpayment. I have brought him now so far that he feels no personal grudge against Schindler and has nothing against it that he participates in the design. To be sure, he apparently wants me to be responsible for everything. . . .

*Richard to Frances Toplitz*

Los Angeles, August 1927

You ask me about my book. As the author I cannot praise it, according to an old-fashioned notion, which however I try to overcome. But it is a success already. It was published in the second greatest architectural publishing house of Julius Hoffmann, Stuttgart.

Hoffmann, as all great publishers, is very conservative and asked different experts when my very radical book was submitted to him. The experts told him it was fine and I must admit that I have produced the most radical thoughts in a polite way, avoiding all kinds of polemics in favor of clearly constructive proposals and ideas. Well, you will read it, because the written part is the most important not the 113 illustrations.

I don't write for architects. I write for educated lay people who are interested in cultural and civilizational problems in general. . . . Otherwise the outlook is gloomy. Perhaps it will be necessary that I ship out as a sailor. This seems to be a calling which is more profitable and of longer duration than this new architecture. . . .

5. Dr. Philip Lovell, naturopath physician and Richard's client in 1928.

*Richard teaches at the Los Angeles Academy of
Modern Art.*

*1928*

*The design and planning of Lovell Health House consume
Richard for most of the year.*

*The Child Guidance Clinic advises that Frank be housed
with an English-speaking family, as his speech is so
retarded. He stays there for two years.*

*In the fall, Pauline Schindler arranges a lecture for Richard
and a concert for Dione in Carmel.*

*Dione to Muetterli*

. . . Every year is characterized by some kind of excitement. First year of our marriage: Mossehaus; second year: trip to USA, Frank's birth; third year: difficulties with Schindler and adjustment to life in USA; fourth year: League of Nations competition, first book, *How America Builds*; fifth year: designs for apartments; sixth year: Lovell House—we are in the middle of it. I want briefly to illuminate for you all the difficulties. Schindler built for Lovell a house on the beach. During its completion there was much vexation. The reason for it, however, lies much deeper. Lovell's annoyance, less on account of the house but more about Schindler's character, was perhaps jealousy. In short, he does not want to have any further dealings with him.

Richard refused continuously to undertake the design of the new house in deference to Schindler whom he defended as much as he was capable of. Then, Mrs. Scheyer[1] appeared on the scene, saying that Richard's consideration was ridiculous. She worked on Schindler, on Lovell, on Richard, and finally, the preliminaries were started. Richard wanted to work with Schindler, tried to involve him, with no success. This you will not be able to understand without knowing Schindler.

Mrs. Lovell's sister has a house by Wright. She detests Lovell, tries to create as much discord in this marriage as she is capable of. She is Schind-

---

1. Galka Scheyer, a painter in her own right, represented the "Blue Four," the Bauhaus painters Vasily Kandinsky, Alexey von Baulensky, Lyonel Feininger, and Paul Klee, hoping to sell their paintings in the United States.

ler's friend and is furious that he is not getting this commission. Yesterday, Lovell spent several hours with us to look at the plans and to discuss this situation. Mrs. Lovell is rich, her sister is poor. This causes an everlasting contest between the two sisters. Whatever Richard does is being criticized and ridiculed behind his back because Schindler would have done it so much more beautifully. He remains taciturn and smiling.

Lovell's advice is not to pay the least attention to whatever Mrs. Lovell has to say because it is he who makes the decisions. The more his sister-in-law speaks against it, the more he would be for it. However, even if he says so, who knows what the outcome will be? It is surely not an atmosphere for creative work. All these matters are very subtle and understandable only for the initiated. It is impossible to talk about it. It is a tangle like in a Dostoyevsky story.

*Richard Added a*
*Postscript*

In this letter Dionerl has made it sufficiently clear why I do not have the peace of mind to write you at length, which I *so much* would like to do.

*Richard to Muetterli*

Los Angeles, August 1928

It is late evening and this shabby writing paper lies on a heap of drawings and plans I should work on. A cricket chirps in front of the door. Instead of working or going to bed, I sit and think. The cricket chirps again, very loud. It really is a grasshopper, like in a Greek novel *Daphne and Chloe* or something similar. I return to my steel construction drawings. . . .

*Dione to Frances*
*Toplitz*

Los Angeles, Fall 1928

Next week Richard will give a lecture in Carmel and I will give a recital. This means one week's vacation, the first in two and a half years! Both of us need it badly. It will be especially good for Richard because for many months he has been concentrating on one building.

I am still trying to earn some money with my music without much success. I send letters to clubs, to movie stars, and to rich and influential people in the hope of getting some private engagements. I also work with a trio and we may, perhaps, get an engagement with Vitaphone. I enclose a letterhead I use for such occasions.

*Dione to Her Parents*

Los Angeles, Fall 1928

I would like to describe to you our trip to Carmel.

"No Richard, our car is too old, is already acting up. How dare we undertake such a long trip?" However, while I say it, I am already dressed in pants and sweater, the back of the car is filled with a mattress, blankets, cushions, and groceries as if we were preparing for a North Pole expedition. "Oh well, let's stop at the garage and have everything checked before we leave" says Richard. That's the beginning of an American vacation!

Neutra design for proposed Lambs Club. Los Angeles, 1926.

The roof porch at R. M. Schindler's house. Los Angeles, 1927.

# 1926–1932

Early Neutra design for League of Nations Palace design competition in Geneva. Los Angeles, 1926.

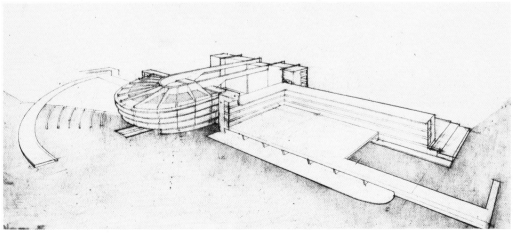

*Opposite page*: A 1928 announcement of a course in architecture to be taught by Neutra.

Neutra with Dion at R. M. Schindler's house. Los Angeles, 1927.

Dione and Neutra on the roof of R. M. Schindler's house. Los Angeles, 1928.

Dione, Frank, and Dione's sister Doris at R. M. Schindler's house. Los Angeles, 1927.

# ACADEMY OF MODERN ART

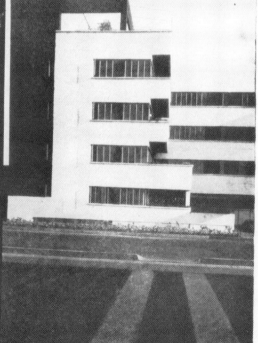

GARDEN APARTMENTS, LOS ANGELES
RICHARD J. NEUTRA, ARCHITECT

## A PRACTICAL COURSE IN MODERN BUILDING ART
### DIRECTED BY RICHARD J. NEUTRA

THE DRAFTSMAN OF TODAY IS THE ARCHITECT OF TOMORROW. EVERYTHING THAT WILL BE PRACTISED TOMORROW AS VITAL IN BUILDING ART, WILL HAVE ITS ROOTS IN TODAY'S TECHNICAL EXPERIENCE. BECAUSE MODERN ARCHITECTURE HAS ITS FEET ON THE STRUCTURAL GROUND OF PRACTICAL CONSIDERATIONS.

TWO YEARS AGO A BOOK WAS PUBLISHED WITH THIS VERY ASPECT OF ARCHITECTURAL POSSIBILITIES WHICH FLOW OUT OF THE TECHNICAL CIVILIZATION OF AMERICA. THIS BOOK AROUSED A NEW AND EAGER INTEREST IN MATTERS AMERICAN THE WORLD OVER AND WAS COMMENTED UPON IN ALL CIVILIZED LANGUAGES.

AMERICA MAY BE CONSIDERED THE MOST FERTILE GROUND OUT OF WHICH THE ORGANIZATION OF THE FUTURE CITY PLANNING AND BUILDING WORK WILL GROW.

RICHARD J. NEUTRA, A.I.A., Z.V.B.D.A. INTERNATIONAL AUTHORITY ON MODERN ARCHITECTURE, AUTHOR OF "HOW DOES AMERICA BUILD," CONTRIBUTOR, THE ARCHITECTURAL RECORD, NEW YORK, WILL PERSONALLY DIRECT PRACTICAL EXERCISES IN ARCHITECTURAL DESIGNING AND DRAFTING TO BE COMBINED LATER WITH A LECTURE COURSE ABOUT THE ESSENTIALS OF MODERN ARCHITECTURE AND ITS RELATION TO OTHER CREATIVE ACTIVITIES.

THE CLASS WILL BE NECESSARILY LIMITED. FOR FURTHER INFORMATION APPLY
## ACADEMY OF MODERN ART
FINE ARTS BUILDING, 811 WEST SEVENTH LOS ANGELES, CALIFORNIA PHONE METROPOLITAN 3831
F. K. FERENZ, DIRECTOR

Dione with two-year-old Dion; *behind*,
Neutra; *right*, R. M. Schindler.
Schindler's house, Los Angeles, 1928.

SONGS SUNG DIFFERENTL

TO THE SOUNDS OF A SONOROUS VIOLI
CELLO, WHICH THE SINGER PLAYS, OR WIT
PIANO ACCOMPANIMENT: FRENCH, ITALIA
ENGLISH, GERMAN, SWISS SONGS, SELECTE
FROM THE REFRESHING AND HUMOROUS FOL
LORE OF SEVERAL CENTURIES, PERFORME
BY A YOUTHFUL, DELIGHTING FEMALE VOIC

DIONE NEUTRA

Letterhead designed by Neutra for Dione
to solicit musical engagements. Los
Angeles, 1928.

Neutra watches as Frank plays with
blocks at R. M. Schindler's house. Los
Angeles, 1928.

Neutra explaining construction of Lovell Health House to students
from the Academy of Modern Art. *Extreme right*, Gregory Ain; *behind
him*, Harwell Harris; *kneeling at left*, Barbara Morgan; *behind her*,
F. K. Ferenz, director of the academy. Los Angeles, 1928.

Lovell Health House after completion in 1929. Los Angeles.

ノイトラ氏新建築講演會

主催 國際建築協會

（土浦亀城通譯　幻燈説明）

RICHARD NEUTRA
BESUCHT JAPAN !

Japanese poster announcing a Neutra lecture in Tokyo in 1930.

Neutra is introduced at his 1930 Tokyo lecture by Kameki Tsuchiura whom he had met at Frank Lloyd Wright's Taliesin.

Neutra sketch of a Japanese man wearing an American straw hat. Tokyo, 1930.

Neutra sketch of prostitutes in Shanghai, 1930.

Neutra sketch of boats in Canton Harbor, 1930.

Neutra sketch of a puppet theater in Singapore, 1930.

Neutra sketch of a street fight in Colombo, Ceylon (Sri Lanka), 1930.

Neutra with students at Bauhaus. Dessau, 1930.

Bauhaus students greet Neutra on arrival in Dessau in 1930.
*Left to right*: Heiner Knaub, Dione, Neutra, Renee Mensch, Fritz Ertl.

Neutra bus design for White Motors Company. Cleveland. 1930.

Neutra's prefabricated Ring Plan School show in model form at the Museum of Modern Art exhibition in 1932.

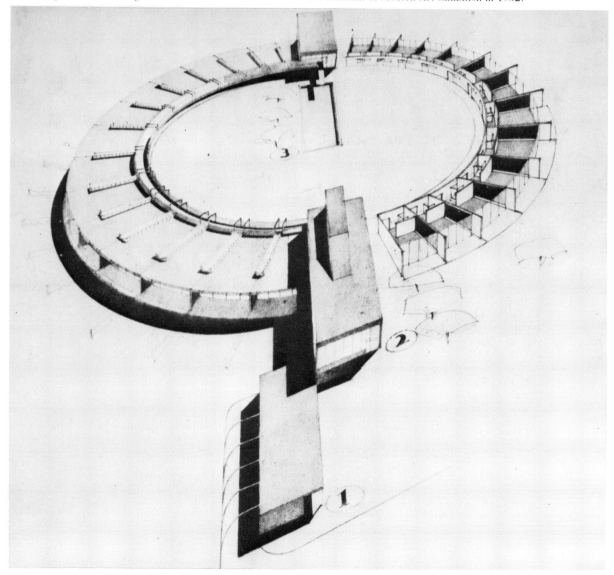

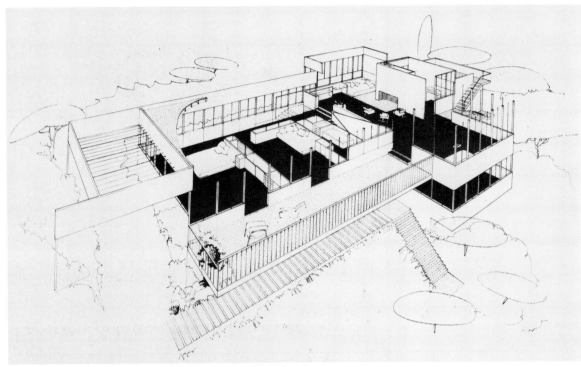

Neutra's isometric sketch of Mosk House 1933 floor plan.

Mosk House. Hollywood Hills, 1933.

Pretty soon we're driving comfortably along. We have decided to drive no faster than thirty-five miles an hour. That gives me a marvelous feeling, as if time did not matter. The early morning landscape looks dewy fresh and the hillsides show a green tinge, the result of a beneficial rainfall. We coast along in a happy frame of mind. The car always plays a role in our conversation as if it were a beloved, somewhat unruly, unpredictable child having to be praised when it behaved well.

The road, of course, is excellent, a smooth ribbon of concrete winding over mountains with marvelous vistas or along hills or riverbeds. We stopped and had our first picnic, later finding a niche in the road which looked suitable for parking and sleeping in the car. We slept quite well until 8:00 A.M. and watched the sun break through the clouds. Towards evening when we reached Carmel we were glad to have a real meal with Pauline Schindler and a private room to ourselves.

On awakening Sunday morning we found it was raining cats and dogs. Our faces became longer and longer with apprehension as we wondered who would want to leave a cozy home to attend a lecture. The receipts of the lecture were supposed to pay for our trip. Well, fortunately, about twenty people showed up in the studio of Dene Denny and Hazel Watrous. The first one a modern pianist, the second a painter and applied artist. The room was airy and uncluttered, quite perfect for giving a lecture on modern architecture.

Richard gave such a clear description of various civilizations and their architecture in comparison with our own civilization and its resulting architecture that even the most romantic listener had to be convinced. His kind, humorous way, his humanity appealed to this artistic public so that a lively discussion took place afterwards as we consumed coffee and cake, sitting around a huge fireplace. The wind howled around the house and the rain drummed on the huge glass panes that allowed a view onto the swaying pine trees. The proceeds of the evening were $20.00.

The next afternoon we were the guests of a very nice couple where we met several interesting people. I sang quite a bit and felt really happy. Among the guests were several young girls and a couple named Blackman. Mr. Blackman immediately started to discuss modern architecture, always in opposition to Richard. The young girls were on Richard's side. Mrs. Blackman nodded her head in apparent agreement, while I, as usual, all ears, full of admiration, was also in opposition to Mr. Blackman, who looked at architecture only from an artistic side, while Richard included the whole modern development like bathrooms, kitchen installations, etc. I looked at the ocean and at my Richard whose eyeballs gleamed white during this lively discussion. Unfortunately, it rained again on the evening of my recital. Again about twenty people braved the rain. The recital was again in a private home which was most appropriate. I sang a few Swiss folk songs accompanying myself on the cello. These everybody seemed to enjoy very much. I also sang an alto aria from the *St. Matthew Passion*, two recitatives, and three bel canto Italian arias. For these I accompanied myself on the piano.

*Richard and Dione attend citizenship school.*

*1929*

*Richard becomes a citizen.*

*Lovell Health House is completed and acclaimed in the U.S. and international trade and public press.*

I have given up looking for further engagements. Having only one car in the family, a small boy who always has to be parked with some friends whenever one has an appointment, it becomes practically impossible because the interviewers let you come so often without results. I have realized the fruitlessness of these endeavors, have resigned myself to helping Richard. There is a lot of typing to do for him and, actually, I prefer to help him instead of looking for outside work.

Los Angeles, August 1929    *Richard to Frances*
*Toplitz*

. . . We are preparing to travel or, better, to be ready to be admitted to traveling. What we do is: we aim for American citizenship and American passports. We are going to night school two or three times a week and study for the really severe examinations, which will allow us to vote in this country to improve the laws. Dione is hopeless to pass those tests, but I believe in my good guiding star and I approve of this citizenship school. It interests me and it only would be desirable that the natives pass such examinations from time to time. How do you feel about this idea? The students of the school represent quite a satisfactory class of people and the instructors are not bad. The best thing is the subject matter: history and the political makeup of an important country in flux, examining its role as part of the world community. . . .

*Frank Lloyd Wright
to Richard*

My dear Richard   Writing Rudolph[1] brings you to mind, and here's wondering how your garden grows.

I've heard some pessimistic reports of your efforts and more of your state of mind. Lloyd[2] said you were engaged upon a book, "History of American Architecture," I believe, in which you proposed to leave my name out entirely. I think this is a good idea. It would make room for a lot of others that otherwise might not have enough.

And from someone—I forget who—that you were importing foreign draughtsmen from Corbusier et al. and with them starting a school of new-thought in Architecture in Hollywood, which is a vigorous enterprize and likely to be successful, if the crowd can be kept well out in front.

I guess you can keep them there long enough to let the show go on to a logical conclusion or a natural end.

But there is better and almost good. The boys tell me you are building a building in steel for residence—which is really good news. Ideas like that one are what this poor fool country needs to learn from Corbusier, Stevens, Oud and Gropius.

I am glad you're the one to "teach" them.

My best to Dione and yourself. Hoping the babies are coming along, and well.   Yours no less, Frank Lloyd Wright

*Frank Lloyd Wright
to Richard and Dione*

Dear Richard and Dione   Of course I was indulging the vein of playful sarcasm that has always been characteristic. I think my friends would love me more if I could overcome it.

Your letter was really a surprise because I had no serious idea that Richard was conducting a school in Los Angeles. I thought it just current gossip. However, I am glad that he is.

Olgivanna and I were glad to have the photographs of the baby. Little Frank seems to be a fine little child to look at. He doesn't seem as though there could be any serious lack in him that time wouldn't remedy.

Taliesin is picking up again. We have been making some improvements. We have seven boys here now. Okami, whom you know, has just come in. We have a great many applications from Europe and may allow several more to join us before the year's end. We are quite busy—two very interesting problems.

We often wish that you were both with us. I think Taliesin never knew nicer times than when Richard and Dione, Werner and Sylva and Kameki and Nobu were here. When the school is on vacation you should come here and put in a month helping us.

I wonder if Richard has seen the April number of the *Record* with Lewis Mumford's review—"Frank Lloyd Wright and the New Pioneers." It ap-

---

1. R. M. Schindler.

2. Frank Lloyd Wright's son.

pears in the *Architects Library* in the rear of the magazine. In the same magazine for July under Notes and Comments they have printed something from me called "Surface and Mass—Again!" I wish Richard would read it. I have at last put on record my feeling concerning a good deal of the so-called modern work which I am free to say impresses me as woeful trash. In the *Record* for August there is an article by Corbusier himself, putting into his language as an address to America the same thought which America has produced long ago and handing it over to us, with sublime disregard of that fact, as though it were a discovery of his own! I wonder if that trait is peculiarly French? Modesty at any rate seems to be far from the soul of the Frenchman.

I have had a great affection for you both and when once my affections are invested, they are quite likely to remain. But I reserve the right always to play a little upon the good nature and with the credulity of my friends.

Read my letter again and you will see there is no very serious matter in it and no intent to more than tease you a little bit.

Keep us informed as to how things go with you. We shall be West again next winter and we may see something of you.

Meantime, believe me    Affectionately and faithfully yours, Frank Lloyd Wright

Los Angeles, November 1929

*Richard to Frances Toplitz*

That I succeeded in such short order with the steel-skeletoned Health House, which was, as a whole, in its philosophy and in many features, so highly unorthodox, seems almost incredible now. It was, in fact, a strange, unheard-of apparition to be conceived in the general scene of 1929. From a distance it was to be seen on a steep, even precipitous, slope, with the looming Griffith Park hills as a backdrop and a wide outlook south, over trees in the foreground, down to the faraway sea. The building loomed over a swimming pool. It was all a very novel "thoroughbred" of integrated design, a never-contracted-for type of construction.

How could I have proceeded from such obscurity and a starvation diet to something like a career?

What has this human and interhuman effort been, and how could it, and the far outpost in which it happened, be described at least in fragments? I was *so far* from the intellectual centers where styles are first conceived or emerge in artistic circles; but real life after all is everywhere close by.

Los Angeles, November 1929

*Richard to Vreneli and Ruben*

I am working 14–16 hours a day.

I see very clearly that if one is not able to achieve some kind of a reputation, one can never escape this involuntary slave work that is so much more distressing and constricting than the mechanical work of a creative, inventive, uninvolved individual.

Of course, I am aware that many famous people had to battle against stupidity until their last breath, but it concerned larger tasks and some kind of recognition did come to them.

I am sending you a few photographs of the Lovell Demonstration Health House. As yet it has not been published anywhere. Do not show it to any architect. It is not necessary to have it published in an architectural journal. Could you possibly send it with the enclosed English text to a Scandinavian or Argentinian illustrated weekly magazine? I would indeed be most grateful.

California, Hollywood-American-modern, architecture finds a certain interest everywhere.

*Richard to Frances*
*Toplitz*

Los Angeles, December 1929

Again a year gone. It was one with a good deal of content and work. As far as I am concerned, I find I do not work for any "purpose," nor for money. It is more like an eruption. When the work is done, I am surprised that I was able to stand all the hardships. So with this new book of ours and with the Health House.

I have also become an American citizen this year, accomplishing what we planned some years ago while traveling in an Austrian railway car at night from Krems or Melk to Vienna. Do you remember? You promised me then, sometime I *would* overcome the barrier of the Atlantic. . . .

*Exhausted and depressed from the Lovell Health House effort, Richard accepts Muetterli's invitation for the whole family to stay with her during his extended visit to Europe. As the American delegate to the Congrès-internationaux d'Architecture moderne, he is to give a paper at the annual meeting in Brussels.*

*Richard sails alone by the way of the Orient. Dione, awaiting her citizenship papers, will join him with the two boys in London.*

*Arriving in Japan, Richard discovers, to his surprise, that he is no longer unknown. Large posters in Tokyo announce his lecture. His book and Lovell Health House have made him famous.*

*The same phenomenon awaits him in Europe where he is deluged with lecture invitations, including a month's stay at the Bauhaus in Dessau—the famous design school founded by the architect Walter Gropius.*

*Richard returns to the U.S. Dione remains behind to consult doctors about Frank. She stays with her parents for six months in Zurich, where she takes cello and singing lessons.*

. . . We had quite a hectic time with the Lovell House. Approximately 1,500 people visited it, mostly on two Sundays. You can imagine the traffic jam, on this narrow street. Right after the inspection the Lovells moved in and Richard has to be there all the time, and it is the most dangerous time in regard to his relation with the owners. That he was able to get along with them until now should earn him a crown. The house is beautiful, although so much is yet missing. No carpet, no curtains, scant furniture, in spite of that they had their first party on New Year's Day with 50 people present, who were mostly dumbfounded but found their bearings after explanations were given by Richard.

Los Angeles, January 1930

*Dione to Muetterli*

Richard suffers from a terrible depression. It is my first experience in witnessing the suffering of an artist, seeing how differently he reacts. Thank goodness, I have enough understanding and love.

It is my impression that Richard needs a change of scene, a spiritual rejuvenation.

Richard would like to go to Germany first. He says he cannot afford to come only as a visitor. He has to learn something and study. Should he decide to stay here, I cannot leave him alone in this frame of mind. But one can cancel the boat tickets three weeks before departure. I don't know whether it is clever to take round-trip tickets. Before all else, however, will you be able to manage? Do you visualize that if Richard gets an offer in Germany, or if he decides to come back here, we might become a burden to you for quite a while?

*Richard to Muetterli*

Los Angeles, February 1930

It is very strange how in your letters intuitively you tune in on my spiritual condition without my having told you anything about it. But not only this, your advice always hits the nail on the head. At the moment I am reluctant to delve again into another adventure like the Lovell House. It sucks too much marrow out of the bones and stamina from the brain. After all, one does not want to end one's life so soon.

California *is* a good place, but the experiment I undertook needs much more penetrating power of the soul as would, for instance, be necessary in Berlin where, at the moment, people are elated with "new building Art." Here, one stands all alone and I had the insane ambition not to falter in any detail. At the same time, I am very superstitious, assuming that ambition goes before the fall. This was not only a physical and mental effort for two years, but a soul's tension under more complex circumstances than accompanying a tunnel breakthrough. You must admit that I voiced no complaint during those two years. Now a few people start to praise me and everybody thinks I should be in excellent spirits. Oh well, one has to let grass grow over a success and start again from scratch. All this pretending of being a famous architect, the constant correspondence with the editors of two dozen magazines, which puts not a penny's worth of butter on my bread, makes me somewhat sick and tired.

Imagine that today I received a notice from a clipping service that an illustrated article about the Health House will appear in nine hundred magazines and newspapers across this country. This is more than I could ever have expected. To tell the truth, such a thing never entered my mind. Pretty soon I shall receive as many letters as our friend Upton Sinclair does, and I begin to understand why he is sick and tired of such a correspondence.

*Richard to Frances*
*Toplitz*

Los Angeles, April 1930

. . . I suffer from too low blood pressure and the idea to start another such venture after my gamble with the Lovell House without any vacation, seemed unthinkable during several moments as the day wanes. This is all very strange. During the past two years my constant thought was, "Should this unusual experiment succeed, it will surely strengthen your character." Well, now it *has* succeeded way beyond any expectations, but I am too exhausted to enjoy the success, as I am afraid to have to start something similar without having had any respite.

*In late May Richard sailed alone for the Orient, planning to join Dione, Frank, and Dion later in London.*

I want to write you a few words before we anchor in Honolulu. Do you know how I remember you most vividly? You will never guess! I remember with greatest love and admiration how you brought Dion into the world. It was wonderful how brave and unassuming you behaved. It is so exhilarating to know that I move towards a reunion with you while at the same time I move away from you. It is much more of a joyous vacation trip because I am aware of the fact that it only appears as if I were moving away from you. If only you can solve everything without too much bother and get on the boat with your two boys.

I hope you were able, by now, to sell our car. This is an excellent occasion to show your business sense. The same holds true for Lovell. Should you, after you have given him my letter and have tactfully hinted that you are in need of the money, not be successful, try to maneuver yourself with redoubled cordiality into such a position that you could receive a personal check to you for at least part of the money, $200–$300, if not the whole amount. Naturally, you will have to follow your own judgment, as I do not know how Lovell will react to the final statement. Perhaps a charming young lady as yourself will be more successful than the worn-out architect.

I find myself in a peculiar soul condition. I feel like a bad guy who lets you do all the dirty work while I am having a splendid time on board ship. I am not only deeply ashamed but downright unhappy that I left you alone to tackle all difficulties, should anything go amiss, while I go making whoopee!

Oh, my darling, how I wish you could be here with me. But perhaps it is wholesome for me to have time to reflect and think about myself, as far as this is possible. For these reasons, as well as an upset stomach, I have been lying awake at night. The weather is very humid. I am trying to come to terms with a problem concerning myself. As I am now idle I have time for introspection. I feel like a human plant or like an animal. I look much younger than I have for a long time and am amazed that I cannot behave as I did when I was twenty-two. In spirit I am surely not at all old, not even grown up. In reality I am childish, but in public do not dare to admit it. I have to play the role of a staid, controlled person. This role is a confoundedly artificial one for me. As commercial and professional architecture is of lesser interest to me at the moment than it normally is (please be sure to keep this letter to yourself) I am sick and tired of the role.

I relish to again play around with oil crayons and have already made several sketches. If I had you here with me I would behave like the greenest lover so that all the passengers would look on with envy. I think I am going to stop behaving towards you as I did when I was up to my ears involved with architecture. To be sure, I could not have behaved younger or more youthful than when I jumped out of bed at 4:00 A.M. to quickly write down and sketch an idea before it evaporated. And while I worked, believe me, I was devoted to you with my whole being. Surely, you are a marvelous woman, my darling Dione child, that you are able to enter into all my lunacies, that you never hold anything against me and that you are no more grown up than I am myself. I come to the realization that somehow I cannot love people who are really grown up. That you never expect me to be grown up, to be "serious" is immensely comforting to me. It seems to me that Frank's character can be explained through the peculiarity of his parents. Let's accept what comes in thankfulness for our blessings. I love to think back when we three hugged each other and little Dion said, "All in Paradise."

I am trying to speculate as to what would happen to me if you died. I am now so accustomed to being happy with a woman of your youthful disposition that I could hardly live without you. Before I met you I managed quite well and that saved me from calamities. I hardly think, however, that like R.M.S. I could have lived as an indifferent sufferer during an unhappy match. I would probably have made an end to it, but would have suffered terribly before reaching such a decision. Come to think of it, I can imagine that an inferior female might have snared me through her charms and that I could have become deeply unhappy. Or, if I had not had the stupendous good luck to encounter you and gain your sympathy, I could, with the passage of time have developed a vile coldness and looked at a female as an object of pleasure without entering a meaningful human relationship. In any case, whether my nature would have bailed me out or not, I shall never forget, day or night, what a gift from heaven it was that I found you and we can be together. I don't forget it. I close my eyes and see you disappear as a green dot in San Pedro. How happy would I be if I could press you to my heart and rest my cheek on yours. Human beings have such a hard time expressing their love except through physical contact. I take a deep breath. What can I say? It seems to me as if only now I said good-bye to you. I suddenly realize that this separation is not such an insignificant one as it first seemed. I am so deeply grateful to you that you sent me on this trip, but perhaps I should not have separated from you. Who can tell how we shall feel later and how long we shall live altogether? I don't believe that one is master of one's destiny. At least the inner workings are manipulated by dark powers. If our separation had not been proposed by you, I would really feel downright unhappy, imagine! I am unable to tell you why, but while I sail, day in and day out over these waters, I notice that plans and travel schedules are really concerned with trivial exterior manifestations. Real happenings follow quite different and ununderstandable rules. During the leisure of this ocean voyage I'm promising myself that from now on I shall devote more time to play and fun. At the same time, I passionately wish you could be with me now. If you were here, I would hardly pay any attention to our travel companions but concentrate only on you, talk with you for hours, listen to you sing, lie for hours quietly beside you, slyly waiting for an opportunity to fondle and kiss you. While I write this I am so in love with you that my stomach hangs like a stone in my body. How can I describe it? Look here, my life's treasure, this is not supposed to be a love letter. But the written word has no power. Just think if one of us would die, or if we should become estranged! I stop my writing for a few minutes reflecting how my whole body pains me in this thought, especially my throat contracts. Choking is the correct expression. How did we ever get together? You came from a different background. Once we were complete strangers to one another. You are a girl and for this reason alone different from me, a man. We are of a different religion, speak different languages. Our temperaments are so different, our endowments, our frailties dissimilar. Perhaps we have already forgotten many things which we experienced together, that which united us. But somehow, somewhere, the memory of it lives on in us, we organic, concentrated human beings. To cut this out would be nearly fatal. I cannot imagine how anybody else, perhaps not even you, will read and understand these sentences. They seem to be mere grammar, an exercise in writing skill. Only my heavy heart and the pressure on it are unbelievably real.

But, my Dionerl, you are still alive. Hopefully, you still care for me. As long as this is the case I shall be thankful.

*Dione to Richard*

Los Angeles, June 1930

What do I have except you and my belief in your architecture? With me you come first, then comes architecture, finally the children. With you architecture comes first, then me, then the children. Although you *believe* I come first, you must know in your innermost heart that you could not be happy with me if you had to give up architecture. However, I fully believe you can be completely happy *if* you can combine both of us. I am proud and deeply glad when you jump from your bed at 4:00 A.M. to record your thoughts and I understand with all my heart that you feel united with me at such moments. I am profoundly grateful that I have been given the capacity to feel with you and to understand what motivates you. . . .

*Richard to Dione*

On the Boat to Japan, June 1930

I stood at the ship's stern as the sun sank behind a cloud bank. We are, perhaps, 150 miles from the Japanese coast, but the horizon has as yet no shoreline and is empty as it has been for the last nine days. To look backward is as beautiful as to look forward to the part of the horizon we are approaching. Here, in front, one does not hear the engines, but only the rush of the broken waves. Yesterday I saw a flying fish. A strange bird with a long neck fell on the deck. The sailors attached a string with a little lead emblem around one claw. The bird hissed and opened his long beak.

Yesterday we had our good-bye festivity. As there were very few women on board, I dressed up as one. I danced and behaved coquettishly so that everybody followed my movements with amusement.

I start to count the days, Dionerl! Where you have time only for me and I am not distracted by silly business considerations, what a fine time we will have together. Oh dear me, I am beside myself with insatiable longing. I am plagued by the fear that if something happened to you I would have to be put in an insane asylum. Altogether I am, perhaps, not quite normal. Also, I become overly exuberant when well nourished and without competition.

I remember how I walked up and down on a hilly path in Waedenswil during the lunch hour and again, how desperate I felt without you in my basement workroom. Only when I'm near you am I halfway normal. You can see how easily I can be the father of our poor Frank. The main difference between us is that he shows little interest in other people while I really love them as long as they don't step on my toes.

*Richard to Dione*                                                                Tokyo, June 1930

In Tokyo five persons fetched me from the boat after a photographer had photographed me and a reporter interviewed me. In the newest architectural journal they printed a whole page of photographs about me. "R. J. Neutra visits Japan." Five hundred persons, or even more are expected to attend my lecture. Tonight the architects are giving me a big reception and a banquet. A trip to Kyoto is planned. . . .

*Dione to Frances*                                                             Frankfurt, July 1930
*Toplitz*

Rush, rush, rush since our arrival. Richard came to meet me in London; hence we moved to Paris where we met Doris and her husband. Then we stayed at Muetterli's house for two weeks without much rest. . . .

. . . We are quite tired seeing so many things, but especially Frankfurt was very interesting. We are on our way to Vienna and the train is moving out of the station. . . .

*Richard Added a*
*Postscript*

Yes, Dione is right to say that what Europe offers us is: Rush! I am longing for the quietness of North America!

. . . I gave a well-paid lecture here in Frankfurt and Dione and myself were celebrated like the Prince of Wales and his bride (if he had one). We lived in a marvelous guest apartment in one of those luxurious old Frankfurt residences.

All the way from Japan to China, to Switzerland and Stuttgart, I try hard to create a good reputation for the USA and nobody is checking what I am saying, believe me!

I probably shall also lecture in Prague, Berlin, and possibly Rotterdam. . . .

Although I pride myself of a good deal of receptivity, I find my brains somewhat clogged by all the things I have swallowed through eyes and ears during these last months. I suppose you have received my letters from the Asiatic journey. The deepest impression was that of the coming China. In Egypt I became mixed into the riots against Sidki Pasha.[1] In Naples I arrived after the earthquake and in London at the eve of an unsuspected bank holiday.

1. Prime minister of Egypt, 1930–33.

I have talked with publishers and editors all around the world and found them sweet and flattering, but much smaller men than their publications lead you to believe. In several points the world became more transparent to my intelligence and insight.

*Richard was also invited to lecture in Berlin (fall 1930) in the impressive new auditorium of the Metal Workers' Union which Erich Mendelsohn had designed. In 1970, shortly before his death, while he taught at the California Polytechnical University at Pomona, California, he gave a lengthy interview for an article that was published in the student magazine (January 27, 1970). In it he mentioned his stay at the Bauhaus in Dessau:*

"In the front row sat Mies van der Rohe, and after my talk he invited me to the Bauhaus as a guest professor for as long as my time might allow. On this occasion I made the acquaintance of the most interesting personalities there. I also was familiarized with all the problems of such a school situated in the Germany which had then begun to totter under the onslaught of nazism, suspicious of it. There was already the first inkling of what was to happen in the coming decades.

"I remember the first day I spent in Dessau with Mies. He took us to a fine restaurant downtown and we had a wonderful conversation when we came home pretty late that night. Discovering that he had misplaced the key to let us into our guest quarters in the main building, we walked around and around but couldn't drum up anybody who was awake. Finally we found an open basement window. With combined muscular forces we lowered my bride into the basement in the hope that she would be able to find a way to open an entrance door from the inside. She tried her best, making her way over cellar stairs and through dark corridors, but she did not succeed. While she spent the greater part of the night in the dark basement of the building, we two were walking around outside discussing the future of world architecture!

"So this was my first experience with the Bauhaus. Later on I found very much to learn and exchange there, both with lively students and worthwhile teachers. They were a manifold lot and Gropius had really not forced on them uniformity, in spite of all programmatics pronounced.

"I hadn't been experienced at all with European students, but there were all kinds of young people from all parts and I sensed a feeling of restlessness among them which lingered on after the last head-master and top man had left. Hannes Meyer had been the preceding director between Gropius and Mies. He was a declared Communist and all his favorite students had become quite politically colored.

"In my own study group there were quite a few of these students, and it was interesting how political issues were often superficially understood or mixed into the tendencies of the Bauhaus. I would like to emphasize the hopefulness of the Bauhaus movement, which actually believed that modern technology could give us humans all we need. The people I knew, saw and learned to appreciate in the Bauhaus, were the most diversified characters one can imagine.

"It was supremely characteristic that Walter Gropius had succeeded in building master houses for these great men of manifold contemporary art—Paul Klee, Kandinsky, Muche, Moholy-Nagy, Jawlenski, Feininger, Young, Herbert Bayer, Marcel Breuer, too, I believe—standardized and identical abodes, accommodating the most diversified people who were certainly not compatible as artists! They were very, very personal and individual in their outlook on art and life. These people *could indeed live in identical dwellings—when we rightly worry whether or not one can frame normed habitations, or prefab them for quite ordinary families of coal miners or steel workers in Pittsburgh or East Germany! What a demonstration! And a typical characteristic of the Bauhaus at that!*

*"If these so very diversified artist personalities, with all the self-expressionist attitudes which distinguish creative humans of our time, could be thus housed, then this is a demonstration of the immense skill of Walter Gropius, wizard of fusing the most contrasting metals. With the steady flame and heat of his enthusiasm he alloyed them into one pot, one could say, by inviting them to the same spot. That he could do this goes way beyond my own abilities and comprehension, and perhaps this is the reason why I admire him so much. I may have tried similar things, but never with so distinguished personalities as he did and never with any comparable success.*

*"I saw in him a man playing an important role in the cultural scene of our era. Balanced collectivity and team spirit was his forte. This was not quite so pronounced in Mies, in spite of all the other timeliness of his work."*

*At the Bauhaus Richard worked with his students on a competition for a theater in Charkov. Virginia Weishaus, wife of composer Imre Weisshaus, teaching at the Bauhaus, wrote Richard what she had been told about his seminar at the Bauhaus.*

*Virginia Weisshaus to Richard*

Berlin, August 1931

. . . I knew from Dione that you had lectured at the Bauhaus and so I asked at once some of the older Bauhaueslers what they had thought about it. I was surprised at the cautious replies (I asked three), the way they looked at each other and said: "Well, well, oh yes, of course, very valuable, but—." One of them said: "Well, of course, he made everybody work. We never had to work so hard for anybody else." Sometime later, my enthusiasm a little dampened, I asked a young fellow named Buske, and he explained that the three I had asked first belonged to the faction that you had eliminated when you divided the class to work on the Russian project, and that they had ever since had a grudge about it. But he was tremendously enthusiastic about you and said that your working tempo was marvelous, that many of the students you worked with hated to be forced to go at such a working pace as you made them do.

It was terribly gratifying to hear that America has learned a wholesome respect for Richard Neutra, and all about the success of his lecture tours. But gosh, Richard, I hope you aren't going to turn into a *talker* and let it take time away from your valuable *doings*. America is always so idiotically eager to listen to lectures about everything. What I mean is, that I hope these social successes will really bring something of substance in the way of more opportunities to build fine buildings. . . .

*During Richard's lecture trip through Europe, his friend Ernst Freud in Berlin received a wire from Philip Johnson, then trustee of the Museum of Modern Art in New York: "Where is Neutra? Have a job for him." In New York he learned that Johnson's father, a prominent lawyer in Cleveland, asked him to be a consultant for the White Motors Company in Cleveland to design a bus with an aluminum frame.*

*Richard accepts a commission to design buses for the White Motors Company of Cleveland.*

*He leaves Cleveland for Los Angeles, lecturing along the way in New York, Chicago, and San Francisco.*

*As Dione relaxes with her parents, she reflects on the stressful impact the work pressures of the last five years have had on her marriage. In her letters to Richard she expresses her inner turmoil about their life together.*

*She takes Frank to Vienna to consult with various physicians, including Sigmund and Anna Freud and Richard's psychiatrist brother, Wilhelm. They convince her not to leave Frank in an institution but to take him home.*

*In June, Dione and the two boys join Richard in Los Angeles.*

*Richard lectures and writes articles, but no commissions materialize.*

*1930– 1931*

On the Boat to the United States, December 1930

*Richard to Dione*

. . . I am slightly seasick and am swimming in the direction towards USA. I have a few hundred dollars at my disposal and a few chances. Also chances to squander. What is in the offing? Lectures, playing a role with nothing to back it up. The famous modern architect has no office, no organization, no jobs. Where can he rest his weary head? Just as I did in 1923, so I do now. I swim towards USA. It has a width of 2,000 miles and a length of 3,000 miles. New York has many skyscrapers' stories where my name is unknown and a few editorial offices where one has made a note that I am supposed to be a West-coast sensation. I am a little seasick and lame in the head. How shall I start in New York? If I did not have this ridiculous prestige, it would be perhaps easier. On top of all there is this depression and fear of a crisis. I feel as if I was one single man against a continent. However, I have sowed so diligently, I should at least try to harvest.

Cleveland, December 1930

*Richard to Dione*

I achieved excellent results in my talk with the directors of the greatest motor bus manufacturing company of America. I spoke like a book, like an experienced sales expert. I had my hair plastered down smoothly, wore light gray gaiters, and Roncagelli clothing. After dinner I was asked to show some slides. I explained them during the showing with the greatest success. It was a combination of American know-how and cosmopolitanism, which I successfully imitated. Ladies and gentlemen were carried

193

away. Therefore, it is mainly a question of contacts. I am absolutely sure that no one later asked whether I was a fool. Contacts—so important and so difficult to achieve. I desperately play the role of an ambitious young man.

During the last four days I lived in style in Cleveland's most exclusive club with breathtaking service. I adapted a dozen times better than you would have done. In fact, if people do not know me from before, I fit practically everywhere. One day into a soup kitchen, one day into a Communistic one, an Episcopalian one, an aristocratic or a Serbian, an Irish one, into a group of people behind the settings of a Berlin theater, on another day I can travel in all classes, can work as a gardener's apprentice, or lecture as a professor.

*Richard to Dione*                                                                         Cleveland, December 1930

At the moment I lead a life of fantastic seclusion. It is a very strange experience for me to have to adhere to strict office hours. I rise early, in the dark, and three-quarters of an hour later, in an unaccustomed cold train, I travel along a suburban line. Schoolchildren, Negroes, on 79th Street, Cleveland.

At the corner where I wait for the yellow streetcar every morning filled with Negro girls, there is a dark Gothic Calvary Presbyterian Church right beside the Greek Christian Science church, number so and so. You know, these churches have a number in each city and the archangel Gabriel carries each number in his notebook. At the Calvary church I read about the forthcoming sermons, dance evenings, and a sign: "Mr. Pollock, *Spiritual Surgery*." (This signifies simply surgery to improve the spiritual religious life.)

I walk across the street, pass quickly one drugstore after another, ascend the stairs of a house at the northeast corner. What I found in the upper floor astounded me: "Sylvia's Charm School—Entrance." What in heaven's name is a "Charm School"? Too bad that it is dark behind the glass door. I would have liked to ask the price of a cram course. I speculate whether Sylvia would accept me as a pupil. I was just starting to delve into the subject, but I cut it short realizing that you are interested in my life in Cleveland.

I have long office hours. I consider it correct to adhere to them strictly. For two days I waged a furious battle concerning the bus bodies. Now I have an excellent idea, while I asked for more and more huge blueprints. However, it is doubtful whether my ideas will convince those who make the decisions.

I must present a front, must appear very impressive, confronting, everybody thus, *if I want to accomplish anything*.

*Richard to Muetterli*                                                                     Cleveland, December 1930

*Read what follows at breathtaking speed.*

The situation in Cleveland is as follows: Outwardly everything is calm. I tell you, I have drawn up beautiful buses, but the most important fact is my attitude. Only an undoubtedly world-famous authority can push through such a model against the involved interests of the various bureau chiefs. Each one of them, for heaven's sake, would not condone any changes. The chassis specialist advises me to round it out, make the rear look exotic. This concerns only the "body" designer, not him. However, the radiator cannot be tampered with, under no circumstances. (It looks awful covered up.) It has been excellently designed and constructed for cooling purposes. However, "could I change the outer shell." "For heaven's sake, not! We have tremendous backlog of old models." Whenever one wants to tackle one part, the resulting changes go through and through. I have discussions with the bumper specialists, the aluminum seat and upholstery experts, when and how I can pierce this maze! How does one open up, how and where does one store the standardized hand luggage which I want to store underneath the fold-up seats? What happens if a lady sits there, what if she sits by the window and her suitcase is 19½ inches high? Therefore, one cannot make the windows higher, ergo we lower them. I beam, the center of gravity has been lowered. The whole thing has been reduced a few inches, which means heightened stability. The high joint between roof and supporting beam does not come apart anymore. The chief engineer thinks my proposal has merits. Well, dear Muetterli, do you think I am a bore writing down such stuff? It give you insight into my brain activity as long as it cannot be combined with my heart activity which is with all of you.

*Now slow up.* This whole matter is only tiresome if, unexpectedly, boiling hot, your whole body is inundated with it. If you can follow me step by step, I, who do not understand a thing about buses (or for that matter about bank buildings or theaters or whatever else), who undertakes this assignment with a beating heart but pounces on it with searching eyes, quick elastic brain equipment, who after a few days, radiating with joy, lets my wife or you put your hand on my belly to feel the preliminary movements of what is to be born swelling like an avalanche. Finally at 3:00 A.M. I wake you up from your first sleep, embrace you passionately and tell you: "I have a marvelous idea. Go back to sleep, but I *had* to tell you *right now*! However, as you can see my glowing eyes even in the dark, you *insist* that I tell you *hot off the griddle*, because you love to hear my voice at such an occasion, and such a happening is wonderful every time it occurs.

Well, dear Muetterli, you are married to a musician. This is much less perilous. The composer's output is not dependent on officials connected with him by twenty telephones. The linoleum contractor does not have the brashness to quickly drop by as late as 10:15 P.M. Dionerl knows that fresh guy! Oh, oh, oh, it is *wonderful* to be married to an *architect*; *that* you have missed. I do not communicate? Ask your Dionerl *what* I tell her. Only when I am very weary I stop talking. I discuss with her every check someone is supposed to pay me but has no intention of doing.

Cleveland, December 1930

*Richard to Dione*

It is my last day in Cleveland where I have seen and experienced a lot. I lie in "my" bed, room 334, dawn of a Sunday morning.

195

I have dined with very rich people, in clubs and in mansions, where I was invited and celebrated. At other times I ate in an *American diner*. You know it is an imitation of a railway coach where one sits on a long counter and watches the cigarette-smoking cook while he prepares hamburgers. The principal customers are taxi drivers, occasionally an old prostitute. The already well known Viennese architect is an unknown habitué in this place, economizing so that his beloved Dione, if she feels like it, can join him again, the money for the trip being at hand.

Today I presented my work in elegant fashion to the president of the company, who seemed visibly impressed. Your husband has again pulled the chestnuts out of the fire and you really should give him a kiss. Tomorrow I shall decide what to do next.

*Richard to Dione and*
*Muetterli*

New York, December 1930

I have seen more in the past year than anyone could desire, under more unusual circumstances than anybody I know. To work one's way as a sailor is adventurous only to somebody who has never tried it, or who has never traveled with limited means. A researcher, a traveling literary expert, an engineer representing his firm, a newspaper reporter, a diplomat, an owner of a Dollar-Line round trip ticket, a poor devil looking for a job, a lieutenant guiding a military transport, these are the usual typical travelers. What I have just now experienced and am still experiencing appears to me completely *unbelievable*; I don't know! I traveled around the world without money, only with a clearly defined use of time, being excellently advised and guided, receiving hospitality, publicity, and continuous recompense, which tops what I could have earned had I remained stationary. All of this improvised without any security, any particular goal in mind. All arrangements indefinite like a gentleman's.

The whole trip has cost us an immense sum of money considering our circumstances. In reality, to be correct, not us, because when we started this trip I had only a small part of this sum. Now I have reached the conclusion that I am not slow in making decisions or in taking advantage of a situation. However, when I consider how others of my acquaintance would speak about this whole matter, it becomes clear to me how little self-confidence I possess. Modesty is a very weak expression for it. Take this bus adventure. On the spur of the moment, without preparation, I make bus drawings that surprise even me, good-looking designs. At the same time, I was able to create the impression that I really understood something of the highly complicated technical aspects of the matter. I truly know only very few architects who could undertake such a venture without being a total flop. After all, it is a completely different medium! As if Vaterli, who is a pianist, would accept a position as a flutist in the Cleveland Orchestra, trying to impress the conductor who since thirty years is an expert on wind instruments. Not to break one's neck in such an effort is quite a success. Don't you think so?

I really know very little about automobiles, which Dione can confirm. But everything went much better than I could have hoped for. And this

happens at a moment when I am in dire need, because my financial calculations were as childish when I set out on my world trip as when I arrived here. I surely am not a passive creature, but I am in greater need of a
guardian angel than anybody I know of. Everybody I know tries to play it
safe, seems to me compared with myself. And we were fortunate to escape
being sick.

An immense, unlimited optimism, a monumental self-confidence of an
aggressive nature should flow out of all this. Why is this not the case with
me? Muetterli? Vaterli? Dione? Is this a deficiency, or is it not? I really
believe that no success could ever blind me to its temporary character. On
the other hand, I hate not being successful, because this smacks so much of
having wasted one's energy, thus having no time to *THINK*!

My belief is that human relations, the flowering of the spirit, are the real
concrete realities. Wherever "success" stands in the way to achieve this, it
is a debacle. . . .

New York, December 1930

I have no light above my bed. It is six o'clock in the morning, thus I
write to you in the early, bluest morning haze. It is the morning before the
Christmas holidays in 1930. It is seven years later. I live four stories high in
the same neighborhood as of yore. A little more north from Irving Place,
slightly west from Lexington Avenue. The room is tiny. To bathe is miserable. I have a dilapidated wardrobe, one tiny shaky table with a light
above it, a metal gas stove. No place to store my papers; I keep them in my
suitcase. I think of you with all my heart in the morning.

I start the day by cleaning my shoes, brushing my suit, bringing and
picking up my laundry, looking up telephone numbers in the huge New
York directory, trying to get telephone connections by throwing in a nickel
and missing connections. Finally, I have filled my whole day with appointments, meanwhile it is already midmorning. I go around the corner to a
cafeteria. After quickly downing a bowl of puffed rice with milk, I descend
into the subway, pass the clicking turnstiles. I do not read the newspaper,
nor a book. I don't write; I do not draw. I travel long distances to get an
address, speak extensively to a vast assortment of people who usually have
no time for me, do not understand what I am driving at; who tell me a lot
of irrelevant matters, are *occasionally* willing to listen in a friendly way,
and write down my telephone number. I write down more new addresses,
look up more people, impress them, talk to them, show them material
from my sample briefcase. Supposedly, this is the way to make contacts.

It seems that in New York alone there are a million unemployed. Yesterday evening I went to lower Manhattan on the East Side to look at some
slum dwellings. Very little lighting, dilapidated fronts with dirty windows,
rusted fire escapes; many shiny automobiles quickly traverse this huge
proletarian quarter towards the Williamsburg Bridge. I could not see a
sidewalk on this two-story bridge at night and had to be careful not to be
hit by a car. I wandered towards the Bowery. Not one female in sight, only
men, men, men. Some drunk, some reeling. Many were vomiting into the

gutter or elsewhere. It is just like the Christmas vacation in Florida of the well-to-do, who have less reason to leave their West End Avenue apartment, corner 104th Street, moving at various occasions to Florida.

This filthy man, between forty-five and sixty-five, who since ten months could not find work, or the rascal who refuses or does not want to accept work that society occasionally hands out to him, this man in his stinking garment can for twenty cents find an evil-smelling place to sleep, but he cannot take a train to Florida, falling asleep in a Pullman car. In a subterranean hole he gets some furniture polish that intoxicates him slightly.

It does not take long to get into the open from the lower East Side. I saw a slightly better hotel for men. On the opposite side I saw two people beating each other underneath the elevator. One of them was very brutal, stepped repeatedly on the face of the other one who was mostly down. On the opposite side one pays thirty cents for a night's lodging that boasts a metal locker. I also visited a lodging where one gets for fifty or sixty cents a cubicle just big enough to accommodate a bed with a screen enclosure, protection against thieves. There does not seem to be any place for dissolute females, and prostitution in the streets seems not to be practiced here. Females who have no place to stay, put a nickel into the subway turnstiles, riding all night from Brooklyn to the Bronx and back again.

I spoke with a small man of my age. I am, by golly, myself a poor dog, but somehow I was ashamed of my white collar and turned the collar of my overcoat up. Until a few months ago he had worked for the Erie Railway, then he tried for weeks to find a pick-and-shovel job in New York, paid outrageous fees to an employment office. Five dollars for a job that would pay twelve dollars a week. I spat and lighted the cigarette I had given him. I hardly smoke anymore. The ladies from the Temperance Movement are of the opinion that one also should not drink but be optimistic and keep looking for work because this is honorable and shows that one wants to make one's way.

Across the street I saw signs advertising corned beef hash for twenty cents. The little man who is good-natured and self-respecting told me that this food was suspect and not worth even twenty cents. He is now selling chocolate. If he sells two cartons a day, he can make a dollar and a half. Thus, he can even pay for his laundry after food and a place to sleep. He positions himself near a department store where the women from the Bronx, Queensborough, and so on, go shopping and may also consume chocolate. In other words, upwards from Thirty-third Street towards Fifth Avenue. "There is no profit in apples. One simply cannot earn a thing. On every corner someone is selling apples, beautiful red apples, and most people of a certain kind seem to subsist on apples nowadays. But even so, this is no business. Chocolate is much better. One gets from the firm an identification card, and if one has worked for a while, even two boxes on credit every day. Of course, one has to know how to handle this, I mean, how to offer, how to be assertive."

All the slums are full of men, men, men, like the kuli sections in Shanghai. Where, I ask myself despondently, are the rundown females? Those older ones or those who possibly have children? Here, one does not think much about women, like one does in Florida, where they are beautifully dressed, promenade and flirt along the beach walk, or alternately dance tango or ragtime with a tanned fortune hunter.

However in New York most poor people are good-humored and understanding. After all, of what importance are the 2,000 Communists who can easily be beaten up if they demonstrate in the streets. All this I write without much criticism or outrage. These are simply facts, 100 percent cheerless except for a well-paid journalist who reports on slum conditions. I simply write down what I observe while I pursue my own important endeavors. In any case, what a comic contrast when I take a meal for which I do not pay in one of those expensive Tuxedo Clubs, put on airs, trying to make an impression.

Now it has become daylight. It is snowing.

During the day I experienced a fantastic variety of people, some similar, others dissimilar. They could not exist together in the same room. However, my flexibility binds them together. It means cleverly changing every half hour. Why should anyone here, especially a lady, take me to her heart? Why should anyone wish me such a doubtful thing?

Oh my Dionerl, you write that you would not mind living in New York and would love to see me successful in this society which dispenses fashionable commissions. Muetterli also would like me to succeed here. I have observed this society during luncheon and dinner engagements. Celebrities abound who twaddle insipid nonsense with seductive females who display red fingernails (probably red toenails too). Dirty jokes are being told. This is a means of being popular in the flirtatious atmosphere where a lot of alcohol is consumed in a smoke-filled room. Oh, the boredom and wasted life. What a way to find work! I carefully look at such a career, trying to imagine how my golden Dionerl would fit into it, whether she could be happy here, whether I could have fewer worries and could be a better husband to her. . . .

Zurich, December 1930

*Dione to Richard*

How you describe the New York high society is appalling to me. But once more, dear Richard, if you feel these circles are necessary for your career, I shall certainly try to participate and can surely learn to accept it. I still believe that for a man of your temperament, your disposition, it is not desirable to have a big office. If you had a school where all business considerations were handled by someone else, where you could train assistants who could help you with commissions, where you would receive a salary that would secure a modest living, but leave you a free hand to design, would that not be a good solution? To be dependent on this society which is torture to you and perhaps even more to me, does not seem to be a solution. Perhaps you can find a job commensurate with your gifts? One more thing, could you not stay in your room one day a week? Otherwise you chase around all week, having nothing to look back upon. If you cannot work, read an interesting book. Surely you could do this for one day. It would help your inner balance. Don't laugh, but seriously think about this suggestion.

*Richard to Dione*

New York, December 1930

Today I was the guest of honor of four of the most influential architects of New York who, together, have a building budget of between forty and fifty million dollars; Raymond Hood, Ralph Walker (New York Telephone Building), Ely Kahn (the prolific), and Joe Urban who is the architect for the New York School of Social Research where yesterday I gave the opening speech in the new auditorium, to be followed by another one tonight and Friday. My fee will be $150.00, which is a godsend.

My financial calculations regarding my stay in New York were somewhat naive; one has to have a front. These four architects dominate the Chicago World's Fair. They prefer to honor me at a luncheon than let me participate in the fair.

*Walter Gropius[1] to
Richard*

Berlin, January 1931

Cordial thanks for your letter of January 8, which arrived only this morning. I take from your letter that you intend to stay in New York for the time being. How long, I wonder? I am quite ready to accept your proposal. It might be possible for me to come to New York in March. I could prepare four–five lectures and would appreciate some suggestions from you beforehand. I would start by laying the foundation with a lecture I could call "Functional Building Design," to be followed by individual themes in which housing and city planning problems would stand in the foreground. Finally, a lecture on the interior decorating of dwellings. May I ask you to help me with the translation? I would have the lectures translated here first, would then beg you to check these translations. Do you believe that the promoters would be willing to assume the travel expense for myself and my wife for a two weeks' stay in New York? At the moment I am without funds and I am hesitant to travel without my wife mainly on account of my poor English. However, I believe I could manage to deliver a well-prepared lecture in English, but would not be able to enter into a discussion. There I would need an interpreter and my wife could be very helpful. This whole proposal interests me very much and I am most grateful that you so forcefully used your influence to further it. At the moment my economic situation colors everything. As far as a time schedule is concerned, I could stay away for four weeks and then see what develops. . . .

*Richard to Muetterli
and Dione*

New York, January 1931

. . . Not having expected any particular strokes of luck, nonetheless, I have achieved as much in New York as could possibly be anticipated. With humor and systematic effort I have managed to procure events, meet more people, learn from various circumstances, and I have received most worthwhile, inestimable publicity than could have been imagined. Behind all this there is a lot of work and inventiveness, a gift to unearth resources which only a person can evaluate correctly who has tried something similar during his lifetime.

1. Famous architect, director of the Bauhaus in Dessau.

In the last few months I have met a thousand people in my profession. I cannot remember *one person* who, without the slightest advantages of personal connections, has tackled so many obstacles as I did continuously, and have to do consistently. If I had a tenth of the contacts that Ernst Freud has, for instance, I would do astounding feats, giving the impression of having excellent connections.

To get commissions in any other way is based on the purest chance, and so far I was able to demonstrate *what* I can accomplish with a halfway lucky break. Such lucky breaks give the possibility for broad publicity (you know *how* little vanity I have concerning this), but it is the only way I could possibly pursue, but it has to have an underpinning of honest work, otherwise it might prove to be a dangerous and artificial sort of publicity. Anything which I produce has to be a masterpiece of progressiveness *and* intrinsic value. Every sentence I write should be exemplary for at least five years, because I foresaw that it would take me double that time to consolidate the impact. Every sentence uttered in public, especially in the presence of the Swiss youth surrounding Giedeon or my audience in Berlin, had to have substance and should, at least, elicit respect.

At each such public exposure I could decidedly do damage to my good cause. My trip through Europe was not only a triumphal one but also a hurdle race in which I could have miserably and irreversibly failed, and thus made a complete mess of our path through life. I say OUR path because when I say *I*, I always think of those dearest to my heart—especially my beloved Dione, who has been such a faithful witness to my rather intelligently conducted endeavors to base our life (and not from free choice but out of inner compulsion) on creative, inventive, ever new, no-routine work that could propel myself and my family forward.

New York, January 1931

*Richard to Dione*

Here, in New York, I have seen an immense array of people who are successful all around, like Mumford, Bernhard Urban, Ely Kahn, Raymond Hood. I have met directors of museums, owners of great publishing houses. Nobody could behave more convincingly than I do. (I don't tell you this with the least little bit of vanity.) It is simply a fact, and it is the only reason for having been the only one so far who was able to *realize* something that obviously is liked and established here and, at the same time, receives daily more free publicity about it. I am such a super salesman that I am admired here, in the middle of New York, that I could—without advance warning—out of a clear sky, sell a white elephant. This white elephant I had drawn up to the minutest detail (each screw hole) and had all its detail prices in my head, while Dr. and Mrs. Lovell squirmed to have this white elephant see the light of day, freezing him out before birth.

Zurich, January 1931

*Dione to Richard*

Well, my Richard, today I have tried to analyze myself, tried to understand why I do not have a clear and happy feeling when I think of you, but on the contrary, feel troubled.

Even if my intellect tells me that I cannot expect from you the impossible, you must admit that life with you, especially after completion of the Health House, was very difficult. I had constantly to comfort you, bolster your courage, try to be of good cheer. I had set all my hopes on your trip around the world, and when I noticed in Vienna that it really had not helped you, I was beside myself.

True, I enjoyed the many sympathetic people we met on this trip and all the worthwhile entertainments provided for you. I have seen and enjoyed a lot. However, if I could have spent the same period somewhere alone with you, where we would have had time for each other, the recollection would be more memorable. I guess I have to recognize the fact that I am a person who lives in and enjoys the present. I do not ponder much about the past or the future.

Can you evaluate sufficiently what it means to me to have this chance to again take lessons and improve myself? The opportunity will never occur again. If I practice assiduously until March, I shall develop a completely new self-assurance.

Please, if my love means anything to you, don't suppress any endearing terms because Muetterli might by chance read them, but write them uninhibitedly. I have a secret place where I can hide my letters. This is the only way in which you can rekindle my memories, because my heart is empty, empty, empty, and I remember acquaintances better than I remember you. But enough of this, I find it absolutely terrible and you must be patient with me and not angry that I cannot remember anything, because you have been so kind. That Dion is my child, and Frank too, how did it happen? Am I not Dione Niedermann, cellist and singer, beloved eldest daughter of the family? Was the life with Richard Neutra just a dream? Oh, what utter nonsense.

We had a wonderful life together; hopefully, shall have it again. I get along with Muetterli when avoiding discussions concerning you. This works well. It is so sad that you two cannot harmonize together. When Muetterli becomes sad thinking of my leaving again, I cannot even give her hope that we may live together at some time in the future. I would not want it so myself. I understand you and I understand Muetterli, also comprehend the impossibility of your understanding her. How strange this is. . . .

*Richard to Dione*                                   New York, January 1931

It seems to me that you now live in surroundings that are unsympathetic to me, that destroy your life with me and all its ideals. I felt this way strongly during my stay in Zurich. It needs a lot of empathy on my part to make Muetterli, whom I have loved for so long, understand me if for any reason I do not have the time to adapt to her view. She is unable to appreciate the real me. That anybody could be totally dedicated to me seems doubtful, even insane, to her. It is her hope that I will eventually make a career. However, in her heart she must feel that despite all inconveniences, I can make a woman very happy. Despite all my efforts, everybody thinks my career is not going ahead fast enough. I should design skyscrapers, give lectures, make contacts, and take it easy! I would like to read books, take a vacation, hear peacefully how my Dionerl sings, and love her with all the fervor that is in me, if only I could catch my breath!

I have always lived up to my obligations, have always tried to secure, not too badly, the material well-being of my family. Actually, it appears to me that this is not my sole obligation. I really believe, when I come to think of it, that I, too, have some "rights"—to fulfill my potential and that one cannot evaluate a marriage this way. I have decided not to bother anymore whether I am a good or a poor family provider. Your father, for instance, had bad luck in this respect. Nonetheless, was he not a worthwhile life companion in spite of it?

It is Saturday evening. Tomorrow is my first speaking engagement. I should cultivate connections for years, like everybody else. I do not want to talk about such matters. They do not interest me, are far removed from what is vital to my Dione. I hope this new year will be kind to you and you remain in good health.

What should I do now? After running around all day, I return to my six-dollar room, lie down on my bed, close my eyes after having carefully looked at your photographs, and I think of you. It is my joy, my relaxation. I looked forward all day to this moment, full of longing. I hoped to find a letter from you. If there was none, I tried to make the best of it.

New York, January 1931      *Richard to Muetterli*

I do not benefit by this separation from Dione. She certainly would not suffer want, as millions of women do, if she were with me. A couple can always manage somehow when living together happily. However, I am glad to share her with you. She is your child and you should have a chance to enjoy her. I am pleased that she has the chance to pursue her music, is happily enjoying her progress. When may I again hear her lovely voice, her playing? It is marvelous for me also that she can have this satisfaction. However, if she dreams of a career as a concert singer and pictures me as a skyscraper architect with offices in two cities, how shall we see each other in peace?

No, I do not care a lot about architecture if I can peacefully be together with your child.

I have also a great longing to hear Vaterli play the piano. It was wonderful when we lived on Kings Road to lie, on a Sunday morning, on our roof porch with a rested brain. Dion would already have fetched my diligent Dionerl and after she had fed and clothed him for his play in the patio, she would sing and accompany herself on the piano. Occasionally it was wonderful to lie in this airy space, watching the sunrays dance on the leaves of our trumpet vine, surrounded by Sunday stillness, listening to Dione sing a Bach song. She also sang a Japanese song which at first I disliked but after a while was attracted to. Afterwards we would take a walk.

There are a few topics I would have loved to discuss with you, and you, too, must have given thought to them because they concern your own life. You surely have pondered these topics during your sleepless nights. What is it that a man and a woman give an offspring of themselves and how does time play with this new biological and spiritual human being? The importance of unsatisfied desire can become disproportionately exaggerated. Where before there may have been doubts, unemotional theorizing, a colorless state, now there is an unappeased appetite. I had come to Zurich in the hope of discussing weighty matters that concerned me greatly with you, but you looked at me sadly, making me feel there was not time enough and you did not have the peace of mind to delve into my problems. Why, my so beloved and cherished Muetterli, which you used to be, why do you now chide me, intimating that I do not have the fullest understanding for you? Why is it only *me* who was "preoccupied"? No occupation, not even one I cherish and pursue of my own free will, could crowd out my love of and involvement in human relationships. On the contrary, my most arduous work brings these relationships to flower. Dione surely should know this, or if she has forgotten it, how did her awareness evaporate?

My dear, treasured Dione-mother, I hope what I write is of real interest to you. What I really should be doing at this time is preparing the lecture which I am supposed to give today at the Art Center for three different associations . . .

However, I do not only want to live in the present. If I cannot find time to commune with those dear to me, life is not worth living.

*Dione to Richard*                                                 Zurich, January 1931

I am in such a peculiar frame of mind. Outwardly I appear happy and content, and as long as I practice, I really am. I guess it was a mistake to marry so soon, before I had achieved a greater proficiency. I never before was so conscious of how deep my happiness is when I notice how I am approaching my idea of perfection. Yesterday we had again a choir rehearsal. Conductor Reinhardt[2] is such an exciting man. He told me that I can again have a singing lesson next Wednesday. I wonder how he will judge my Bach aria, "I Love my Savior Who Now Is Dying." Sometimes I sing it beautifully and I see in what direction my voice is developing.

Imagine, Richard, my cello teacher, Julius Baechi, told Muetterli today that the world has lost a great cellist in me. "Such musicianship, such a good hand." Too bad I could not get farther along the road. All of my teachers have said the same thing, though I cannot at all see that learning comes easy for me.

My conscience bothers me when I write you about my doubts instead of suppressing them. You don't like to hear them and perhaps do not even believe them. Probably you are right and I am mistaken, because you have a clear mind, a good memory, while I live for the day and do not have a good memory. Life is so strange. What will happen if we do not understand each other anymore? What nonsense! But my heart is so depressed and full of anxiety knowing how precarious your situation is at present. Why do I burden you with my fears? Why not suppress them? However, I

2. Walter Reinhardt, conductor of the Zurich Bach Choir.

have the great comfort to feel that you know me better than I know myself. I only hope we keep on communicating. Surely, it is unthinkable that I should suddenly look at you without any illusions. When I openly write you about my doubts I feel less conscience-stricken.

Let's hope, my dear Richard, that all will turn out well. In any case, it should be comforting to you to know how happy I am here, and if I continue to make such progress as I did in the last two weeks, I should soon be a professional singer. I wish I could ship some of my happiness to you.

New York, January 1931

My dear Dionerl, it is not quite true that I married you too soon and, therefore, you did not have enough time for your musical studies. Probe your soul. That the children deflected your course may be true. I don't want to speculate about that, nor that you mention it in nearly all your letters. Strangely enough, Muetterli also has the same attitude. It may not be pure accident that you write me thus from her house. I don't know whether we would have been happier without children, consequently I do not want to speculate about it and, as you know, I am convinced to the contrary. Quite apparently, you now see our whole past differently than I do and it seems you cannot help yourself. Don't worry unduly about it. Continue to practice diligently, enjoying your progress, and continue to do whatever you can to help Frank. Make no programs as to when you want to rejoin me in America. Everything with me is in good shape and although I may be childish, I feel I will be able to take care of you and do whatever else is necessary. Write me about your progress so that my heart can rejoice about it.

May God grant it that my poor Dionerl may not find it necessary to obliterate whole paragraphs in her letters to me, that she remains as happy as she deserves to be. Do not grieve about such matters, dear heart.

I am not an adventurer as depicted in the movies, but my bridge *always* seems to stand on chance supports—my publisher Julius Hoffmann, Leah Lovell—fantastic pieces of luck that I have tried with bleeding fingernails to make fruitful. How many times will I be able to do this? How often can such lucky breaks occur? How does one exist? From what does one live? Can such a man be married? Only with a woman who can be happy with him regardless of everything . . .

Zurich, January 1931

That my family, together with Vreneli, considered me somewhat of a martyr is, perhaps, true and from their point of view they may be right, because surely my life was not *comfortable* compared to Vreneli's. It was, however, not difficult. I don't count the days when I tried to "sell" myself, as I consider them outside of our relationship and a failure, a deficiency in salesmanship. It was disagreeable but of no consequence. What was difficult for me was the last month after completion of the Lovell House, our trip through Europe and especially our stay in Vienna. Whatever you say, the fact remains that I do not like to think of you during that trip. However, I will try to be patient, wait for a change, wait until you are again my enterprising, fascinating Richard. My capacity for love is undermined when for months on end I see you tired and dispirited. However, I am fully cognizant of the fact that life is neither comfortable nor agreeable and that one has to learn to stand up to every situation.

Let me tell you decisively, my only one, *I am not at all ambitious for you or interested in fame!* If it makes you happier to sit behind a drawing board, even if we earn only enough for the bare necessities, this is *much* more important to me than fame. Therefore, do not use me as an excuse. I love to wear beautiful dresses but surely have given proof that I can also live without them. It means a thousand times more to me to see you fulfilled and at peace than to have so-called success.

*Richard to Dione*                                            New York, January 1931

I well remember my gift from heaven, however, only insofar as it was full of love and friendship for me. I remember clearly and distinctly how often you told me, especially these last years while we were lying in our roof porch, that you could not understand your former doubts. How happy we were when we drove along the ocean to Oceano! The sun was shining and we two alone were embarking on a vacation. We noticed the sunny highway, the hills were covered with live oak trees, and we observed together the strange inhabitants of Oceano.

From one of his parents Frank has inherited his paradisical disposition. I can experience such profound happiness when I am near you, my lovely one, when I suddenly have to leave my drafting table in order to give you a kiss, hearing your voice somewhere.

For ten years you have loved me with abandon, without holding back coquettishly. It is said that no male can endure this. It has not spoiled me, and you have had no damage whatsoever. Should we never see each other again, you will not be able to recall one minute when I felt satiated, not being full of love for you. When I kiss your hand, it is not an empty gesture. In my mind I take both hands, press them to my heart from which all my most precious life-force flows.

I have read your pre-Christmas letter and have given it deep thought, although so many pressing matters weigh on me. However, one thing always takes precedence over another. I would rather die on the spot than see you have mournful thoughts about me. . . .

Also I will not tell you worrisome details about my life here in order not to spoil your practice time. I try to imagine how I would feel if suddenly I no longer cared about you. Then I, too, might try to place the blame on external circumstances.

I don't know whether anyone else is more orderly than myself. Just give me time. Give me someone who disburdens me of life's mundane tasks, who, for heaven's sake, gives me some respite. I do not at all complain. I am not the type who blames circumstances for possible failures. I feel I deserve whatever befalls me.

I believe I am most lovable when I lie in the dunes browned by the sun and do not have to present myself in formal attire. Even you have finally come to feel, correctly, that I suffer most from the contrasts between my own inclinations and the demands made upon me. You, who are full of love for me, perceive this.

New York, February 1931

. . . Everything you have written to me during the last few months went through my mind. I have tried to reverse our roles, which seemed feasible as it has nothing to do with our gender but with purely human problems, namely, that I am here in the midst of a battle to make a living, while you have the most heart-refreshing working vacation, practicing to your heart's content. Several times you have asked me to forgive you this or that. Oh, Dionerl, I don't have to forgive you anything, and I hope that I shall never play the role of being superior, thus having the right to forgive. All that is sheer nonsense. I hope that I shall always love you, that I learn to appreciate your being and your worth evermore. I guess it was my mistake to want to see you without any blemishes. Why should you not have some weaknesses too, like any other human being, or like myself?

I guess you will understand that a free, lighthearted life is based on a secure income. It is in the nature of things that inventors, artists, and other free souls rarely can lead such an existence. However, my dear, you never had real worries about me or Frank. Please don't tell me that I should be in a good mood, in a comfortable situation, so that you can continue to love me. This would deepen a possible depression and it is not a loving way to express yourself. It is, for instance, possible that I could contract an illness. That Muetterli feels the same way as you write does not improve matters. I am sure it is all just a thoughtless remark. So many times you have told me, "Why not think of the five million families who have no jobs, of the worrying mothers and welfare breakfasts for children." . . .

There are some careers in existence that are built upon money, connections, a wife's ability, occasionally the wherewithal of a whole family. Marriages under these circumstances can be as happy or unhappy as others.

Without a doubt I could be an enchanting husband if I were not bogged down with having to make a living. Surely, I would always work, but I would work at that which lies on my inner path. Internal rather than external successes would make a radiant companion whenever I succeeded.

Zurich, February 1931

It gives me great joy to re-read the loving letters you wrote me in 1924 while I was in Hagen. Can you remember how important Frank's birth was for us and what great hopes we had for him? You then had such a blind admiration for me. A stranger trying to visualize such a woman would surely believe she was an angel straight from heaven. How is it possible that I changed so radically since then? As far as I am concerned, I feel that I have developed tremendously as an all-around human being. However, because I now experience everything with a much greater awareness, I may possibly have lost a kind of childlike innocence.

*Dione to Richard*

Zurich, February 1931

I feel that whenever you were dissatisfied with me you had just cause. I am really convinced that you love me as much today as you loved me then. I will try to examine myself to see whether I deserved it then and still deserve it now.

One thing I can truthfully affirm, I *never* wanted you to undertake work you disliked because it might be lucrative. I was never stubborn, was never inclined to oppose you, but was always convinced of the wisdom and correctness of your decisions. I was always fervently interested in everything that concerned you, moved you. Further, I was as economical and industrious as any woman could have been under the same circumstances. Well, these are my good qualities. Now I will enumerate my shortcomings: As a mother I was too impatient and too egotistical to find inner satisfaction in my children, and this has not changed. I prefer practicing the cello to reading a story to Dion or taking him for a walk. I am aware of this shortcoming, try to change my outlook, but with little success, I am sorry to say.

As a sweetheart I am not perfect either. However, I have the impression that I could learn more, could learn to approach eternal verities better than I did in the first years of our marriage. I could try harder to be a good mother. I was often hot-tempered and unfriendly, but possibly this may loom large in my memory. What is your reaction to all this, my Richard?

You, on the contrary, have gained in all respects, although at times it seemed you loved me less (during the Lovell House period), which made me sad, but which I now fully comprehend. Oh my beloved friend, as I now deeply probe my soul, a great longing comes over me. I wish ardently to immediately start to become the wife who will measure up to my own evaluation.

I am already afraid to open your next letter because I believe it will echo my previous ones. Would you like to know what I value most in our marriage? It is the certainty that I am developing, am growing, am ever improving humanly in this marriage, and this realization is magnificent. If only I could eliminate the daily toil that chokes up my eternal spring.

*Richard to Dione*

New York, February 1931

When you really loved me I used to be deeply modest, telling myself I did not deserve such love, even expressing this to you. Since you complain about me in every letter, *wittingly* and *unwittingly*, although you try to express it as mildly as possible, it seems to me that I have underevaluated myself, perhaps even—it is *very* difficult for me to write this—put too much credence in your understanding of me because I believed you loved me.

Try to picture yourself how your letters would affect me if I happened to be in a "down and out" period. Would they help me, console me, comfort me? They intimate: I don't much care for you when you are sick, exhausted, and weak. Let's see what will happen when you are halfway settled.

Zurich, February 1931

It is eleven o'clock at night. Peace and solitude finally surround me. Oh my Richard, I lay my head on my arms and close my weary and aching eyes. I think of you with all my might, how you long to have love letters from me. When I read this I can suddenly picture to myself how lonely you are, falling asleep alone, having to take care of innumerable details alone. Then you receive a letter from me which does not please you and you feel doubly solitary. Meanwhile, I also am alone in my bed at night and thinking of you. . . .

Surely, now you are glad that I persuaded you to make this trip around the world. Otherwise you would be sitting alone in Los Angeles and, judging from reports, would probably be subsisting on small commissions while now you are a celebrated personality having a chance to meet a lot of influential people. Oh my Richard, do you think we might return to California?

New York, February 1931

You mention how anxious you are thinking something might have happened to me when you fail to receive a letter. I interpret this with pleasure, that you are concerned about me. However, do not be distressed. It is, of course, correct that all of us are vulnerable. There are more than a hundredfold possibilities of coming to grief than we can imagine, automobile accidents, illnesses, heart trouble, and mentally fabricated despair. Every day when I write to you and you write to me, something horrible could have happened in the interim before the letters are received. It is even possible that we may never see each other again. However, I believe it makes no sense to speculate thus, but rather to have plausible worries. To worry about your well-being I find plausible. I don't want to be late in coming to the realization that you have been a treasure to me. I want always to be aware that you are a life-source to me.

Zurich, March 1931

Oh my dear, kind, intelligent treasure, I am in such good spirits. A great weight has been lifted from me. Now I can confess that I was in real fear of falling in love with Reinhardt. Can you imagine that? I would never have believed that such a thing could happen to me! However, his looks correspond to my girlish ideals. He is blond, blue-eyed, and is a marvelous musician. Today was the first time I had a chance to *converse* with him. Too bad that you could not have been present. To start with, he is a great admirer of Keyserling,[3] a great admirer of romanticism, has confused ideas about free economic systems, future political world order, and lives in a *horrible* chalet-style house. We had a long discussion about modern architecture but were so diametrically opposed in all our views that I could jump for joy reflecting with greatest appreciation on my Richard's clear head. Oh my beloved and dearest friend, my heart soars with happiness, so grateful am I that this spell has been broken. This experience has been an eyeopener for me. I seem to have taken a new lease on life, happily observing how closely we've grown together, how we harmonize.

*Richard to Dione*

Chicago, March 1931

With regard to your teacher Reinhardt I was simply lucky. In any case I am relieved that this cup passed me by! Everything is a gift from heaven. I do not imagine that I fabricate my being lucky, although I am not a passive bystander. My heart's treasure, you are remorseful without even knowing how it would hit me. You could not help yourself and thus there is no need for remorse. Surely I will get over it. It gives me no joy whatsoever to know that my apprehension proved true, namely, that your present comfortable life obscures your earlier life with me. You wrote: "You must admit it was not comfortable to live with you." For me, perhaps, it was even less so. Life with me will *never* be comfortable. I cannot make promises to the contrary.

*Richard to Dione*

Chicago, March 1931

Memory, my beloved Dione, has several facets. There is a romantic way of remembrance which tries to falsify the present, is full of sentimentality and falsehood like a French village on Los Feliz Boulevard. Then there is another kind of memory, the one *I* refer to, one that somehow gives validity to a life that otherwise might be only an endless change of scenery, boring, sensationally exciting. The memory I refer to gives COHESION, gives CONTINUITY to a life which otherwise might seem to consist only of episodes. A life cannot be grasped or perceived as ONE experience. It is fascinating to watch what happens after a child is born, how its life passes through many transformations, how the individual remains, despite changes of scenery or his own metamorphosis, true to his intrinsic self.

To be able to live together with one beloved human being is wonderful for this reason: It provides a memory that is shared and not one that is made unintelligible through continuous change of personalities. "She was a peach," after one had lived with three other girls, is probably one of the romantic remembrances. However, to experience together excitement, luck, depressions, anxieties, secrecies, shared sillinesses, is a wonderful treasure. One sees reflected in the other person one's own wholeness, despite everything.

A man makes your acquaintance today sees in you, as you say, a mature,

3. Graf Hermann Alexander Keyserling (1880–1946), famous German author and social philosopher.

somewhat buxom woman who shows traces of two deliveries which to him are occurences that belong to a past of no concern to him. I see all your present charm, which is inseparable from all former phases out of which it developed for me and for yourself. I do not look at you as a female of a certain age, not even as a feminine human being, but above all as a growing, developing individual, until one day you must die and disappear in the flesh. Then my world will have become dismally empty, not only sentimentally lonely. One can always again find human beings, unless one lives on the moon, as long as one possesses human powers of attraction. But, without a doubt, you carry in yourself a mirror of my own growing and developing, of my own writhing, expanding, withdrawing, encystation, and continuous opening up. Who can see you as I do? Not even your mother, up to your eighteenth year, has perceived you as I see and love you. But I have rebuilt you with the power of my imagination by beholding our small children.

I mirror for you your life as something continuous. . . .

Chicago, March 1931

When you visited me in Berlin in 1921 I was a draftsman for two "architects." Then I told you something of the "New Architecture" consisting of skeleton construction clad with lightweight materials, shining neatness, hope, future. Muetterli knew nothing of this. No periodical relating to this was then in existence, no publication, nothing in our surroundings except what brilliantly lived in my imagination. Ten years later you heard my lecture in Berlin. I shall never be able to project the future far in advance, but you have experienced it with me, my golden mirror. Should I now follow a different path, away from you? If I do you will have lost something of your continuity and I of mine. Is it possible that these hours of turmoil, distress and exhaustion, because they happen to be the last ones that stick in your memory, can obliterate everything else? Were we not prepared to share all sorts of difficulties, despairs, joys, and disappointments in order to give continuity to our lives?

My cello-angel with fingers of a child, I have no intention of exerting pressure on you if you have now decided that you have no memories worth holding on to of our life together. Do you once again want to be the house daughter who sings for Vaterli, is Muetterli's friend, rather than share the days and the friends which have been and will continue to be so dear to us?

Los Angeles, March 1931

. . . Now I want to tell you something in deepest seriousness. You know that I show not the slightest trace of being a tyrant and am a sadist only as far as to be called normal.

It has always been my belief that women are not inferior and it seems to me that the sexual relationship especially rests in equal parts on both male and female.

A marriage may have some camaraderie mixed into it, but it is ridiculous if it does not dissolve right away into love. Not even when they play tennis together are a boy and girl comrades in its real meaning, perhaps more so during a hike. Men may not even know what is happening to them except that a pressure was released, but there is nothing more precious for the girl and what is born than what he has given. One thing, however, is quite evident—he is *giving* and he is not inexhaustible. A girl that falls in love with a he-man, because she thinks he is inexhaustible, will soon be bitterly disappointed if her own lust, in a narrow sense, motivates her, and she either will soon have to find more than one he-man in order to experience satisfaction or will have to resign herself in disappointment. This is expressed in such crass terms in order to make it perfectly clear.

To speak about it more sensitively: A girl who expects from her lover the same share she is capable of giving will inevitably suffer disappointment due to the most innate fundamentals, except in one case: If she loves the boy, loves him as a female human being is capable of really loving a male human being, not demanding, but ready to serve him and be enraptured by his rapture! She cannot harvest from a man any more rapture than she herself is capable of giving, not only what he is capable of *receiving*. In sexual matters the idea of serving cannot be abolished, rather love itself, which is not so difficult and may perhaps happen. (However, from where then shall human beings receive the most common rapture?)

*Voluntary* devotion to serve the rapture of the lover is the female way to *become* enraptured! The most wonderful way for a male is to elevate the *spontaneous* slave, uplifting her from the couch, from the workday, into a "goddess" and give and give, and feel how she receives with almost enraptured thankfulness. It is a pity if a man wants to train his wife to become his enforced slave, a horrible pity if the wife is not satisfied with her husband's "performance," believes to be entitled to demands, does not feel with all her heart that carnal pleasure must be a surprise, *cannot be ordered*, that especially those of a woman must be like a gift, given in radiating ecstasy, but never as a debt to be paid. Only the enthusiasm of the boy to give enables him to bestow what he can give.

Is it possible to explain it in clearer terms?

The fact remains that physical carnal pleasure is of very short duration. It is possible to nurse it along so that it becomes somewhat of a soul impact through adventurous Venetian gondolas, red-colored toenails, outbursts of jealousy, possibly shooting, if one wants to go that far. All this romantic claptrap is an exterior veneer like picturesque or stylized opera decorations. The ultimate interior truth, if felt and recognized, is unutterably greater and full of tragic rapture. How wonderful is the certainty that there is for a time span, if not for eternity, a sweet supplement, a felicitous fulfillment in the midst of the empty universal chaos, a human being that is at times capable to touch our innermost being, and which God has fortunately fashioned also physically in such a way that human beings can experience what is humanly possible. Demands made by a woman have no part in this wonderful dialogue.

It is 11:30 at night. I have just returned from the Crystal Ballroom of Chicago's first hotel, the Blackstone, where my lecture was a huge success. All listeners were clad in evening dresses and tuxedos. At the elevated speaker's table sat the German general consul, to my right the Austrian general consul, to my left, then the A.I.A. president of the Chicago chapter, the president of the Association for Art and Industry, the directors of art institutes, senators, ladies, millionaires, philanthropists, magnates from the steel industry. An unbelievable hubbub. All during the week the newspapers wrote about me, in the art section, in the society section, news stories with unprecedented, exaggerated eulogies all about your husband, who has a cold. In two speeches, also in the City Club, I was introduced as one of the greatest living personalities. The previous speaker had been F. L. Wright. I praised him and Mr. Sullivan. Everybody told me that this meeting had been the high point. I have no idea when to depart. All sorts of things seem to be in the offing. No time to go into details. Possibly it is all idle talk, one never knows.

While I lecture, I worked myself into a concentrated frame of mind and spoke excellently, as everybody assured me. Nowadays I always tackle a new topic.

You said, "I better give up this crazy endeavor of trying to draw you towards me from the distance. . . ." This drawing of you towards me is no longer necessary because I am completely with you. It is, of course, devastating to me if you don't like me as I presently am. Can you visualize being able to bend me back into shape so that we can again harmonize? I promise to be like putty in your hands. I wish so *ardently* for you to be again satisfied with me. If this is not possible in letters, then hopefully it will be when we are united.

I surely had a hearty laugh when I read that you wanted to be like putty in my hands. Ho, ho, ho, you are as tantalizing and changeable as a serpentine dancer! However, I gleefully look forward to this putty. I think we two are the most childish pair of the family. Be it so. It is magnificent that you again voice a longing for me. I can now take a deep breath. However, do not complain continuously that you are not of a passionate nature. *As far as I am concerned*, I don't demand it but want you to remain true to yourself. Do not think too mechanistically—materialistically—otherwise you will get into competition with those women who consistently think in that manner. What do *your* feelings tell you?

I have tried to depict to you how a girl can be permanently happy with a man. Human beings are not naturally materialists but superstitious, spiritualistic believers in ghosts. If love did not exist, it would have to be invented.

I am in Vienna.

Today I walked to the Berggasse thinking continuously, "This is the city in which my Richard grew up." *My* Richard. How wonderful it is to know that somewhere in this world a human being exists who is completely devoted to me! I try to imagine how you must have felt when you started to notice that I was slipping away from you. Human beings are so different from one another. Perhaps a woman has a stronger belief. Although your letters now sound disappointed, I am convinced that once we are together again we shall understand each other as well as we previously did.

I have now consulted various physicians; the consensus seems to be that Frank's brain was damaged at birth due to lack of oxygen when I could not push him out.

Anna Freud told me today that her father concurs with Willy's[4] opinion that Frank has a brain injury in his speech center which, however, has a chance for improvement. Both think I should keep Frank due to his great attachment to me.

Today I felt very happy as I returned along the Ring[5] in the sunshine with increased hope. Frank's speech is decidedly a little bit better every day, and I seem to have a good hand in managing him. How this is going to work in combination with Dion, but especially with you, I shall have to wait and see. Let me tell you how I visualize it. I guess neither you nor I assume our responsibility is at an end when I now decide to take him home. I am aware that with this decision I turn my back to a life that could have been reasonably free of worry, but on the contrary, I will have many difficult months ahead of me. What depresses me most is the impossibility of pursuing my musical activities. Of course, I still hope to find time to practice, but to earn any money with it will be out of the question.

We shall have to arrange my time in such a way that rush work is minimized, and that you will know beforehand what has to be typed. It will not be possible to have a lot of dinner guests and I shall not be able to go out often, in order to conserve my energy. The most important aspect in the treatment of Frank is that I must not be preoccupied. I must always be calm, friendly, humorous, and not hurried. Thank heaven that Frank is often a lovable and charming boy. If any chance of slow normalization exists, all the efforts I shall have to put forth will be worthwhile. This training in becoming patient can only be beneficial in my relationship to you and Dion. Therefore, I look forward to this challenge with joyful suspense and would be overjoyed if I could solve everything well. This I am writing to you today so that you understand my metamorphosis. I am quite conscious of this momentous step. To leave him here would be simpler and cheaper, but as a mother I would be a failure and the undertaking attracts me. I have the feeling that all sorts of inner happiness possibilities

4. Richard's brother Wilhelm, a famous psychiatrist in Vienna.

5. Ringstrasse, the circular road surrounding interior Vienna; it is considered one of Europe's finest city boulevards.

are inherent here and, hopefully, will reflect upon you. In moments of weakness you will help me, dear husband and father of the unsuspecting Frank.

Vienna, April 1931

Oh my dear Richard, yesterday was simply awful. I cannot remember ever having been so desperate. This decision making without being able to ask your advice is so difficult. Yesterday was an especially desperate day. I consulted the speech specialist, Dr. Froeschl, who told me very pointedly after a ten-minute examination: "Either you stay here for four weeks and I teach you how to make Frank speak, or I can only give you a very poor prognosis for improvement." Twenty-eight sessions at thirty shillings for each amount to $840. I would have to burden your relatives for another four weeks and I would not be able to see you for another two months, as an inexpensive ship leaves again only in June. Well, I was really desperate as Willy also advised me to stay. In the midst of my despair the entrance bell sounded and the maid brought me a little basket full of enchanting toys and a silken housecoat with the most loving note from Mrs. Freud and Anna Freud. Is that not touching?

I was so wrought up that I could not fall asleep until about 2:30 A.M. and at 9:30 I had to be at the hospital as Frank had to be X-rayed. It is hoped that this treatment will stimulate the speech center and reduce his restlessness. Also, while there I tried to get information regarding Dr. Froeschl. It was negative. Also Professor Freud thinks I should not go to him, considers him a stupid person, something which I intuitively felt. He thought Frank was, at the moment, not capable of absorbing such speech instructions. I really disliked the man. Therefore, I have decided to ignore Dr. Froeschl, leave here tomorrow and join you in a month. I only hope that later on you will not reproach me for not staying and are in agreement with me that I did the right thing in not leaving Frank here.

On some days everything goes smoothly. On other days, for instance today, Frank was absolutely impossible. Occasionally I shudder at the thought of what I have burdened myself with.

Have I sufficiently stressed the fact that both Willy and Professor Freud believed I could do better than an institution because they gained the impression that I regard this problem objectively and unsentimentally? Don't you think we could observe Frank together and figure out what would be beneficial for him?

Vienna, April 1931

With a heavy heart today I walked in the warm sunshine. I have tried to probe my soul, which pulls me hither and yon. On one hand I would like to take Frank with me and take care of him. On the other hand, will I be able to manage considering my impatient makeup? Will he not completely usurp me so that I will have no time for you and Dion? Will I not be so exhausted in the evening that I shall lose all the musical skills I have regained through hard work? Will my sense of duty, which tells me Frank is your child, a soul that possibly can be saved, help me to say: "It is of no importance whether you can sing or play." Shall I be able to consistently think thus? It would be so much simpler to leave him here to his fate. And still, when he looks at me with such an adoring and loving expression, I imagine that his love for me, my understanding for him could be the key to helping him more than any doctor or treatment could. I would like to try to help him and would pray every night to find the necessary patience and insight to do this.

I have to think through all eventualities in order to come to a quick decision.

*Dione to Richard*                                                    Zurich, April 1931

I am back in Zurich. I have suddenly found an inner equilibrium that lets me endure all outer difficulties and agitations with unruffled equanimity. Do you think it is possible that without my being aware of it Frank's sad condition has preyed on me more than I was aware, and that I am now happy to have a chance to help him myself, discovering that I have the inner strength to do so? Although all authoritative experts have told me that my upbringing has nothing to do with his condition, I know in my inner heart that I made mistakes and I don't like to remember them. Now to know that I can perhaps help Frank makes me deeply happy.

From whence do these mysterious transformations in a human being come that enable him to cope with a situation he formerly thought impossible to deal with? Only a few months ago music was of greater interest to me than my children. Now I am filled with an objective gift of observation and I am interested in solving the problem confronting me. Still, I do hope to squeeze in some time for my music. It will all depend on how well I can organize our life.

I am so happy to hear about your successes. Too bad I could not be present. How will your relationship to Schindler be affected? Oh my, I wish you could pry yourself loose from him. I am really interested in knowing what influence your success on the East Coast will have on the local scene, whether they will bring us into a different strata of society. . . . In any case, I will have suitable garments for any occasion and surely shall be able to fit into high society.[6] For the time being I cannot, but when I contemplate how much I have already learned, I surely could learn this too. I am now so impatient to join you and so happy anticipating our reunion, but at the same time sad when I contemplate how lonely Muetterli will feel knowing that I would not even like to have her live in the same city as we do. To see you two together is simply too much for me. I do not want to experience this dissension again.

6. After living for five years in clothes bought secondhand, Dione was enjoying the luxury of new dresses made especially for her by a dressmaker—courtesy of Muetterli and Vaterli.

Today as I returned from the dressmaker I heard Frank scream terribly. He did this because Dion ran behind him threatening him with a stick. "Only for fun," he said. I took him by the hand and put him in the bathroom whereupon he started to scream in the same way Frank did. I am really the only person who is able to manage Frank. But even with me he suddenly throws himself on the ground in the street if he does not want to go in the same direction as I do. Unfortunately, I must admit that with Dion the impetuous Dione has not yet disappeared. It is especially difficult because Dion, the quicksilver, and Frank, the screamer, are exhausting for Vaterli and Muetterli. Thus, I spend most of my time in the upper apartment. Once on the ship I shall have ample time to master this combination, so that upon my arrival in Los Angeles I will be able to add you as the third in this equation and have my housework as the fourth to come to terms with. At the same time my heart demands to be alone with you, to have time only for you. How is all this going to work out? Hopefully I can keep my equanimity. If not, I will have a very difficult life in front of me.

Formerly Dion looked more like an episode. Now in combination with Frank he cannot be overlooked. Presently I am not only your wife but also a mother.

Day by day we come nearer and nearer to each other. Will you receive this letter? How does it get to Panama? I hope your expectations concerning Los Angeles are not too high and thus will not suffer disappointments. If only I could be without worries when my universal friend, comrade, playgirl, Dionerl, arrives. Well, well, she will arrive with many beautiful dresses, as she writes. My former old Dionerl will, hopefully, be the same despite all this finery which conceals the most precious soul.

Look here, my Dionerl, is it not splendid to love one another, to want to give joy, love, and a reason for living to each other? I am so deeply thankful that you want to be happy with me in the right way and that we will educate the children in this spirit. Surely, it is not a fool's paradise. It will require much sagacity, patience, and, before all, an understanding of my difficulties. They are exceptional and for that reason harder to understand than, for instance, yours. However, I hope that *nobody* will understand them more profoundly than you who were sent to me by heaven!

I am practically separated from Schindler. I am busily working on many projects with only the faintest hope of realization. Life is so short! Who knows how little time we may have with each other, how lonely we still may have to be in this life? But not now! Your ship must not founder. Los Angeles must not be rocked by an earthquake.

Oh, your letters are now so different. They make such wonderful reading. I enjoy them with a full heart and think how loving, kind, and beautiful you are. I am full of good resolutions.

*During the Neutras' stay at the Bauhaus, they had become especially friendly with the U.S. modernist painter Lyonel Feininger and exchanged several letters. Only one has been preserved.*

*Lyonel Feininger to Richard*

Halle, Museum Monkburg, March 1931

Many thanks for your friendly letter of January 24, and the catalogue of the Bauhaus exhibition with your accompanying lines. I have been *wanting* to write you, took your letter along to Halle where I have again my marvelous workroom in the six-cornered tower of the old castle, way on top. It can be reached only by a small winding stone stairway and not even that if I lock the door below. Did I ever tell you about it? I am drawing one picture after another of this entrancing, unknown old city. Nobody believes me how beautiful the town is until my paintings "demonstrate" this fact. Don't people have eyes? These paintings—of which I have already completed twelve—will be exhibited in two special rooms of the museum with thirty charcoal sketches of the town, and the city wants to buy ALL of them. Imagine my studio thus: a room with ten Gothic windows, two and two in five or six walls. On the sixth wall a low Gothic door leads to the stairway. Therefore, *light* from five sides. It has been my dream to paint in such surroundings. I relish all the magic of light influx, counter reflections, the sun in its daily travel. In the middle of the room I have three large drawing tables so that, finally, I have room for everything. From each window I have another view over city, castle grounds, far reaching hazy landscape. On one side an old chapel with an organ whose sound I often hear. When I go to Dessau around Easter, I will try to get for you a few postal cards. I also take a lot of photographs of the old town. My path to my tower passes through three sides of the museum courtyard until it ends at the spiral, stone, stairway, then I pass through wonderful old rooms filled with paintings and ceramics, stone figures and altar saints. Glass cases filled with reliques from the 13th and 14th centuries, vaults, etc.

We think very often of you and of your dear wife. We *always* knew you. Are you in good shape over there? Are you in good spirits? I will send you copies of the photos I took. Your wife liked especially the one where you smile. Belatedly, our best wishes for Easter to the two of you.

*Richard to Muetterli*

Los Angeles, July 1931

Since early morning I am riding southward on the bus and it is now 5:30 P.M. I am coming from San Francisco in the hope that I can, by nightfall, connect up again with your daughter in Los Angeles. I did send her a wire. It will be magnificent to see her again. Matters stand thus: In San Francisco I had every unearned success and all sorts of people proclaim they would like me to fulfill their architectural needs. Every time I reach San Francisco I become more intelligent.

It is wonderful to travel by train, not to smoke, not to eat, not to read silly newspapers, but simply have time to think. This travel tempo, the feeling of which is so different than going by car, walking, or riding. Finally, all these means of transportation are stimulating our brain musculature. Ultimately, for the time being at least, all of us somehow remain on this globe.

There is bankruptcy in San Francisco too. I spoke with the well-to-do and with those down-and-out, had lunch with radicals and with a Communist leader. "End of an epoch" is a frequently expressed comment! Everybody expects further trouble. I am really curious to know what shall await us in 1933.

My host was Joseph Goer, a writer with radical tendencies who created the San Francisco Forum. Every month another personality of importance is a guest speaker. The last one was F. L. Wright. Dione wrote you already that we became reconciled. At our last meeting when I brought him to the railway station, he leaned out the window and said: "You have been described to me as my most subtle enemy, Richard." I replied: "Well, do you need any description by others? Can't you use your own judgment?"

He answered, "I have always used my own judgment—and frequently it would have been better I had not! You don't mind that I kiss your wife, Richard?" Whereupon I answered, "Never did, Mr. Wright!"


Los Angeles, December 1931

*Dione to Vreneli*

The prospects here are miserable. We do not know anybody who has any connections in the building field. After Richard's success in the East, which, however, did not produce any tangible results, it is doubly difficult for him to sit without work. There is not the slightest indication that the situation will change except by a lucky break, and who knows when it will come. Can you imagine the following situation? Twice a week Richard participates with Schindler in an evening seminar. For two months the school advertised all over the country. The net results are eight students. This gives you a slight indication of the chances modern architecture has here. However, where is it better? Perhaps in Germany Richard's work would be appreciated.

An example: An acquaintance, a physician, phoned that he wanted a design for a small office building. Richard spent many hours to convince the man, worked at least two weeks on the drawings, wanted the doctor to sign a commission letter that would establish his modest compensation. The man does not want to sign. Richard keeps on calling; he tries to bargain Richard down. The fee is, anyway, so modest that it barely covers our living costs for two months, but if Richard tries again to design something experimental it will take him four months.

Yesterday, after the evening seminar, Richard visited this man again. In order to bargain Richard down, he treated him with such strong alcohol that Richard was quite intoxicated when he returned after 2:30 A.M. We felt lucky that he had had no accident. All day today he felt dizzy and nauseated.

This is happening to my Richard whose brain is full of beautiful building plans and ideas. Instead he must do battle with this kind of person if there seems the slightest chance.

There is never a client who comes and says: "I believe in you. Build me something beautiful." Should a possibility to build arise, Richard would first have to diplomatically try to convince and persuade for hours, perhaps for several weeks.

Marvelous is the nearby park. Altogether, the natural landscape surrounding Los Angeles is magnificent. The city itself strikes me as ugly and disorderly. I am very happy to be again united with Richard and, being capable and efficient, can somewhat soothe his worries. Please try to imagine a little his present situation, otherwise your European conviction that he will be rich one day is too painful at the moment. He is not a fashionable architect. He is an experimenter, way ahead of his time and, for this reason, not fashionable. Should he try to design in today's fashion, cater to the prevalent taste, he would experience such a disgust that he could not adequately solve a given task. It is a problematic situation. Nevertheless, we often are very happy together. It is surely a fact that women here work much more than in Europe. On the other hand, we live a kind of picnic life which I like. . . .

*Dione to Muetterli*

Los Angeles, December 1931

Unfortunately, I cannot report anything worthwhile. Richard was able to save some money in Cleveland and has a small income by giving occasional lectures and writing articles. We save every cent.

However, do not worry about us. As long as we love each other and are happy, as long as we are not starving, worries are superfluous. Occasionally, I fantasize what we really would do if all the savings were used up. But most of the time I enjoy the heavenly landscape, enjoy my children, try to keep my balance, let Richard's depressions not weigh me down so that I can bolster up his courage. For the past few weeks his mental condition has been better. At the moment he is again down. He sleeps a lot and looks, on the whole, very well. All in all, he is a courageous fighter and I admire him with all my heart. . . .

*Dione to Frances*
*Toplitz*

Los Angeles, December 1931

. . . This life without any work is difficult to endure for Richard. He is always very busy, but not with something that would earn some money. The waiting for a possible miracle makes us nervous at times. . . .

*Richard to Muetterli*

Los Angeles, Christmas 1931

Remembrance is such a strange phenomenon. I am curious to know whether other people, too, live continually with the memory of their past. I hardly ever hear them mentioning it, while I am continually aware of it and, at the same time, I am fully involved in the present and the future. It is actually a part of my life! Credo that one's own historical past should have some kind of relevance for one's whole life.

There seems to be a limit, a boundary for a person's comprehension. As soon as I observe someone in distress, I try to understand, to be helpful, but my interest in a general conception of misery is of a different kind, like my interest in aerodynamics or the construction of a new kind of airplane. In the social-planning field, emotional involvement should be carefully avoided. Even the feeling of social justice is an emotion one should preferably not indulge in. Such sentiments have, perhaps, no place in a Christmas letter, but they are ideas that occupy my mind. Whatever happens to me is justified. So it looks to me, except when I am especially lucky as was the fact, for instance, that the oldest Niedermann daughter married me.

*Richard brings the New York Museum of Modern Art's first
exhibition of "Modern Architecture"
to Los Angeles.*

*Richard receives a loan to build his own home
and office.*

*At the end of the year Richard is commissioned to design a
building on Hollywood Boulevard for Carl Laemmle's
Universal Picture Corporation.*

*The first decade of the marriage ends on a hopeful note,
and the fulfillment of Richard's promise as
an architect begins.*

*1932*

We had the great joy to spend an evening at a friend's house together with Professor and Mrs. Einstein. This was a great experience because this great scientist revealed himself as a human being, full of humor and a philosophical outlook on life, so that both of us felt deeply happy. Richard involved him in an hour long lively discussion about the philosophical background of modern physics and produced such telling and uncommon examples that Einstein became very interested and finally agreed with Richard. All of this was much too complicated for me, but it was fascinating to watch these two men, watch their gestures and facial expressions. During the evening a postcard was signed by all present and sent to Erich and Luise Mendelsohn in Berlin.

Los Angeles, March 1932

*Dione to Muetterli*

An important happening in January was the opening of the Museum of Modern Art exhibition, "Modern Architecture," in New York. This was a great event because the country saw for the first time a collection of the best modern work. Germany showed examples of Gropius, Mies, and Haesler. France showed Le Corbusier, Holland showed Oud, USA showed the works of four architects unknown to you except Wright. The selection was, of course, arbitrary, many were left out, but the space was limited. A catalogue contained a short synopsis with photographs and descriptive text of each participant, and a short history describing the development of modern architecture. It is the first time that the American public heard about it in the English language. The exhibition, which was modeled after the one in Stuttgart, was very homogeneous and was a great success in New York.

As Richard was the only invited participant from west of Chicago, he tried his utmost to bring this exhibition to Los Angeles, entailing a lot of effort, as the cost was a thousand dollars. The museum and the library here showed no interest. Finally, a department store, by putting pressure on various suppliers, was able to procure the money. This was really a great success, because the public here is truly quite unaware about the new building art. Unfortunately, the exhibition arrived here in July, at the same time of the Olympics, but it created quite a stir. Richard had invited the president of the conservative university USC to accept the chairmanship of the honor committee, as well as thirty of the most prominent citizens, mayor, governor, bank presidents, newspaper people, and members of the upper ten thousand; in short the most conservative, albeit the most influential, elements.

Richard's reasoning was that through this assemblage he could blunt or minimize attacks in the newspapers. At the opening, a few hundred of these upper ten thousand were present. No rotten eggs were thrown, no disparaging remarks were made, at least not publicly, and the ten exhibition models and photographic enlargements were stared at as one gazes at exotic animals. A model of Richard's prefabricated Ring Plan School was his contribution to the exhibit, besides an impressive enlargement of his Health House.

The exhibition has the advantage for us that Richard is now everywhere introduced and known as an internationally famous architect. That makes it somewhat easier for him to execute his radical ideas or, at least, make an attempt in this direction. The interest in modern architecture has grown tremendously in this last year, and the exhibition has helped materially.

*Richard to Muetterli*

Los Angeles, July 1932

Although I have slowly become accustomed to the nearby park, I am still enchanted with it. How such a Californian city is constructed may not be ideal, but it is a noteworthy step forward in comparison with European cities where some parts are in annoying contrast to each other. This is an ideal spot for people out of work, for those down and out, in short, for those who do not have a secure source of income.

With a few others helping me, I am trying to start a school for social research. The famous radical historian, Charles Beard, known also in Europe, whom we visited recently, is going to address our group tomorrow. I too, will have to make a speech. Should this attempt succeed, I might have a chance to do constructive propaganda for a large-scale planning in the interesting corners of the world.

Not only is it the financial lethargy that stands in my way of realizing any of my projects, so laboriously conceived, but it is a titanic soul effort to start ever anew. Finally one becomes exhausted.

Los Angeles, July 1932

My relationship to Schindler is, unfortunately, not as I would like it. It is not in his nature to be candid and open. Whenever he can, he tries to ignore my efforts. Even so, I could be his true friend, especially regarding the promotion of his work.

Los Angeles, July 1932

Richard has not had any work for a whole year. You can well imagine that he has had some trying hours, days, and weeks to see time slipping by, to become older, to forget, that is the worst of all. But all around us many are in the same situation. On the other hand, I feel more hopeful because we have made many more contacts with more influential people and Richard is more and better known. The architectural exhibition is here now. Richard worked very hard to raise money for it, and there were some very stunning write-ups in the papers here. Richard will give three lectures in connection with this exhibition and I, at least, hope that it will help us. (You know Richard is always more pessimistic.) Richard has become a figure of importance, is invited to dinners, openings, and such occasions, has to wear his tuxedo quite often.

Los Angeles, July 1932

Finally the miracle has occurred, most wonderful news. A patron has loaned us money so that Richard may demonstrate in a small house what kind of progressive materials are available pricewise, and that such a small dwelling need not be "uncomfortable" or have a "hospitallike" atmosphere. In this manner we will acquire a house and an office designed by Richard where he can demonstrate his ideas. Not having had this has been a great disadvantage and we set great hopes on this project.

I have been driving around for weeks to find a suitable lot, which was not at all easy because the combination of office and living quarters poses a problem, as the office should be readily accessible, not too distant from Los Angeles or Hollywood, located in a suitable neighborhood. Finally, we found a small plot of land facing an artificial lake called Silverlake with a view over water and mountains.

*The "patron" referred to above, "Dione to Her Parents," was C. H. Van der Leeuw, Dutch industrialist, philanthropist, and architectural enthusiast, whom Richard had met while lecturing in Europe in 1931. Van der Leeuw, impressed by Richard's* How America Builds, *made a special trip to Los Angeles to see the world-famous Lovell Health House. When he discovered that Richard lived and worked out of a rented bungalow, Van der Leeuw offered him a loan with which to build a home and office.*

On Board the North German *Lloyd Bremen*, April 1932

. . . Just a few lines to thank you for your kindness in L.A.—They were delightful days and I was so interested in your work and so glad to be able to like the house of Lovell still more than I thought I would have. I appreciate your work *even more* after meeting Lovell here on board. How on earth did he find you? And how was it possible to carry through the work? I suppose Mrs. Lovell has been a great help, because I cannot imagine he understands anything about it! . . .

*Richard to C. H. Van der Leeuw*

Los Angeles, July 1932

I had started various letters to you, while circumstances changed in a constant flux and I feel quite unhappy if I should have taxed your patience too much.

Meanwhile the $3,000 you loaned me has been lying safe on the U.S. Postal Savings Bank. I cannot conceive of a safer place. Meanwhile my own situation has brightened in other ways, and particularly my appointment to conduct the graduate course at the University of Southern California seems to give some stability. (It is in fact the first time that a great American university offers a degree on the basis of modern work.)

I looked again for lots in a new neighborhood and decided to build a small house to be enlarged later. The thought became very dear to us, and I am convinced that at the present low level of real estate costs and cost of construction such a house could not possibly mean anything of a loss, but rather a very sound and even promising investment. Despite a shortage of creative work I am extremely busy following up a dozen preliminary prospects and inquiries, and just now am discussing with two leading architects of the Chicago fair who are visiting, as well as with city officials an exhibition during the Olympics now in town. Is it not strange that such a high-powered activity should as yet not yield a comfortable income, but this seems part and parcel of the general situation today.

I have never before been hesitant to make decisions, but being surrounded by hesitants it takes a triple effort to recognize what is sound action. Under no circumstances can I accept your waiving of the interests which I owe you as per our clear agreement. . . .

*Dione to Frances Toplitz*

Los Angeles, November 1932

At the moment Richard is extremely busy. He works from 6:00 A.M. to 11:00 P.M. He is also occupied with his first small residence. It is the first time that an American family WANTED to have a modern house. Many people are interested in the outcome as nobody here builds like that. Schindler, with whom we lived for several years, has developed in a different direction.

The clients for the little house, Ernst and Bertha Mosk, had visited the Museum of Modern Art exhibition and have commissioned Richard to build their house. As they were enthusiastic about modern architecture, he had no need to convince them of its advantages. . . .

*After living in the house for five years, Mrs. Mosk wrote a letter of appreciation.*

Dear Mr. Neutra, in March 1933 we moved into our modern Neutra house. This gives me five years experience in such a home. Prior to our moving in, I remember you telling me, "this place will give you new experiences, open up new unheard-of channels, will make your life richer, etc." At the time I just vaguely understood what you meant by this. Now I believe I am in a position to not only understand but definitely to know what it is you meant. This kind of a home is more than the word implies. It is an instructor for one's own development and after a while this development becomes quite conscious. We are always having the feeling that now we have freedom to breathe and grow. The house is alive and so we too feel vital. To you we will be and are grateful for this vitality. It was a great privilege to have been closely associated with a person who is so far ahead of his time and also who has given us an instrument so that we can keep up with his vision.

Having a modern home the kind that you built isn't just a fad or should I say an ultra fashion? It is a slow and most positive growth, I would consider it an outer expression of an inner progress. People who are sensitive to the changes taking place around them express this in their own environment.

This house has a vitality which is so pronounced that those living here cannot fail to feel and even observe it. There are no dead corners to take up your precious energy, there isn't much furniture around to take up the valuable space, so that the people in the home have a chance to expand and also to know the value of living in space, that thing which we all need so much of on the inside of us.

New perspectives have opened up to me, new interests and most of all I have a positive feeling of being an integrated person instead of split into so many small pieces not knowing where I am.

As we happen to live not far away from two universities, we have quite a few classes up here to study the modern architecture. I was pleased to learn later that many of these people went away with a real interest in the modern home and its advantages. From this I know this place has a social as well as a personal value.

I am happy to tell you that I made quite a lot of music this year. At first I played regularly with a pianist, then sometimes in an orchestra. I also joined the newly constituted Philharmonic Choir group. We gave four concerts in the Hollywood Bowl. Although only five rehearsals were scheduled in the space of six weeks, we rehearsed nearly every day. One good thing about these many rehearsals was that I learned to sightread. Due to financial difficulties this choir has ceased to exist, but I now sing in a double quartette and we are preparing programs for the radio. I will, as well, be the alto soloist at a midnight mass. In addition to all this, I am also doing a lot of typing for Richard.

Regarding Frank, he is surely the main success of the year. He is so much better that I give thanks to God every day. He is already able to read and repeat simple stories. He can solve simple arithmetic problems, sing a few songs, and recite a few poems. Now he has started in a special class at the public school. He takes the bus at 8:00 A.M. and returns at 4:00 P.M. As the first part of the year was very strenuous for me, I really enjoy my newly found peace and quiet. Frank loves school. His outbursts have diminished, but he is still unable to answer a question. His speech is very much below par. His tenderness and devotion to me, however, are touching and he is my great joy.

*Richard to Dione's Parents*

Los Angeles, Christmas 1932

. . . Your oldest son-in-law earns more at the moment than most other architects. In fact for the next two months we are out of the woods and I am contemplating buying myself another pair of shoes, when they are reduced in price after Christmas!

As yet I have not touched the loan money except to buy the lot. I cannot find a minute to work on the plans, it is really ironic. You must understand that it is not my ambition to become a property owner. What I do want is to build and live in a house designed by me and am building it for this reason. That's the real situation. It is a commission, only one under particular circumstances of full trust, and by God, I want to fulfill it. Dione tells me I should not rush but wait until full concentration is again possible and as usual she is right. . . .

*Afterword*
*Index*

The year 1933 saw the completion of VDL Research House at Silver-lake, which we named after Mr. Van der Leeuw. In the thirty-eight years that followed:

In 1939 Richard brought my parents here for a permanent stay, and I had Muetterli's vital presence and help for the next twenty years. Vaterli even learned to drive a car at age seventy. They both became American citizens, voted enthusiastically, created a large circle of devoted friends, and thus enjoyed life to the fullest.

What happened to Frank after so many frustrating years of hope for improvement is rather sad. After living with us for twenty-nine years, he finally had to be committed to a state institution. In 1970 I was able to place him in a halfway house, which the state of California had established in the meantime. He leads as satisfying a life as can be expected, visiting me twice a month for a few days.

Dion pursues his career as an architect, not only continuing the father-son practice but also developing his own new ideas on "nature-near build-ing." He serves on commissions, giving lectures both here and abroad.

Raymond, our third son, was born in 1939. He studied medicine at McGill University in Montreal, Canada. For three years he served on a Na-vajo reservation in Arizona and spent three years as public health re-searcher in Cali, Colombia, and as an assistant professor at Harvard and UCLA. At present he is chief of the epidemiological studies section of the California Department of Health at Berkeley.

Yes, Richard did achieve both fame and fortune during his lifetime, and his architecture can be found all over the world. But he also became known for developing a totally new concept of what architecture could be—a style of design that could be a means of bringing people back into harmony with nature and themselves. This he called "biorealism."

Richard functioned not only as an architect but as a writer who pro-duced fourteen books. His best-known, *Survival through Design*, was translated into German, Italian, and Spanish. A paperback edition was published in English and French, and another paperback edition of 30,000 copies was published in Dresden, East Germany. In 1984 an edition was also published in Hungary. Now Dion has published a thirtieth anniver-sary edition. The extent of Richard's influence is best expressed in a letter received from the author of *African Genesis* and *Territorial Imperative*, Robert Ardrey, who wrote to Richard on January 27, 1967:

"There is probably no city in the world where the influence of your work and your ideas cannot be read in stone and stucco realized by men you never met. This is the genuine immortality, when what a man has done so thoroughly imbues his time that it takes on a kind of anonymity. Like a sperm in a gene-pool nobody quite remembers who was the donor, but there it is a portion of a population's resource forever. Your concepts of living have in many ways been like that. I can remember times in Los An-geles in the 30's when there was only one man, Richard Neutra, and you said, 'that's a Neutra house.' Nobody else could have built it. And then later you looked at a house and you said: 'Look at the Neutra influence.' But then later on unless you were a Neutra fan and connoisseur you wouldn't say it because your concepts had spread so widely and deeply into domestic architecture that they had become part of the modern way of life. That's where like a mutated gene you entered into our gene-pool, improving the stock for all time."

And I, Dione? During Richard's lifetime I accompanied him everywhere. I was his secretary, his publications editor, his troubleshooter. My life now is almost as busy as when Richard was alive. I began cello and singing lessons shortly after he died, and I try to practice three or four hours daily. For the last few years I have been a guest lecturer on college campuses as well as for civic and social organizations. For my program I sing folk songs in a half-dozen languages while accompanying myself on the cello.

I think Richard would have been pleased to see how his Dione has blossomed and was able to create her own rich life, so that now, after his death in 1970, I am fulfilling what he told me as an eighteen-year-old girl, namely, "happiness is to fulfill your own potential."